the FINDHORN COMMUNITY

The 'Universal Hall'

the **Findhorn Community**

CREATING A HUMAN IDENTITY FOR THE 21ST CENTURY

CAROL RIDDELL

Findhorn Press

© 1990 Carol Riddell
First published 1991 by Findhorn Press, The Park, Findhorn, Forres
IV36 0TZ, Moray, Scotland

ISBN 0 905249 77 1

Set in Palatino on Mackintosh SE.
Design and layout by Philip Mielewczyk, Bay Area Graphics.
Cover illustration by Marianne Kersten; chapter illustrations by
Harley Miller; photographs by Findhorn Foundation
Visual Arts Department.
Printed and bound by Billings & Sons, Worcester, UK.

Printed on recycled paper

To Eileen Caddy

The Findhorn and Kinloss Community Council has asked us to make clear that the 'Findhorn Community' referred to in this book is not the local community of Findhorn village.

Other books by Carol Riddell
Approaching Sociology (with Margaret Coulson)
Gifts of Divine Love (with Marianne Kersten) (in preparation)

Acknowledgements

At one time or another during the writing of this book, I have received love and support from practically every member of the Findhorn Foundation, and from many members of the wider Findhorn Community. So my heartfelt thanks go to everyone.

I also want to give special mention and appreciation to Jean Prince, who went over the book carefully in draft form and pointed out much clumsiness of wording and not a few mis-spellings. Others who have made helpful comments on the text are Michael Hamm, Mary Inglis, Renate Suzuki—my daughter, Rhiannon Hanfman, Eileen and Peter Caddy, Alex Walker and Craig Gibsone. In spite of the fact that he does not always agree with my interpretation of events, Peter Caddy gave me much help on the early parts of the chapter on the history of the Foundation—Chapter 5. Sandra Kramer has done a wonderful job on the final editing.

However, the opinions expressed in the book, unless otherwise ascribed, are my own. The Findhorn Community has no official 'line', and there is almost always someone to disagree with any point of view. As I have tried to refer to commonly expressed or majority beliefs or practices, I have usually referred to 'we' throughout the text, but readers should remember that other community members might not always agree with what I have written.

Special thanks are due to Harley Miller for the line drawings, Chris Giles, Dieter Bartholomaï and Ron Parker of the Visuals Department for the photographs and Marianne Kersten for the cover picture, inspired by the Findhorn Community.

My Kaypro 2 computer, 'Charlette', and 'Brother HR', my printer, have been indefatigable, and never let me down once.

Carol Riddell, February 1990

Some of the material quoted in this book is acknowledged in the text. Other sources for which the author and publisher are grateful are:

Pg. 93: E.F. Schumacher, *Small is Beautiful* (Abacus/Sphere)
Pg. 111: Alice Walker, *The Colour Purple* (Women's Press)
Pg. 21: Carlos Castaneda, *Journey to Ixtlan* (Penguin Books)
Pg. 181: Bhagavan Sri Sathya Sai Baba, *Discourses on the Bhagavad Gita* (Sri Sathya Sai Books & Publications Trust)
Pg. 69: Vladimir Mayakovsky, *Poems* (Progress Publishers, Moscow)
Pg. 37: Pablo Neruda, *Five Decades: Poems 1925-1970* (Grove Press)
Pg. 129: Hermann Hesse, *Narziss and Goldmund* (Penguin Books)

Contents

Foreword

A few years ago it became clear to us at the Findhorn Foundation that a new book on the community was needed. Much had happened since *Faces of Findhorn* had been published in 1980, depicting in words and pictures a flavour of the community in the 70s. Since then the Foundation had weathered a period of spiritual, financial and leadership crisis that had brought its very survival into question. It had emerged stronger, clearer, and with both more humility and a more realistic commitment to translating its spiritual principles into an enduring lifestyle. Not only did it now own the caravan park on which it had come to birth, but also a flourishing diversity of concerns, individuals and businesses had sprung up alongside the Foundation, associated with but not directly part of it. What was emerging was much more than a community or educational centre; it was something more akin to a village or neighbourhood. Previous books had talked of putting spiritual principles into practice in growing plants and growing people; now, it seemed, these principles were extending into social, cultural, political and economic spheres as well.

Recently David Spangler, guide and mentor to the community in the early 70s, was revisiting the Foundation and led the members in an exercise in which he asked them to respond to two questions. What, he asked first, was the spiritual and philosophical heart of the community? And secondly, what was the absolute minimum, in physical, material and practical terms, that the community needed in order to ensure that its principles were embodied and worked out?

The answers were, as usual in this community, varied and diverse. But there was also a common theme to them, and what it came down to in the end was that both the spiritual and philosophical heart *and* the absolute minimum required was two or more people gathered in the name of spirit—and there would God be, in the midst of them. Almost everything physical, in fact, could be taken away, and the gift the community offers would still remain, for what it represents can be embodied and expressed in very simple conditions.That gift, that heart, is the opportunity to discover and recognise the sacred in our midst, in all aspects of our ordinary everyday lives—and to connect with and give expression to it.

At the same time, all the forms—be they physical, social, economic, political—are important too, for they are the vehicles through which that heart can be expressed. The forms of the community have shifted significantly over the years, and will no doubt continue to do so in the future. The nature of these shifts, the hows and whys and wherefores, can be and often are open to a variety of interpretations. When the idea of a new book on the Foundation surfaced a few years ago, a group of four or five long-term members got together to explore it and discovered to their astonishment that they had very different perspectives on and interpretations of what had happened in the past ten years, even when they had been intimately involved with the same issues. Sometimes when two or more are gathered, there is no agreement at all!

Part of the strength of the Findhorn Community is the space it allows for differences. At its best the community functions as a vital, dynamic, synergistic body which reflects both the unity *and* the diversity of spirit; its interdependent parts, whether individuals or groups, reflecting uniqueness rather than uniformity. The differences add to rather than detract from the whole. Of course, this has its challenges too, and there are times in community life when it seems that when two or more are gathered, there's not a damn thing gets done! But despite the length of time things can take, it is generally held to be richer and more worthwhile to learn not to suppress the differences but rather to deal with them in ways that nurture both the individual and the whole.

Ultimately it is not the forms or interpretations of the Findhorn Community that are important. In years to come the community may not be remembered very clearly for its specifics; it may not even be remembered by name. But if it has fulfilled its promise, if it has done its work well, there will be a new spirit alive on Earth, brought to birth both by this community and by the ever-growing multitude of people and groupings seeking to embody a new consciousness in their individual and collective lives.

Any book about the Findhorn Community is a personal statement. This one is Carol Riddell's. Her connection with the heart of the community is a deep one, which makes her statement in many ways an expression of the collective—a unique, individualised shaping of the spirit that moves in and through what is happening here. As you explore her book, may that heart and spirit find a deeper expression within you too, and bring you into a greater sense of the vast and purposeful and loving community of life of which we are all part.

Mary Inglis

Findhorn Bay
Looking towards
Forres

Introduction

Noiselessly chimes the morning light
In litanies of angel bells
Refracting silver and gold
The silence reverberating.
Far away, remote, forgotten,
Timeless blessings streaming
From an inward life
Filling the world
Till all that sounds
Sings to one Heart.

Now does the air smell sweet
Now is there life and living
Now does the cock crow
And the sky shine blue.
—Don Turner

The north-east of Scotland is one of the remaining quiet areas of Europe. The only large towns are Aberdeen to the east, and Inverness to the west, separated by 160 kilometres of gentle, rolling farming country dotted with villages and small market towns. To the coast flow several rivers from the Highlands. The river Findhorn, as it leaves its beautiful wooded gorges, reaches the sea via a wide landlocked bay, about 40 kilometres east of Inverness. At the tip of the eastern arm of this bay lies the little village of Findhorn. It was once a small port, but now, due to silting from the sand-dunes that surround it, it is an attractive summer haven for yachts and a few tourists who come to stay in local caravan parks.

Looking south from the narrow spit of land beyond the village a broad panorama of gently rising wooded hills is to be seen; a few fields are in the foreground, with the little town of Forres eight kilometres away in the centre. This countryside radiates peacefulness, and on a quiet summer evening, the dusk light colouring the ever-changing cloud patterns reflected in the bay, blessedness would describe it more aptly. Sheltered on three sides by mountains, the area has more sunshine and less rainfall than almost any

1

other part of Scotland, and is in considerable contrast to the wild mountains and misty grandeur of the western coasts.

The local people are friendly and welcome strangers, but they are as proud of their local identity as of their Scottishness. A Scotsman once gave me a lift into Forres. "Are you local?" I asked him. "No, I've only been here 14 years," he replied. The area is quiet and law-abiding, with little crime, although a drug problem has emerged among a small number of young people in the towns. Unemployment is high, yuppies rare.

A little inland from Findhorn village, but still on the bay of the Findhorn river estuary, is a large, active NATO airbase, whose roaring jets disturb the peaceful atmosphere and are a constant reminder of 'the world outside'. In between lies the Findhorn Bay Caravan Park. It was here, in 1962, that Eileen and Peter Caddy and Dorothy Maclean were guided to start the community which is the subject of this book, and which is at present visited by several thousand guests every year, from all over the world. The setting is appropriate for a spiritual community: the peaceful landscapes are matched by the sound of big jets taking off to scour the Atlantic for Soviet nuclear submarines; one lives straddled between two worlds of experience—one might say, the world that God made for us and that which man has made for himself. Indeed this contrast illustrates rather precisely the reason for and the significance of the spiritual community at Findhorn. At the time of writing, the community has expanded from the Caravan Park where it began, to occupy a large old hotel, Cluny Hill Hotel, now called Cluny Hill College, on the outskirts of Forres. Most of our guests stay here. At Cullerne, a large house near the Caravan Park, are our main gardens. Self-governing sister communities exist at Newbold House, a little outside Forres, and on Erraid, an island off the west coast of Scotland.

In 1972 the community was registered as a charitable trust, under the name 'Findhorn Foundation'. Until the early 1980s the Foundation and community were virtually co-extensive, but then a community wider than the Foundation began to form.

We have co-founded and still support an independent Steiner school in Drumduan House, a beautiful old mansion which was donated to us. Independent small businesses and groups are developing, working in cooperation with us—the New Findhorn Directions group, our trading company, operates the Caravan

Park, the Phoenix Shop, selling books and crafts, and a Trading Centre. Other independent small enterprises spiritually connected with us include Meadowlark, a beautiful home for old people; Minton House, a retreat and small conference centre; Alternative Data, a computer software business; Bay Area Graphics; and the Weatherwise solar energy and housing construction company. We have exchange and networking connections with numerous other groups across the globe.

The first part of this book deals with the significance in the world today of the Findhorn Foundation and the community which has grown up around it, and with the spiritual principles upon which it is founded and by which it can be understood. This section is more abstract, more challenging reading than later parts of the book. Some readers, particularly those wanting to know 'how things are going at the community', may like to start with the second part. For me, our day-to-day life only has meaning in the context of more general issues, which is why I have felt it right to place them first. The second part describes something of our life here and how we attempt to put spiritual principles into practice, as the core of an experiment in living together, an experiment which is itself constantly changing and developing. The third part sees the community through the eyes of a number of members and ex-members, and the fourth examines perspectives for the future. The approach is my own.

Each member of the Findhorn Community would write a book about their experiences and their understanding of what they are living through in their own personal way, with their own emphases. However, I believe my six years at the Foundation—the six most inspiring years of my life—have given me a viewpoint that is not greatly at variance with our collective consciousness.

I suppose that I have always been a seeker—in search of understanding of the contradictions in my own identity as well as those of society. In earlier years I sought to change the world through left-wing politics and feminism; and had to transform my own identity in a dramatic and unusual way. It all taught me a great deal, but my first real sense of a spiritual integration of the personal and the social came when I learned Zen Buddhist meditation in the early 1970s. Three years of Re-evaluation Co-counselling, Gestalt and Bioenergetics assisted the rearrangement of my psychology, and gave me the strength to give up my job and trust in a

3

then uncertain future. I cashed in my pension in order to study in California for three years, learning techniques to open for myself the intuitional faculties we all possess. Only then was I ready to be drawn to the Findhorn Community. I came here in 1983, having given up my job as a sociologist five years previously.

For three and a half years I worked in our gardens, then for a year in our shop. After another year directing ('focalising') the Personnel department with Cally Miller, came the time to write this book. At the Findhorn Foundation I have been able to live, for the first time in my life, an inner spiritual harmony, and have found a genuine happiness, of a kind that is very close to bliss. In 1985 another Foundation member introduced me to the teachings of Sathya Sai Baba, and He has become the perfect spiritual instructor for me. This book is a small way of giving thanks for these incalculable gifts. Most of the examples I have used come directly from my personal experience in the community.

I have been supported by the Foundation to write this book as an independent, individual statement about the community, a trust which I deeply appreciate.

Nowadays we are constantly featured on television programmes, but no book about the Findhorn Community has been written for several years. Eileen Caddy, who still lives with us, has published several volumes containing the channellings she has received and, recently, an autobiography. They provide a wealth of authoritative guidance on how to live a meaningful and joy-filled life. In them is given the spiritual purpose of the Findhorn Foundation. David Spangler's writings situate the community in a world context, but he has withdrawn his earlier books from publication. An account in journalistic style of the first years of the community was given in *The Magic of Findhorn* (1975), by Paul Hawken. This book has introduced thousands of people to us, but it no longer accurately reflects the balance of our daily lives here. He also has indicated that he does not wish republication. *Faces of Findhorn* (1980), now out of print, showed something of our life in the 70s through pictures, while other books—*The Findhorn Cookbook* and *The Findhorn Garden*—have related to particular aspects of our work. Peter Caddy is now writing his memoirs, and we all await their publication with great interest. They will form an invaluable complement to Eileen's autobiography in understanding the history of our community.

4

Among other things, this book examines the significance of the Findhorn Community in the contemporary world. Our story is not just that of another utopian community. It is urgently relevant to the problems of modern civilisation. The community does not exist in isolation. It is part of a world-wide movement for personal and social transformation, expressed in channelled writings such as *A Course in Miracles*; in the teachings of contemporary spiritual Masters, like Sai Baba; and in the strivings of a multitude of individuals and small communities the world over for a change in consciousness. We are part of a gentle wave of transformation that is moving across our planet.

Before proceeding, it is necessary to make a note about the use of the word 'Findhorn' in this book. To the yachtsmen, the villagers and many local people, Findhorn refers to the village and the bay; to the anglers who yearn to snare the salmon that each year enter the bay, it refers to the river; but for the thousands of spiritual seekers who visit us and the millions more who see the frequent television presentations, or read articles in the mass-circulation magazines of many lands, Findhorn refers to the spiritual community which, as I write, has existed here for 27 years. Thus it means no disrespect to the village, or the river, or the bay, when I use the term Findhorn about the Foundation—it merely recognises the area's internationally most widely-known feature. Perhaps it would have been better if there had been another name, but it is normally clear which identity named 'Findhorn' is referred to. Some local villagers would prefer that we always say 'Findhorn Foundation' when talking about ourselves but, with the flood of visitors and international presentations about us growing, we can no longer control what name is used. Furthermore, the Findhorn Foundation only came into being when we were already ten years old and the Foundation is now just part of a growing Findhorn Community. It seems better to accept the inevitable. For spiritual seekers, the Findhorn Foundation or the Findhorn Community is just 'Findhorn'. Generally I have spoken of the Findhorn Foundation or the Findhorn Community in this book, only using Findhorn on its own where the context is absolutely clear.

Part One

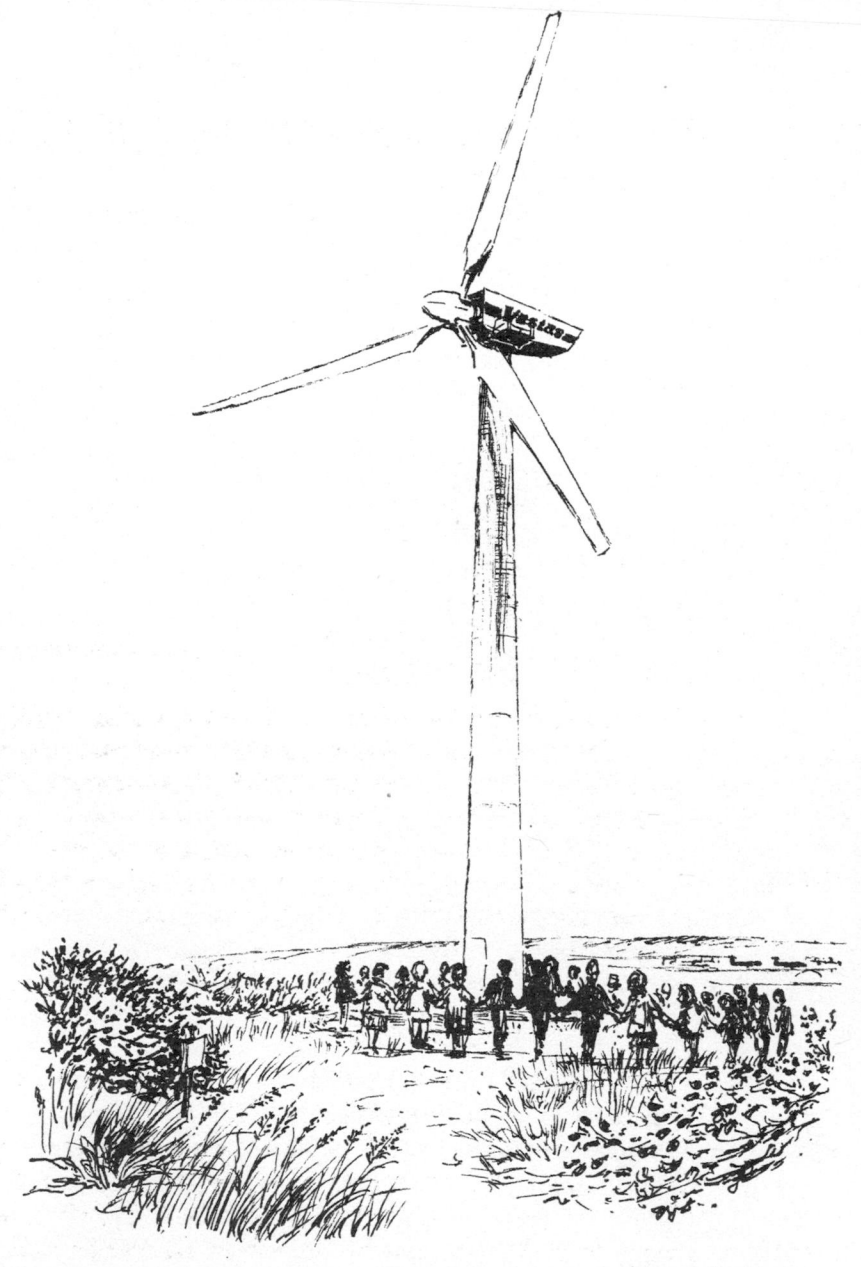

The blessing of 'Moya' the
wind generator

Chapter 1
The Contemporary World
and Its Challenges

Out across the pallid sea arm, winter rain
combing dirty marshes
The big factories transmute labour into profits
and pollution
joining the clouds
raining dirt into my flat
Sewering the sea
Sleek Jaguars in the suburbs or further out
Smog and scum around, we remain human and
defiant—
wispy little flames . . . .

—A Liverpool Poem

The World Needs a Spiritual Way of Life

In an interview at the end of this book, a Findhorn Foundation member describes how he arrived from a great city to our very small community. In a dream on his first night, he saw himself coming from a very small place to a very large one. In appearance, the community is small indeed, but its social significance is very large, as this book attempts to demonstrate.

The Findhorn Community plays a significant part in a revolution that is gently changing the world. It is not one of the noisy revolutions or 'isms', of which there have been many in our turbulent times; we do not stridently seek converts for a new ideology. We are in the mainstream of and contributing to an older, an age-old, way of experiencing the world, whose time has now come, and without whose ascendance humanity cannot survive the challenges of its own civilisation. It is, simply put, a revolution of love, whose aim is to put spirituality back into the centre of human identity where it belongs, so the world can enter a new era based on mutual understanding, cooperation and harmony. This revolution does not 'do' anything, it does not normally make headlines

9

in any of the news media, but it creates the conditions in which the above qualities can flourish among human beings. Perhaps it is responsible for the rather extraordinary changes that, at the close of the 80s, have laid the basis for the end of the Cold War and the transformation of Eastern Europe. But it has much more still to do . . . .

The Findhorn Community is not based on dogma. Yet its practices express a simple theology, one which underlies all major religions:

God is Love; God is omnipresent. God is therefore our essential Self. Seeking to make this essential Self our experienced reality is the spiritual approach to life.

By taking this approach, life's meaning is discovered, and our awareness, creativity and vitality begin to be released.

The philosophy of life that has evolved at the Findhorn Community differs from that of established religions in that, like their own mystics, we do not place emphasis on outer form, ritualistic observance or customary obedience to revealed codes of behaviour. We seek to discover Self behind self; as we become Self-oriented, we become selfless. Unlike most earlier mystics we do not withdraw into caves or hermitages, but see ordinary life as the setting for our Self-discovery. Thus life in the community is not monastic. It is relevant to people in any situation, of any religion, class or colour. The most important thing is that the 'theology' works, and even with our modest degree of commitment to the spiritual, it works rather well. There is a famous saying that if you take one step towards God, He will take ten towards you. But in which direction do you take that one step? We have discovered that it is towards your own loving essence. The story is, indeed, true!

The world in which the Findhorn Community exists has become more and more secular. Materialist civilisations in the past have justified themselves in the name of imperial power, banditry, or cultural or racial superiority; but all have come, after a while, to nothing. The driving force of our current civilisation is material gain. During the past century a world civilisation has emerged, one of great cities and ever-accelerating technological change. Communism is only a rather unsuccessful variant which substitutes state for private accumulation. Materialist civilisation has, in the West at least, made traditional religion marginal, but it has not created human happiness.

10

Is it possible to create a fulfilling civilisation which is not dominated by material acquisitiveness, but which does use human technological inventiveness sensibly? At the Findhorn Community we believe it is possible. Our own practice over the years is like a workshop preparing for such a civilisation. A spiritual civilisation is in the making here and in other similar centres, with a spirituality appropriate for human beings brought up in the pell-mell world of the twentieth century.

It is actually *essential* for an alternative civilisation to become predominant. A large number of people in the West and a few elsewhere are, in material terms, doing very well, but from a global and historical perspective we are living in a very dangerous situation, perhaps the most critical humanity has ever faced. Major changes of perspective are not only beneficial to individuals. They are necessary and urgent for humanity's secure future. Although the new technologies have created one world and undermined all old national and cultural boundaries, human attitudes have remained age-old. Greed, envy and suspicion are promoted —under other names, of course—to stimulate our chaotic civilisation. They have fed enormous social problems—of alienation, criminality and drug taking. Underlying them are the three great challenges of our times: the arms race, ecological destruction, and world poverty and debt.

Everyone is gradually becoming more and more aware of these problems, but attempts to solve them are still piecemeal. Each individual, company or government tends to put material 'progress' first, while hoping others will deal with the crises it gives rise to. At the Findhorn Community, however, we explore a human consciousness based on love, trust and inner suffiency; we recognise and care for each other as part of one human family; we live modestly, and try to take loving care of what we have; and we care for the earth which sustains us. Simple enough, but unless international civilisation too bases itself on these values, can humanity survive?

Our great materialist civilisation has created devastating weapons systems. It is destroying our global environment, and it has damned two thirds of the world's population to searing poverty and indebtedness. At the Foundation we do not feel despondent in the face of these challenges. We are optimistic that they will be resolved. But we do not try to pretend that they do not exist.

11

The Dangers of Deterrence

At six in the morning my caravan shakes as a huge military jet takes off from the nearby airfield. It is going to search the ocean for a Soviet nuclear submarine. We cannot really ignore deterrence in the Findhorn Community; it gives us earache. If deterrence works, the world's vast nuclear stockpile will not be used. If it does not, we die, for even with a 50% reduction in nuclear arsenals, there is plenty left to remove all of us. Nuclear war, chemical war, biological war, genetic war; all of these are much, much more dangerous to make mistakes with than were old wars and posturings with swords, spears and muskets. We live a hairsbreadth from death by computer misreading or political disaster. But how can one make the nightmare of megatons into something personal?

In 1986 I visited my daughter, who lives in Japan with her Japanese husband. It was only a short train ride from their home to Nagasaki, and I wanted to make a pilgrimage there. I was not quite nine when the atomic bomb was used on Nagasaki. I cannot remember my reactions at the time. Probably I accepted what we were all told, that it shortened the war. Perhaps it did. The nuclear explosion took place in the air over the city. At its epicentre on the ground stands a simple marble monolith, surrounded by a small garden with paths and neat hedges. Coloured streams of paper —prayer symbols—are piled to one side, and local children, brought to see the site as part of their education, crowd the garden. Above this point an atomic nucleus was split, and seventy thousand people died in a matter of seconds.

I sat down at the monolith and tried to meditate—a typical Findhorn Foundation reaction. As soon as I closed my eyes, uncontrollable tears started to flow, and my body was shaken by deep sobs. Embarrassed to be seen weeping so in front of all the children, I stood up and opened my eyes. The tears subsided. It was as if the agony of that instantaneous extinction still hovered as energy in the atmosphere of the place, waiting to find catharsis through compassionate hearts.

It would be good not just to have disarmament agreements while retaining our fear and mistrust of others, but to have peace. I cannot do much about the twists and turns of the negotiations in Geneva and elsewhere, but as a member of the Findhorn Foundation I work with considerable success to develop inner peace. I do not think I can legitimately harbour great expectations about negotiations between statesmen and states, if I cannot in my own personal life find some inner harmony and express it in my immediate surroundings. It is empowering to work in this way, for I am no longer an alienated spectator of decisions I cannot control. I have something practical to do, and one is also happier if peaceful. I believe our collective attempts at acquiring personal peace, which is part of the divine reality within us, contribute to an atmosphere in which disarmament negotiations can succeed again and again, till the only remaining mega-weapons are models in museums.

Caring for Our Earth

As I write, the 'red' empire of communism is collapsing all around. Green has become the fashionable colour and there is a tinge of it in the corner of every politician's eye. That is a good thing, because our earth needs a great deal of loving attention.

At last our technology has enabled a select few to observe our earth from outside the atmosphere. Some of their pictures and comments have been collected in a wonderful book, *The Home Planet.* They are very revealing:

> For the first time in my life I saw the horizon as a curved line. It was accentuated by a thin seam of dark blue light—our atmosphere. Obviously this was not the ocean of air I had been told it was so many times in my life. I was terrified by its fragile appearance.
>
> After an orange cloud—formed as a result of a dust storm over the Sahara and caught up by air currents—reached the Philippines and settled there with rain, I understand that we are all sailing in the same boat.

(Ulf Merbold, astronaut from the Federal Republic of Germany, and Vladimir Kovalyonok, cosmonaut from the USSR, quoted in *The Home Planet*)

We may no longer take for granted the natural environment in which we live. Our civilisation gives material benefit to only a few of the world's inhabitants, but in its destruction of the environment it knows no boundaries. In spite of scientific enquiry, nobody really knows the extent of the damage that is being done, how dramatic it is, or how long its effects will last. Multiple pollution of earth, seas and skies; holes in the ozone layer; ever more toxic chemical waste to dispose of; radioactive waste; pollution from gigantic accidents; destruction of forests for cash crops; desertification; global warming; the extinction of animal and plant species; the potential exhaustion of mineral resources—the list is long and frightening.

At the Findhorn Community we live beside an early example of the ecological results of commercial greed. As the tribal chiefs and landlords of the 18th-century Scottish Highlands discovered the potential financial return of sheep farming, they destroyed the remaining natural forest cover of the land, and drove the population out. The wild, highland wilderness is actually a man-made northern desert. Once the main forest stands had been destroyed, the mineral content of the soil was quickly leached off, and grazing by sheep and deer made sure the forest could not regenerate. The land ownership structure eliminated peasant farming, except in far-flung corners of the worst land. The population of the northernmost county, Sutherland, was 300,000 in 1830; today it is only around 25,000. The devastation of the Highlands is often ignored, as it has become a paradise for wanderers gasping for solitude in our overcrowded, overstrained civilisation. But it is an unnatural wilderness. Among our community's current activities is a project to regenerate regions of the old Caledonian forest.

During the early years of the Findhorn Community, in the 1960s, well before the appearance of the Green movement, ecological consciousness developed in a rather unusual way. Through their meditation work, the founders of the community rediscovered that it was possible for humans to contact and communicate with the energy forces controlling the growth of plants, and that these forces respond. The extraordinary organic gardens of the early community were the result. Some of our current, similar work with nature energies is described later in the book. We have practical experience, on a small scale, of how to co-create with nature to make a desert flower! It may well be very helpful later when humanity has ceased to destroy its own environment and is beginning to repair the damage.

In recent years, the community has developed a more conventional ecological programme. In doing so we have found that one of the deepest wounds that industrial civilisation has inflicted on us has been a reduction of sensitivity to nature itself. Everyone is

14

horrified by stories of city children who have never eaten any-thing other than tinned or frozen vegetables. However, if we are really going to save our planet and become co-creators with nature rather than its attempted conquerors we are going to have to do more than eat fresh vegetables. A new humanity will have to fall in love with the wonder of God's expression in the natural world, as St Francis once did. If we can reconnect with the sacredness of the natural world that the native Americans and other 'earth' peo-ples know, its rapine in the interests of greed will be unthinkable. Even the Foundation's very-willing guests and members often have to be re-trained to make this loving connection.

Attempts at ecological regeneration without a sensitivity to the delicate balance of nature can be more disastrous than the prob-lems which stimulate them. The Hopi Indians say that every prob-lem the white man solves with his technology creates a worse one, an observation it is sometimes hard to deny.

The great ecological crisis of our times has been well document-ed. Already it is probable that drastic collective action crossing all national frontiers is required in order to reverse the process. The root cause is a gross distortion of the human relationship with the earth we live on, caused by the unceasing stimulation of material desire. Thus the real solution requires a major personal and collec-tive re-evaluation of the meaning of human life on earth, and of the source of happiness. More sensitive, inwardly directed people make less demands on natural resources and have a much greater appreciation of the wonder of human interaction with the planet. A new lifestyle is needed.

Without this re-evaluation there would be a steady deterioration of conditions of life, expressing itself in a disaster here, a chronic problem there, till the pollution and destruction of the environ-ment and the ability of the human body to resist it reached a cross-roads of no return. The Findhorn Foundation provides a working alternative lifestyle, spiritually based and holistic, which demon-strates the direction humanity must take, and some of the prob-lems we must solve if humanity is to survive.

Affluence and Poverty

As an inhabitant of the wealthy lands of the earth, I used to watch, horrified, the endless catalogue of famine, poverty, instability, nat-ural and man-made disasters, war and civic strife shown on my television screen from the Third World. It seemed to have no relevance to my comfortable life. Later, in my profession, I studied the so-called 'sociology of development' and realised that Western wealth and Third World poverty are very much two sides of a coin. We may accept that the upsetting of nature's balance has widespread consequences, but it is harder to believe that our wealth is intimately tied to another's poverty, for it arouses uncomfortable guilt feelings.

Yet the historical study of relationships between nations shows quite clearly that, as some became richer, others became poorer. For instance, Australian aboriginal and Native American peoples were decimated in the take-over of their land for farming. Dutch commercialism was fuelled by pillaged wealth from Central and South America, passing through Spain. Indian wealth provided much of the capital for the first British industrial revolution and so on.

At present, the poverty of the Third World is not merely alleviated by charitable aid, but also *maintained* by international relations between rich and poor countries, as Third World leaders constantly complain. Extensive foreign ownership of land and industry exports profits. The best land is used for cash crops purchased by the West, expropriating peasants to hopeless shanty towns. The terms of trade are dominated by the rich nations, so raw material prices are very low. Debtor nations cannot repay the interest, let alone the capital, on their debts, which swallow up huge proportions of national wealth. Transport is monopolised by the wealthy nations, who reap its profits. Income differentials are so huge—up to 15 to 1—that educated people are constantly tempted away.

As a result, the rich nations monopolise the world's resources. At present their political strategies depend on an ever-increasing material standard of living. Yet Third World populations are more and more beginning to demand similar standards, as are the peoples of the ex-communist world. The tendency is to fall deeper and deeper into debt.

This demand for more is insatiable, a false dream of happiness. There is an inherent global economic instability. Banks are trying to write off Third World debts because they realise they will never be paid. Yet more and more people and governments become caught up in the dream. China, for instance, using older technology expects to build 300 million refrigerators in the next five

16

years. The result will be an increase in fluoro-carbon emission as great as that saved by all the efforts of the rich nations. But who will pay for the new technology the Chinese would need to make their refrigerators 'environmentally friendly'?

Debt is not confined to the Third World. The level of debt in the wealthy nations themselves is already astronomical, and a default in Third World debt payments could trigger the kind of economic crisis the thought of which makes stock market analysts jitter. On my recent workshop tour in Germany I saw a bank advertisement—'How to spend your next year's income this year!' Our much-vaunted market economies are a house of cards, but in order to stop the progression of the dream, there has to be a viable alternative to a greed-based economy.

Uneven socio-economic relationships between rich and poor groups of nations are not merely unstable and destabilising. As the communications revolution brings us all closer and closer together, gross distortions of wealth and poverty are reflected in all kinds of moral and ethical problems. Those who have may become unconsciously guilty, developing insecurity and reactive behaviour patterns. Those who have not may envy those who have and exhibit even more exaggerated materialism; or they may turn to crime to achieve what legitimate business seems to deny them. These problems occur not only between societies but also within them, for wealth is unevenly distributed here too. Another reaction, from wealthy and poor alike, is to turn to drugs to 'blot it all out'.

Frankly, a piecemeal solution is hardly likely. As one poor nation recovers from a debt crisis through some manipulation or re-scheduling of loans, another falls into one. A fragile advance is destroyed through some natural disaster, crop failure or political instability. Each individual manufacturer seeks the cheapest of raw materials for his products to maintain his profit margins. In an extremely competitive world economy, he is forced to create the crisis he may personally deplore.

A spiritually oriented life attacks this problem at the root. If we realise that the basis of happiness is within us, not in material things, material goods become less important, not an end in themselves. In the Findhorn Community we try to live frugally and comfortably, taking care of what we have as an expression of love. In my view it is probable that the earth as a whole could sustain its population at the level of our current lifestyle. One can hardly expect people to give up the frenetic search for happiness through material possessions unless we can demonstrate something else which works better. But we can. In the community we live a lifestyle which teaches us the harmony and balance between individuals and groups. We become more and more aware that other people's interests are, ultimately, our own. We are a laboratory where solutions fundamental to the problems of poverty and affluence are being explored.

* * *

Added together all these problems are pretty overwhelming. Humanity just has to re-examine its motivating principles. For 27 years the Findhorn Community has been doing this by practising a different way of life. We continue to do so, expanding our community and seeking to share the resulting experience more and more widely. Thankfully, we are not alone in this task. Many other groups and individuals have reached similar conclusions and are following a comparable path. We are all interacting, generating and sharing energies which indicate the way to overcome the crisis that the whole of humanity faces.

Mere adjustment of external conditions won't solve the problems. The crisis of humanity is too severe for that alone to succeed. We need a reorientation of the motivation for living—from an external, materially directed, *extrinsic* search for fulfilment, where action results from the stimulation and satisfaction of material need, to an internal, spiritually oriented, *intrinsic* search for fulfilment. In the latter, action results from the discovery of love and wisdom *within*.

One day, the airbase down the road, our alter ego, will either be eliminated in an apocalyptic denouement, together with the rest of us, or it will be quietly dismantled, as a transformed consciousness on the planet becomes dominant. At the Findhorn Foundation we are exploring this transformation. If humanity succeeds it will reach a new stage of development, one in which war and the threat of war is made redundant, the environment is cherished, and people live sustainable and mutually-caring lives. After living in the Findhorn Community for six years, I am confident that the necessary transformation will take place.

18

In the next chapter we turn to a more philosophical discussion of the crumbling basis of materialism, and of the alternative that is being asked of us now, introducing the basic spiritual ideas of the Findhorn Community.

Pluscarden Abbey

Chapter 2
Materialism or Essence

"We're not talking about the same thing," he said. "For you the world is weird because if you're not bored with it you're at odds with it. For me the world is weird because it is stupendous, awesome, mysterious, unfathomable; my interest has been to convince you that you must assume responsibility for being here, in this marvellous world, in this marvellous desert, in this marvellous time. I wanted to convince you that you must learn to make every act count, since you are going to be here for only a short while, in fact, too short for witnessing all the marvels of it."
—Don Juan, from Carlos Castaneda's *Journey to Ixtlan*

Is the World of Our Senses Real?
Nowadays, most ordinary people learn that the world of our senses is the 'real' world. Growing up in this 'real' world gives rise to desires, and the attempt to fulfil them seems to give meaning to human existence. Advertising stimulates this view and commercialism provides for it. Finally, materialist philosophies which propose that the world of ordinary sensory perception is the only real one, legitimise it. However, the very scientific discoveries that underlie the technological civilisation of our time also indicate that the world of our senses is remarkably limited. Indeed, it is best described as a limiting framework which allows a measure of security in an incomprehensible universe, alternatively too vast or too tiny to understand at all. Scientists operate with frequencies of electromagnetic radiation which our senses cannot directly perceive. From them they gain a vastly expanded image of the universe. They use, for instance, radio waves, microwaves, infra-red rays, ultra-violet waves and X-rays. We all know that they exist and that they are used in our technology, but we cannot 'see' them. Each frequency gives a very different picture of the physical world than that of our senses. Which picture is true? If we saw with X-rays, people would appear as skeletons. If we saw with radio waves, they would not seem to exist at all. Our senses

provide us with an 'arena for action'—they do not tell us the truth.

As I sit here writing this, I *feel* still and relatively stable in my small caravan. Yet the Earth is spinning on its own axis at 1600 kph at the equator, and moving through space around the sun at 115,000 kph. The sun itself is whirling around the centre of our galaxy at some enormous speed, while the galaxy is moving away from other galaxies even faster. The scale of these movements, the enormous distances which they represent, make our human endeavours seem absolutely infinitesimal. Our senses eliminate almost everything, allowing us to exist comfortably and enabling us to give importance to the little things that surround us. In the great oceans of space we are never still, nor would our endeavours make any impact, even if we managed to destroy life on our planet. On a material level, human existence is actually insignificant. It is only our senses that enable us to build up a delusion to the contrary.

The alternative end of the spectrum investigated by scientists is equally demoralising for those of us reliant on our senses. Like everybody else, I have a sense of my own physical reality, of that of others and of the world I live in. But this, too, appears to be a delusion provided by my sense perception. As scientists use increasingly remarkable instruments to translate the actual structure of matter into understandable forms, my experience of physical reality seems more a phenomenon than a truth. We descend into the microscopic level of cell, then molecule, then atom. Compressed, the nuclei of the atoms of the human body would cover something like the head of a pin. What remains might be described as energised space. I am nothing more than a pinhead plus energy—poor ego! But techniques have been devised to enable us to 'look at', or infer, the inside of the atomic nucleus itself. And here things become very curious indeed. There is a lot more energised space, and lots of even more infinitesimal 'particles', which, the scientists tell us, may be conceived of 'as if' they were matter or 'as if' they were energy. Some of these particles or vibrations even appear to be travelling for short moments backwards in time, from the future to the past, while others are 'anti-matter', perhaps indicating the possibility of a parallel universe, 'in reverse'. Notice that I have to use inverted commas to try to translate this reality so that the mind, activated by normal sense impressions, can comprehend it. Materialist philosophers base themselves on the 'real world'. But this 'real world' is merely an epiphenomenon of the vibratory frequencies ('wavelengths'), on which my senses operate. It is actually the result of an extremely effective way of limiting what appears to be an endless nothingness, orchestrated by constantly changing energy, so that we can exist (relatively) comfortably.

Modern physics and astronomy inform us that we are certainly not what we think we are, and that our efforts are minute in the scale of things. The length of our individual lives is equally minute in the timescale of the universe, although the whole of our physical body, at cellular level, is renewed every eight years. Actually, if one really accepts the discoveries of modern science, even up to the present, answers to questions such as 'Who am I?' and 'Why am I?' which are based on our everyday sense impressions seem totally superficial. But the scientists, with all their answers, give us none of the answers. They only make *Homo sapiens* seem more and more insignificant, clinging to his little fantasy world. To understand modern scientific discovery itself demands a new level of consciousness, a new structure of intelligence. The world view of *Homo sapiens* is no longer adequate to live with the new awareness that our sense perceptions do not tell us the truth.

Science actually only increases the mystery. It contributes to the anxieties of living if, on top of everything else, we are aware of our utter minuteness in the scale of things, or of the non-material nature of the material. But there has always been another way of looking. It is time for those experiences which have been the property of the mystics and the 'rishis', the inward-turned wise people of the East, to become the property of us all. For the mystics understood the awesome vastness and minuteness of creation. They knew that everything that seems to be so real is not reality. They found the key that unlocks these secrets—and it is time for all of us to put it on our key ring.

By quietening outer activity, including that of the mind, they learned to 'listen' to what is to be 'heard' behind the ordinary sense experience which seems to define our world. *They discovered that all the incredible multiplicity of form is an emanation of Oneness. There is an ultimate vibration that underlies all others. It is present everywhere. This vibration consists of what we call LOVE—a love, however, that is unconditional and unattached.* No one can prove this to another person; there isn't a machine that can measure it. It has to be experienced. That happens as a result of trying to find what is real, as opposed to what is phenomenal, by seeking it in ourselves. The techniques for doing this are all the various forms of silent meditation and contemplation; of training in various kinds of movement and sound; of prayer and devotion; and of the cultivation of unconditional love in everyday life. During a Zen Buddhist meditation retreat in 1974, at one point my entire normal perceptual reality dissolved; there was no longer an 'I', only an experience of truth, and that truth was Love. The experience changed the whole direction of my life.

Some physicists have taken note of the writings of the mystics and the oriental sages, because they partly describe the sort of things the scientists investigate. However, the mystics go further. The method of internal enquiry is superior to that of science because it leads to the ultimate truth that Oneness, the Divine Essence, is present everywhere—omnipresent. The conscious attempt to unify with that reality gives life its meaning. Instead of allowing the outer world that we experience to define who we are, we may rather turn inward and discover who we *really* are. Then we can learn how to experience the outer world properly, and to relate to it blissfully. We can describe this as understanding the outer from the *inner*, instead of trying to understand the outer from the outer. A spiritual path requires that we learn to make the transition from a world we define by the outer experience of our senses, to one defined by the inner experience of reality. We can then express our discovery in the limited world of the senses. It gives that world a different significance, changing the motivation of our actions and ways of relating. Christ expressed it by calling on us to love our neighbour *as ourselves*.

In the Findhorn Community, we have all to some degree committed ourselves to this path. Occasionally on the way come powerful experiences of the truth that Love is the Essence behind form. In modern psychological jargon they are called peak experiences. However, it takes time and spiritual development to 'capture' them, to live consistently from the reality that they express. Time spent in inner space prepares one for the test: what rules in the 'outer' world of our perception—our limited, confusing sense impressions or the inner truth? Our challenges lie in the restricted world of the so-called physical; for to embody truth in this arena we have to be able to see through the delusion of reality that the sense-experienced world presents. The Indian teachers have called this delusion 'Maya', the belief that the limiting experience of sense perception is the truth, instead of a mask over the reality hidden in it.

Finding Reality Inside, and Expressing It in the Outer World
In the search for spirit, the meaning of life is twofold. Firstly, we are trying to discover who we really are—to experience the Divine within. Secondly, we are trying to express what we discover, through our actions in the perceived world. People who are adopting this twofold path as their purpose in life are transcending the stage *'Homo sapiens'*, and are the early representatives of a new human development—*'Homo divinus'*. The expanded consciousness of *'Homo divinus'* will enable us to resolve the problems of our current civilisation.

It is not necessary to accept this without question. In order to see whether it is true that the ultimate knowledge of Love lies within you, try adopting the same methods as those who have already discovered it. You will find that you get the same results. The Findhorn Community is an ongoing workshop in which this 'experiment' is being practised. That is why it came into existence.

In what way do these views differ from the arguments of established religion? All major religions have two aspects. The first propagates belief in the existence of God, and provides a basic moral code for right conduct—righteousness or dharma. This code operates, more or less modified, through social customs and laws. One response to the crises of our times has been to emphasise these outward functions, leading to the growth of fundamentalist movements in both Christianity and Islam. The second aspect is the mystical current, also present in all religions. The experience of the nature of the Divine is sought through contemplation, or through practices which turn one inward. What is discovered becomes the source of the morality of action. The more you know who you really are, the more your actions will be righteous, for you are expressing Love in the outer world of sense perception.

The world religions have not, up to now, succeeded in preventing any of the crises discussed in Chapter One. This is not because they are essentially wrong, but because they have become 'secularised'. They have emphasised the first aspect of their activity at the expense of the second. As a result, they have accommodated

25

themselves to materialism and its philosophy, rather than providing an alternative, rich way of life. Through this accommodation they have, at least in the West, been reduced in significance in comparison with previous centuries. The present, potentially terminal, crisis of our civilisation requires that the churches emphasise the discovery of God's presence within each of us as the basis of the good life, rather than the pursuit of the material with a belief in religion added as an ameliorative influence. We are happy that more and more people from the established churches are visiting the Findhorn Foundation to experience the effects that even only a week of working from 'the inside out' has on them.

As we change our orientation to life, so we experience a profound change in character and in the way we perceive the world. The older mystical philosophies strongly emphasised renunciation, often speaking of the extreme difficulty of the task of discovering inner truth. The state of 'enlightenment'—the experience of full embodiment of Divinity—has been confused with the process of spiritual transformation—how one goes about the change. To arrive at a place involves the journey there. Without the journey you cannot arrive. Consciously setting out upon the journey already changes things. Going in the inner direction gives meaning and purpose to life; the more one does it, the more meaning and purpose one finds!

At the beginning of the process of self-discovery, the world of the senses seems to be objective and separate—something to be defended against, or to be overcome. As the experience of inner oneness begins to take hold, this 'objective' world seems to become more flexible, as if it, too, is adjusting itself to the change of emphasis. Strange coincidences begin to occur; the so-called real world starts to relate itself to your new awareness like a sleeping being, slowly awakening. As you go inwards the energy frequencies from which you view things change. The outer world is no longer solid, but begins to dance with you, stimulating you, testing you, assisting you in your transformation. As the inner connection develops further, and awareness deepens, you begin to take the lead in your dance with the world—you gradually become the creator of what happens. A Self oriented towards the Divinity within becomes increasingly able to reshape outer reality. But this Self no longer has the same identity as when it began the transformation—it no longer wants the same things.

The process of reorientation towards inner awareness involves excitement, joy in living, growth in creativity, a relative release of material needs, increased ability to accept people as they are and a determination to resolve problems. At the Findhorn Community we do, to some degree, demonstrate all of these things, which is why so many people want to come to be with us. These changes develop the type of identity which humanity needs if we are to survive the present global crisis. This new lifestyle and the requirements for a new civilisation are in harmony.

The Teachings Received by Eileen Caddy

Eileen Caddy, who in 1962, with Peter Caddy and Dorothy Maclean, founded the community that later became the Findhorn Foundation, has long received messages from an Inner Source, or heard a Voice, as she sometimes says. This process and its significance are described in more detail later. Some of the messages have appeared in her various books, listed at the end of the chapter. They consistently emphasise that the source of wisdom is to be found *within the seeker:*

I was shown the earth infilled with great light. I saw that the light was coming up through the earth, infilling every thing and everyone. I felt a tremendous joy and upliftment at what I was being shown. I heard the words, I AM THAT I AM. I AM the alpha and omega and all life. Rejoice, My beloveds, for you are all part of the glorious wholeness, all part of that glorious oneness.

(Dawn of Change, p. 1)

Seek and find your direct link with Me. Retain that link no matter what is going on around you. For it is through that link that all things are possible.

(Foundations of Findhorn, p. 112)

Relax! Give yourself over completely to Me. There is much to be done but it can be done better in a less desperate hurry. Enjoy everything you do. Savour every action like a connoisseur. Be satisfied only with perfection.

Start this day with 'summit thinking'. Let your thoughts dwell on Me; feel yourself in My presence, walking with Me, talking with Me. Let the wonder of our Oneness sink into your consciousness. Stay in this raised state of consciousness. You can do this when you live fully in the moment, not giving a thought to past moments or future moments but just to this one moment in the Now ....

Your close relationship with Me is more important than anything else, for all stems from that relationship. The more time you spend with Me, the smoother will be the running of your everyday living. From that centre, where you will always find Me when you seek, the ripples go out in ever increasing power.

(*God Spoke to Me*, pp. 16, 18, 19)

Expand your consciousness and know that I am all there is. Then go on and on expanding it and see the all-inclusiveness of the I AM, and see clearly that you are the I AM of the I AM, that there is no place where I am not. Keep stretching, feel every atom in you ache with stretching, feel yourselves growing, breaking all bonds which have held you in bondage and have stifled your growth and expansion.

(*Footprints on the Path*, p. 96)

Similar guidance fills Eileen's work. When read as a whole, it is clear that through her is being presented not a new theology but a theology which emphasises the 'mystic' connection with Oneness as something available to each of us. This connection is the source of the qualities of a joy-filled life. There is also a strong sense of the inexorability of the process—it is an energy transformation whose time has come:

Step by step My plan is unfolding, and nothing and no one can hold it up. All your needs are being wonderfully met now; all your problems are being solved now; all My wonders are unfolding now. Now is the time. Live fully and gloriously in the ever-present glorious now, and behold Me in everything.

(*Dawn of Change*, p. 13)

This is an historic and momentous time in the progress of man. At this time the veil is being rent in two and that which has been hidden through the ages is now to be revealed. The secrets of the sages will no longer be secrets, for all shall know about them.

(*God Spoke to Me*, p. 81)

This is an exacting time for each of you, a time of deep changes within and without, a time of seeking and sorting, of moving into new realms and new dimensions. This period of transition is not easy. You can help by accepting change without resistance . . . . You will see the seemingly impossible become possible, black turned to purest white, evil intent changed in mid-

28

stream, man at last beginning to see the error of his ways . . . . He will become awakened at last to the things that really matter in life, the things of the Spirit.

(*God Spoke to Me*, p. 110)

Another major theme in Eileen's guidance is that God is Love, and that Love is the essential identity of each individual. It exists as reality behind all the moods we put on. Knowing that you are Love enables you to see the other as essentially Love, too:

My love is limitless. Nothing stops the flow of My love except the little self which is free to choose its own way. It turns its back on My love and demands its independence and so cuts itself off. When man chooses to go My way, to walk in My footsteps, the floodgates are released. Once again he can become aware of the wonder of My love.

(*God Spoke to Me*, p. 63)

Banish forever all these false teachings and false concepts of Me. I AM love. I AM within each one of you. I AM THAT I AM.

(*Dawn of Change*, p. 145)

If these messages had been given in isolation, they could perhaps be dismissed. But the teachings of the Indian Sathya Sai Baba, believed by many to be an avatar—an exemplary incarnation of God—are surprisingly similar. Furthermore, the remarkable spiritual book, *A Course in Miracles*, also channelled, has the same theme—as have many others that have appeared in the last ten years.

If we are open to seeing, it is clear that something important is happening. Humanity is being given a spiritual reorientation course, to enable us to rise to a new level of human interaction. The emphasis in all these teachings is not on the difficulty and unattainability of the goal, *but on the immediate benefit of setting out on the path*. Divine Grace is directly involved in our affairs, as it was when Jesus Christ was on earth. The 'second coming' is the availability to all, on a global basis, of the consciousness of Christ, rather than a new physical appearance of his body. By crucifying the ego of our materialistic desires, we can be resurrected into the Christ consciousness of the true meaning of life, and live in happiness and harmony together.

All Religions are Ways of Approaching One Truth

In today's world, the parochial belief that there is only one 'true' religion, whose job is to take over all the others, finally has to be abandoned. If God is the Indweller, the reality in us all, then how we seek to discover Him is a matter of cultural background, of personal choice. Our job is to find that means of Self-discovery that best leads us forward from our present starting point. That may lie in Christianity, Hinduism, Islam, Buddhism, Judaism, or some other path. It may be found outside the established practices of the major religions, which often place more emphasis on the promotion of a code of outer social morality than on discovering the basis of morality within. Equally, one may talk of the Indweller as 'God', 'Jehovah', 'Allah', the 'Atman', the 'Essence', the 'Oneness behind all diversity', or the 'Christ Consciousness'. What we find does not differ; the various names and forms in worship are labels and practices to help us.

We are being asked to adjust to a world situation in which, for survival's sake, we need to learn that culturally and spiritually we are like flowers in a garden, each with its own particular shape, colour and fragrance, each equally valid. We can no longer judge other cultures or religions as either better or worse than our own. At the Findhorn Foundation we have consciously chosen to be an international community. We accept the validity of each person's method of finding their path to the inner truth. Our success demonstrates that it can be done.

Ignorance is the Basis of Evil

The idea of God as the Essence, the Reality of all that is, omnipresent and omniscient, is a monistic one. There is only God, only the 'Atma' or Essence. Everything that seems otherwise is the result of the way it is viewed, not its reality. The notions of evil and sin and their accompanying feelings of guilt have led to a widespread sense of inadequacy and worthlessness, especially among some Christians. But ultimate Good is not a quality that can be defined by its relationship to that which is perceived as not-good, its negation. It is, simply, the truth, that which *is*. The opposite of that which is, is that which *is not*, i.e. non-existent. There is therefore only Good, and its discovery is the discovery of the truth. That which is not good, which is evil, is not something different from God—an alternative, inherently evil universal force—but behaviour without a knowledge of the truth. The devil does not lie outside us, hoofed and horned; he represents that in us which has not discovered the truth, and therefore does not act from truth, but from ignorance. The temptation of Christ, for instance, does not involve some nasty being approaching Him and offering Him the things of the world in place of those of the spirit. It lies in His own *inner* temptations to lose God-consciousness and take the material world for reality, desires which substitute the ephemeral for the real. Jesus did not succumb to these temptations, and today we also have to learn to resist them.

Having arrived at this understanding, 'wrong action' may be defined in three ways: Action in contradiction to the laws of society may, in the short term, seem to bring material benefits. Action in contradiction to divinely revealed laws, such as the Ten Commandments, is usually accompanied by guilt and inner conflict, but may also seem to bring material benefits. However, action in which the Real is confused with the unreal stems from loss of identity with God, the Indweller. Sai Baba uses a simile to help us to understand this third concept of wrong action. In the half- dark (ignorance or confusion) you may mistake a piece of rope for a snake. Then you act inappropriately (evil or fear). If you take a light (seek truth), you will see that it is not a snake but a rope, and be able to act appropriately (know who you really are). Since nothing else really exists, this loss of identity with God leads to a sense of meaninglessness, of inner despair.

As a result of the changes happening to humanity at this time the third experience of wrong action is becoming dominant. As it does so, we shall have to help one another regain consciousness of the truth we may have momentarily perceived but then turned away from, for the consequences of this type of wrong action are psychologically devastating. Many lost people turn to drugs to try to find a moment of truth amidst the meaninglessness they experience, and they destroy their lives in their desperation to recapture bliss.

The Embodied Self, the Soul Self and the Real Self
A view very widely held in the Findhorn Community is that of the separation of the identity of body and soul. When we talk of life we are referring to three aspects, as if they were on different 'frequencies': the individual life in the body; the 'life' of the soul,

using individual incarnations as a means of training in self-discovery; and the 'eternal life' that the soul is in the process of discovering—the universal, unchanging, timeless Essence, Divinity itself.

Once we understand that what we think of as matter results from the way that our sense organs limit our experience, the concept of a non-material soul, entering and re-entering the physical world, becomes much easier to understand. Indeed, the medieval Christian view of a soul existing in a body only once, and then being sent to heaven, hell or purgatory for eternity on the basis of that one life seems naive. The idea of reincarnation has been a keynote of the Hindu religion, and was current in very early Christianity. The path to self-discovery provides too much evidence of previous existence in human form for it to be denied out of hand.

Each individual personality is largely unaware of its earlier existences, but on the inward path there are opportunities for enhanced memory of such incarnations, which may be applied to releasing blockages in present life. Such recall has even been used as the basis of historical novels, and is available to all under deep hypnosis. As we experience these memories, we realise that we are not merely our current identity, but a soul in development, operating through many incarnations in the material frequencies of the sense organs and learning from the law of cause and effect (karma). The consequences of wrong actions that we perform out of ignorance return to us as lessons, giving us a chance to seek another way. At some time all of us have experienced lives lost in the illusion of immediate gratification or dominated by the energy of base passions. Those who have had a problem and resolved it are usually much more understanding of someone who is currently going through a similar difficulty. When we learn that we, as souls, are not merely saints but have also been sinners, we can operate on a higher level of compassion to assist those still living in confusion. In the Findhorn Community, no one is asked to believe in reincarnation in order to become a member or to visit us; we have few dogmas! But people are asked to search for the God within. As their awareness expands, they usually begin to experience something of their 'soul self' and its previous incarnations. There is no point, however, in dwelling overmuch on the past when the present is so exciting, or on the partial when the whole is available.

'Homo Divinus'

With the realisation that God is the Indweller, the True Self, omnipresent, His nature unconditional Love; that the purpose of life is the soul's conscious reunification with its truth; that the physical reality of this world is the stage on which the ongoing drama is set—life, as well as death and suffering, comes to be perceived as something very different than if we mistake the material world of our senses for reality. Death becomes the conclusion of a particular scene in the drama; birth the opening of one. Suffering is a result of taking the phenomenal world as real, and compassion is giving others assistance on their path to truth. Seen in this way, life is a wonderful, ever-changing adventure, and one can become filled with a boundless inner happiness and peace. Even people who have only partially reached this state find life more interesting and enjoyable, worry less, and care more about others —we find.

We may sum up this chapter by characterising two types of people. The first seek fulfilment in the external world, either through what they do, or through what or whom they possess. They experience themselves as limited and needy people, whose requirements have to be met in order for them to be happy. They are subject to unhappiness if they do not have what they think they need, or if something is taken away, or if their performance is criticised. Strength for them involves qualities of aggression or dominance. Their endeavours are directed towards controlling, or defending themselves from, the environment. If they are religious, they believe in an external God who regulates their conduct through a revealed moral code. Many do not find the satisfaction they seek in the external world, and may be frustrated and sometimes bitter. These are outer-directed people, individuals characteristic of the civilisation we are leaving behind.

The second type of people centre their lives on the discovery of divine inner truth. They see their needs as transient and the things they have as secondary; the experienced world reflects to them what they need to transform in themselves to find who they really are. As they discover new aspects of themselves, they are excited to share them. They find life fulfilling and exciting, but sometimes suffer from impatience, very conscious of the gap between their present state and where they hope to go. They find strength in calmness and clarity of vision. The things of the material world are a means, not an end, to them. Their religion is inward-directed and contemplative; they tend to seek transcendental states, and in their behaviour they attempt to communicate the experience of these states to others. These inner-directed people are developing the characteristics necessary for the new human civilisation which will have to replace our present one. We are working on the development of such individuals at the Findhorn Community. They will become more numerous and, eventually, dominant. They represent emerging *'Homo divinus'*.

Books by Eileen Caddy

Guidance
God Spoke to Me (1971), *Footprints on the Path* (1976), *Foundations of Findhorn* (1976), *The Spirit of Findhorn* (1977), *The Dawn of Change* (1979), *Opening Doors Within* (1987), *The Living Word* (new edition 1988). *The Spirit of Findhorn*, published by Fowler, is out of print. Others are published by Findhorn Press.

Autobiography
Flight into Freedom. Element Books (1988)

Findham Community
Meeting in the Universal Hall.

Chapter 3
The Need for
Personal Transformation

The child's foot still doesn't know it's a foot,
it wants to be a butterfly or apple.

Later, the stones, bits and pieces of glass,
streets, stairways
the packed earth of the road,
go on teaching the foot it can't fly
can't be round as a fruit on a branch.
The child's foot,
defeated, went down
in battle
a casualty
condemned to live in a shoe.

Little by little in the dark it began
to interpret the world after its fashion
never knowing its other foot, still enclosed
groping for life like a blind man.
                              —Pablo Neruda

Individual Frustration in a Materialist Society

A social value system in which success is defined in terms of ability to get to the top is built on an obvious paradox. There are only a certain number of positions of wealth, power and influence. No matter how clever, ambitious or able people are, they cannot all be political leaders or captains of industry. As the old saying goes, 'you can't put a quart into a pint pot', and the fact that most people won't reach the 'top' has nothing to do with their own individual abilities, but simply reflects the reality of social organisation itself. To accept an ideology based on such a contradiction is bound to create frustration. Some have a measure of success and consider themselves superior to others. Others bemoan their fate as less adequate human beings. Some try to opt out into an

37

escapist dream of drugs, or into an endless, meaningless observation of the activities of others—usually fantasy people—which television provides for them. Yet others try to satisfy their frustrated ambitions in non-legitimate ways, turning to the criminal world to seek fame and fortune.

In socialist societies the vision of 'true communism' has been unable to mobilise enough of the idealism needed for collective action, except during short periods when material frustrations with the old order have boiled over. A world of propagandistic make-believe has been created in which people have become cynical about everything. Now the leaders of the Soviet Union are calling for spiritual regeneration. Mikhail Gorbachov has compared his vision of socialism to a 'temple on a green hill'; meanwhile the entire façade of 'socialist' Eastern Europe has collapsed like a house of cards. Neither socialist nor capitalist materialism has provided real human satisfaction.

It cannot be said that even those who derive the greatest material benefit from our current social structures have found much fulfilment. A new car is a joy, but not forever. The pleasure of a second new car palls more rapidly. So it is with material wealth in general; the pleasures it provides are of diminishing value. Of course, it is pleasant not to have to worry about material needs. The unhappiness of the wealthy, however, provides a hunting ground for therapists. The dream of material wealth has been an effective stimulus, working on the most primitive levels of desire, but its realisation does not live up to its promise.

As the scale of modern society grows and it becomes increasingly transnational in scope, more and more people feel powerless and frustrated. Mass housing developments provide unbelievably unstimulating environments to live in. People may undergo bouts of mental or psychosomatic illness and withdraw, by opting out, or project their bitterness onto those nearby who seem different. Racism, religious and nationalist fanaticism, football violence and hooliganism are all symptomatic of a sense of disempowerment that, in appropriate circumstances, erupts into extremist political movements. Democratic choice is often confined to the occasional right to vote in increasingly huge constituencies for representatives who themselves are not necessarily close to any real decision-making. Modern therapeutic movements have developed many techniques for encouraging personal development, but all too often these methods are used in vain attempts to help people adjust to ways of living with fundamentally unsatisfying values.

It is unlikely that this kind of alienated lifestyle, reflecting an increasingly common crisis-ridden social situation, can be modified to provide human satisfaction. People can best begin to transcend such a state through the discovery and development of connection with the source of all, the Indweller, the divine reality underlying all forms and present in each of us. Then life becomes meaningful, empowerment develops and effective action can be taken within any social situation. Our job in the Findhorn Community is to explore this change. In this way we can assist people in their transition from a world view which has become inadequate to cope with the situation on the planet, to one which provides both individual satisfaction and the personal resources for the wider social changes our civilisation requires.

The following piece of channelling, which I received for a workshop group, expresses these ideas:

Dear Ones,
You are in the light, the light is in you. When you enter a dark room, you don't grope around trying, in the dark, to discover the dimensions of the room and what it contains. Of course, you turn on the light.

Life is a little like the dark room. You can spend a tremendous amount of time groping around in the dark, trying to find your way around it—stumbling over objects, getting knocks and bruises. Why not switch on the light, so you can see what the room is like, and what there is to do in it?

The light shines on you. The light is in you. At first, you may need to use the light switch, but you can learn to switch on the light in yourself. Then you shine. When you shine, other people who are fumbling around in the dark can find comfort in you. They can see their way more clearly. Some may realise that they, too, have their own inner light that they can switch on. So helping yourself in life by lighting up your light is a help to others as well.

To keep your light burning bright, you need to connect with the current. The current is also in you, but it connects you with the power station. In life, the power station is truly the whole of creation itself, buzzing with energy, humming with vibration. As you make the connections, so your light lights up. All the different lights are powered by the same current which flows in you, around you, above you and below you. The current underlies and gives meaning to all the lights. What would be the point of a light without any energy to make it glow?

A life without light is really a chancy affair. One moment your hand may feel something nice. The next, you knock yourself against a sharp object and get hurt. There may be lots of maps and ideas for getting around in the dark, but basically none of them are much use, because it is impossible to orient. Actually it is much easier to put the light on, but lots of you never bother to think about that. Some of you are even afraid of what you might see.

In fact, the room of life is a very wonderful one, a treasurehouse of beauty and variety. With the aid of the light in you, you can have a wonderful time in it. It is also a very big room. There are long walks to take, steep places to climb. But with the aid of the light you will see that it is worth taking the walks, worth making the efforts to climb, because the results are very beautiful indeed.

You are the Light of the world. The time has come when everyone is going to discover that they have a light in them, and to learn how to switch it on. When a light is to shine, of course the connections need to be made. Some workmen will come along who know how to connect things up, so that all the lights can work at once. You are a little bit like the workmen, preparing the place for lighting up time.

Now it is the Earth that is going to be the place where the lighting up takes place; so you are the workmen preparing the people of the Earth for the switch-on. Humanity has spent enough time experiencing what it is like to go blundering around in the dark; now the wiring up for the big switch-on is taking place. In order to see to be able to do the work, you first need to connect yourselves to the source of energy.

When the lights go on, a lot of people are going to be dazzled. They will try to find dark corners to hide in. But when the big switch-on occurs, everybody will have to get used to the light, and a lot of people will need help. This is also your role. You are not only fixing up the light, but you are going to help people get used to it, too. That is the after-sales service.

Do not be afraid, but do light up the light in yourselves and make it burn more strongly. I am with you, supporting you, blessing you. I run the power station, but I am also the light in you. In fact, I am the whole show. It pays to get closer and closer to Me. People call Me many names, and I am happy with all of them, if they want to find the light.

Have trust, confidence. Learn to see. Be Blessed.

Channelling, the ability to receive inner guidance, has been much mystified and romanticised but it is an easily learned technique, available with a little training to all who turn inwards for translating God's energy, always there, into communication. 'Speaking in tongues' was a common practice among the early Christian apostles, while the Koran and many other sacred texts are channelled works.

Changing 'Human Nature'

As we transform ourselves, learning to work from within, traditional external morality ceases to be a rule by which we ought to act, but becomes a guide as to whether our inward listening is effective. For as we start the process of working from 'the inside out', we immediately come up against all the old ways of thinking and behaving with which we have lived for years and which are very familiar to us. They can be described as the personality as we know it, or our everyday sense of self. It is the transformation of this everyday self into the Self within which provides the challenge of the new spirituality. This transformation needs to be dealt with delicately and lovingly, but it needs to be dealt with. Some seekers may undergo an overwhelming experience of what it means to be real, but even such glimpses, while intensely motivating, are usually brief. The task is still to embody the experience, to create an identity and a lifestyle that express it. For this we all need inner work, support and guidance. In the Findhorn Community we support each other and use all sorts of techniques, including therapy and self-development workshops, as well as those we have developed ourselves, to move us along this path. Our aim is not to adjust to the old, but to facilitate the discovery of the truth behind appearances, and to live from that.

One of the conditions of human development is that we must use survival strategies. We are born innocent and unconditionally loving, but helpless, without the ability either to look after ourselves or to communicate anything other than the most basic needs. The love that we receive in return, however, is by no means totally unconditional. It is mixed up with our parents' conception of how we ought to be. In turn the child's unconditional love is modified. The dialectic resulting from this interaction provides the dynamic of personality formation. Where the demands are too difficult for a child to accommodate, he or she may even be battered in frustration by a parent and die. A child who is expected never to cry, or to be nothing other than a sweet living doll, may develop a mutilated personality and emerge as an adult suffering from deep frustration and inner rage. But, extremes apart, each of us as a little child has had to evolve a strategy for coping with not-well-understood demands from the parental world.

Many of these strategies dating from the earliest pre-verbal levels become adopted unconsciously and structure the developing

41

identity. It is not merely, for instance, that we may feel unloved. Little children may, in their innocence, define non-love as love, and spend their lives seeking the rejection they experienced from their parents. It is for them the only real satisfaction, although as adults they are merely aware that their relationships 'go wrong'. Some, seeking to please, come to feel that they are real only when they do what others want. As they begin to try to discover who they really are, they may experience a deep angst, as if there is actually nothing to them at all.

As we progress from being babies to children, what we want —basic love and nutrition—becomes differentiated and defined in our developing consciousness: we want sweet foods, we cling to Mummy, and so on. We take into ourselves, through our parents and other significant figures, the ideas of satisfaction prevalent in our culture. They do not *seem* to belong to others; they are 'ours'—what we like or don't like, what gives us pleasure, what gives us pain. Much of our self-evaluation—our judgement of ourselves, our levels of self-confidence, aggressiveness, insecurity—is actually an introjection of other people's views, accepted before we had the ability to evaluate them. Adults may find comfort in the belief in God's forgiveness of us as sinners; we may use a strict moral code to hold all our deep frustrations and violent impulses in check; we may use our reason to try to provide explanations for why we behave as we do, and to ameliorate the judgements that crowd in on us; but we are all reacting against an essentially *imported* concept of self which we have unconsciously adopted as our own. So we get by, adapting with more or less success to the immense changes going on around us, living a life of pleasure and pain, satisfaction and frustration as our survival patterns are constantly activated and re-activated.

There is, however, a deep yearning built into our identity—the psychologists tend to call it a 'curiosity drive'—which lies at the root of all the strategies described above. Such yearning can underlie, for example, compulsive acquisitive behaviour, though it is never satisfied by it. I want: women, men, cars, a yacht, everything to be in order, freedom, pleasure, excitement, to be noticed, and so on. The 'I want' is their root. It underlies them all. In fact, what I want is to know who I am. Finally, nothing else will do. Either I die frustrated and the search goes on; or fulfilled, merged with the divine source. Eileen's inner voice says:

42

As you raise your consciousness and realise your Oneness with Me, there is no duality. Love flows through you in ever-increasing power, and you see only the perfect and good in all. How necessary it is for you to do this. Really understand that mankind is made in My image and is therefore perfect. If I am your Father, I am the Father, Mother, God of all mankind. Accept this realisation.

(*God Spoke to Me*, p. 77)

To acknowledge this deep yearning, a personal shift in identity from the sense of ourselves which we learned in our psychological process of development, towards our Essence—who we really are —is necessary. It is the reason why the Findhorn Community is here, and why it is so successful. For anybody can make such a change, whether they be rich or poor, intellectual or practical, complicated or simple, believer or agnostic; whatever their nationality or religion. And, as they change, the great 'I want', father of all the other 'I wants', begins to be satisfied, and life becomes exciting, fulfilling. As the change is made, the problems of alienation and disempowerment diminish. We become calmer, stronger, clearer. We begin to release our frustrations, we grow less needy, less compulsive. A calmer, more loving, aware and considerate identity begins to emerge. It is a simple and effective process.

This process is the social 'paradigm shift' that humanity has to make to overcome the problems which beset us. Furthermore, it is not only the successful completion of this task which is fulfilling. The attempt to change, itself, provides a full agenda for life. Far from attempting to escape from a dispiriting reality, we engage with life because it is so interesting. There is so much to be done; doing it is so exciting!

In the Findhorn Community we live without major stress in a beautiful environment but we are very busy people. The days are always too short. Developing a relationship with the Real involves a new relationship with all that we have known, seeing it with new eyes, ones that become increasingly more loving and compassionate, and less judgemental. On our journey to the Self, we are assisted by two kinds of techniques. The first kind relate to inner development, and many of them are meditative in quality. "*Be still,*" said the Voice to Eileen, "and know that I am God." Such techniques, which can be adapted for simple group work, take us on the journey inwards, to our 'higher' self. Contrary to common belief, they are not difficult or demanding, and do not have to be undertaken for hours at a time. Their purpose is the discovery of Love within. To go deeper into meditation techniques is a personal decision which may be made as one becomes aware of the benefits they bring. If it is undertaken as a result of other people's opinions there will be an inner conflict which reflects itself when one becomes still. Inner discipline develops as a means, not as an end in itself, but it does require application. In this it is no different from the discipline required to acquire a skill. You cannot be a musician, a doctor or a carpenter without training. Why should the ultimate skill require none?

The second set of techniques is for when we get stuck; for when we are afraid to let go of the old. They make use of the various therapeutic practices. At the Findhorn Community we are happy to use anything that works, and there are usually plenty of qualified practitioners available. But the use of these techniques is also a means, not an end in itself. The community is not a therapy centre, and therapy is not the solution to the human predicament. Our aim is to release what blocks us from becoming Self-identified rather than selfish as quickly and as economically as possible. We are concerned not with contemplating our navels, but with finding the Love that lives in us, and with freeing ourselves to embody it in ever-increasing quantity. The challenge is to *practise* it. To pretend to be loving when one does not feel it is the utmost hypocrisy. When we find that we are not feeling loving, it is sensible to investigate what is blocking the love, and to use an appropriate technique to release the block. In this way, the psychological structure of the identity can be reformed, step by step.

Reason as Servant, not Master
Another aspect of the process of restructuring the identity to come 'from the inside out' involves reconsidering our attitude to reason. Reason is the mechanism by which we learn to give order to the incomprehensibility of the world. It is the basic working tool for the understanding of phenomenal experience. By learning to predict what will happen when we act, we acquire some measure of control over our environment. But reason soon becomes a tyrant instead of a servant. For, as well as enabling us to have some control over the world, our developing reason limits what 'can' happen in terms of the perceptions it organises. "What is not seen

can't be real," it says. "What we know with our senses is the only truth." We have already challenged the objectivity of the view of the world that our senses give us. And we have talked of guidance, channelling, 'going within' to discover Reality. None of these are available if we adhere strictly to a definition of the world propounded by reason. Neither Eileen's guidance, nor the founding of the Findhorn Foundation, nor indeed Sai Baba's or Jesus Christ's miracles are easily explained by reason.

To find who we are, we have to learn to put our critical faculty on hold, for it is too dependent on inadequate definitions of what is real. Many people are rather fearful of this. Reason, for them, seems to keep their unresolved unconscious desires at bay and guards against possible craziness. We are not trying to deny our existence in the phenomenal world. But, rather than being the determinant of truth, that world provides the framework in which incarnated beings operate. As such, it is an excellent 'reality check'. The behaviour of deluded people will spread not love and wisdom but unhappiness for themselves and others. Such people have not found the frequency of truth, but have lost themselves in another level of illusion.

Reason has its place, not to limit reality, but as a checking mechanism which enables a relationship to be made between claims and results. Divine Grace as well as intuitive modes of seeking knowledge operate through the physically-experienced world, where the consequences of their application can be checked. But without grace and intuition, the door to self-discovery is locked.

In my earlier life, I adopted a very rationalistic social science perspective to provide security against my chaotic emotional life. Much later, as I learned clairvoyant reading, I was deeply sceptical of the possibility of my receiving information concerning others about whom I knew nothing, simply by closing my eyes and, after meditating, just allowing myself to speak. Yet again and again I found myself saying things about people which I could not have known. My poor rational self had to admit that its definitions were inadequate. Gradually, as I prepared myself well, working only from the 'highest', constantly invoking divine truth, I began to trust my intuition. I have found I can often by-pass long sessions of psychological diagnosis by directly intuiting the basic problem which blocks people who come to me for help.

The innumerable 'coincidences' which happen at the Findhorn

Community also quickly undermine the overweening rule of reason. One, or even two, coincidences can be accepted as such, but when they come in a stream, we must, if we are 'reasonable', begin to allow for the possibility that 'reality' is much more flexible than our reason can envisage.

A small model illustrates this way of describing human identity. Our perceived self—who we think we are—is in centre position. Below it are our unconscious wishes, or impulses, which we may uncover with therapeutic techniques. On the left side is our past, not that of our current life, but an immense area of experience in other lives. It may occasionally be useful to become aware of this through past-life regression techniques. On the right is our future. Time is the best agent for discovering this aspect of ourselves, though we may get some indication as to general trends and problems from astrologers and clairvoyants. Above is our Higher Self—and above that the Divine Self. By contacting the Higher Self we can understand the world of our perceptions, and look at our problems in a new way. Moving in this 'upward' direction constitutes the spiritual path. None of the areas that lie outside the self-experienced personality, the ego-self, are immediately apparent, but they are very real. Sai Baba says, "You are three people: the one you think you are, the one others think you are, and the one you really are." The search for the latter identity gives humanity its true raison d'être. We will just have to get down to it, in order to cope with the monstrous problems of our materialist, externally directed civilisation.

DIVINE SELF
(Who I really am)
▲
HIGHER SELF
(Getting there!)
▲

┌ ─ ─ ─ ─ ─ ─ ─ ─ ─ ─ (Spiritual development techniques)

PAST EXPERIENCE   PERSONALITY   FUTURE
(May need releasing)   (My current sense of my-   (May make me anxious)
(Regression work) ──   self—who I think I am)   ──────── (Time)
└ ─ ─ ─ ─ ─ ─ ─ ─ ─ (Therapy techniques)

UNCONSCIOUS
(Keeps tripping me up)

The Energy of Transformation

If we look at a candle burning in a darkened room, we can see its flame. But the candle also lights the room. If we look at a computer screen, we can see what is written there. But the computer screen also gives out energy (the 'tempest' effect) and it can be read at a distance with the appropriate equipment. Firms are now worrying that people will be able to steal their secrets that way! In both cases, an energy is being given out. In the first case we can see the flame; we also see by the light emitted. In the second case we can see what's on the screen, but not the emitted energy. When we have an X-ray, we cannot see anything, but the energy may have an effect on us.

By extension, it is not too difficult to imagine that everything we are and do gives off energy. When someone is angry, for instance, our senses observe the way they behave, and from that we infer that they are angry. We cannot see the energy they give off, but we may feel uncomfortable and want to keep out of the way; or our own angry feelings may be triggered and we respond in kind. Sometimes we may feel angry for no apparent reason. We may be being triggered by the energy of the anger of someone else, whom we can't see. Psychologists have spent much effort in trying to prove that these effects are solely the results of observable stimuli. It is a bit like saying that there isn't anything but the flame of the candle—that it doesn't give off any light. Of course, we can see by the light, so we can't deny that an energy is radiated which affects us. But because we can't see the energy of an angry person, it doesn't mean that it isn't there, nor that it doesn't affect us.

If there is a nuclear accident, such as that at Chernobyl, we do not at the time see or feel anything, but irradiated particles from material released are carried by the wind and their energy is received by our bodies. In a shorter or longer time, depending on the dose, physical effects will result: depression, sickness, hair loss, long-term cancer. We cannot usually feel the energies that human beings give out, but they also have effects on us, for good or ill. As soon as we grasp this, we can move beyond two delusions. The first delusion is that what we do involves merely the physical acts that we perform, the words that we utter, the expressions we put on. Actually, whatever we do gives off energy vibrations, which are picked up by others and affect them, quite apart from our ordinary means of communication.

47

In the second delusion we think that what is not expressed is not communicated. But thoughts, feelings and states of being also give off energies. They are received by others in just the same way as radioactivity although, as with radioactivity, we have not developed sense receptors that allow us to be immediately aware of them. Spiritual teachers have constantly advised us to keep good company and to 'clean up' our mental state, because they know that negative energies *are* received and *do* have an effect. If our life strategies have left us with unresolved inner conflicts, that energy will slowly undermine our physical and mental health. It will also tend to make others uncomfortable around us, or perhaps draw to us those who have similar problems, or who are searching for people to heal. A materialistically oriented civilisation generates many people with such conflicts. They are inwardly frustrated individuals who are radiating that energy outwards.

A group of unhappy people radiates a more powerful energy of unhappiness than an unhappy individual. A group of angry people does the same, and a group of loving people likewise. Human energy waves spread themselves out from their source, just as light spreads from a candle flame. A group of people who are living in the attempt to discover and express inner truth will give off a different energy than that of a group of people who are striving to fulfil themselves by acquiring possessions. The energies radiated by a group of fundamentally happy people may be attractive to a group of unhappy ones, although they may never actually meet. But the energies given off by people who are pretending to be fulfilled when they are not, communicate something different than their observed behaviour indicates.

All this is rather important in understanding the working of the major transformation of which our community is a part. We can describe what has been done physically here, who has come and gone, how people live together, and how endless groups of people who come experience a change of consciousness. But all these interactions involve small numbers in comparison with, say, a football crowd. The real significance of the Findhorn Community is in the energies it generates, and in the energies that those who visit us generate. Fulfilled people have an influence on unfulfilled people, even if the latter do not visit us or meet someone who has. Such people will not know anything about the community, but gradually a feeling that there is something better, that there is

48

another way, that there is hope, surfaces. People are drawn inwards; ideas suddenly become current that were previously 'cultist'—such as that for life to become meaningful the divine is to be sought within.

A candle light may be too dim for us to see by; an arc light may be so bright that it dazzles us. To be able to see well and comfortably, we need a light of just the right brightness. Some people have eyes that can stand strong light; other people's eyes are weak, so they need a gentler light. In a similar way, the quality of energy given off by people like Jesus Christ or Sai Baba may be too powerful for many people. The reaction can be, "They are wonderful, but they are not like me. *I* couldn't be like that." The energies given off by a group of people like the Findhorn Community are not so powerful; they come from fulfilled people, but not perfect ones. The effect is like a soft, pleasant light. We have to make sure that our energy emanations are not too weak for people to feel them, nor too strong for people to relate personally to them.

The Findhorn Community generates energy at a particular vibrational frequency. We work in conjunction with other centres and individuals, some of which are 'brighter' than us, others less bright. We are drawn towards the brighter ones, and the others are drawn towards us. In this way we are part of a network of energy transformation on the planet which is spreading wider and wider and steadily increasing in power. Using the symbolism of light, which is common to all religions, we call it a 'Network of Light'.

We are certain that the community is not an ordinary place in which our personal energies alone are generating a transformative urge. There is an energy source here which amplifies the energy we generate so that we resemble a transmitter. One proof of this is demonstrated by the way the community came into being. We often call this source the 'Angel of Findhorn', and it is one of a number of special energy sources which appear to be operating for the transformation of the planet. We discuss this whole idea further in the next chapter. The energy present in the community tends to stimulate us to change ourselves, so that many of us are often challenged here. We like this and we have chosen it. We tend to attract people for whom our energy level is 'right', but the community as a whole is also in change so that the energy working through us is getting steadily stronger.

We believe that the development of a new humanity will not

come about by the slow multiplication of people seeking a new lifestyle. There is a threshold level, above which new consciousness will simply 'be there' for everyone. A significant event happened in a Japanese zoological research experiment. In the experiment, undertaken in various separate centres at the same time, if a monkey could solve a problem, it received a better food supply. The researchers found that at first one monkey, then a few, in an area learned to solve the problem. Suddenly all the monkeys in all the areas could solve the problem, without any direct teaching. The energy of transformation in relation to this problem had reached a 'critical mass'. At a certain point the solution was simply available to all monkeys. This result is, hopefully, an indicator of the means of human transformation on our planet. Suddenly when enough people have 'found the way', everybody will 'know' that the meaning of life is to be found in the search for the Divine within. It will become the new orthodoxy! Humanity will be able to solve its problems and live with a degree of mutual love, harmony and acceptance, caring for the planet as a whole. Of course, we hope that this happens before humanity destroys itself under the pressure of the problems that its disoriented civilisation has created.

In the Findhorn Community we tend to have faith that there is indeed time to reach the positive critical mass. This is because of our awareness that it is not 'just us'. Divine grace is stimulating the change. We, among many others, are playing our part in reaching the transformation point through our personal transformation and by learning to support the energy that is available to our community to flow out through us to the world. It is a very dramatic and remarkable time to be alive.

New Community Housing

Chapter 4
A Spiritual Symbol
for Western Humanity

Behind all words there is silence—
Behind all action there is stillness—
Behind all creativity there is peace—
In these things we find the Beloved
And know His creative presence.
In the rhythm of this day
Let us find silence in the midst of speech.
Stillness in the midst of action
And peace in the midst of creativity.
                              —David Spangler

The Findhorn Community: An Accessible Model for Change
Exciting times! Humanity loses its way, a divine corrective energy
is applied, and a qualitative change in human behaviour begins to
take place.

To express divinity perfectly in daily life is no easy task but, as
we begin to try, we can make dramatic changes in the quality of
our lives, our happiness and our comprehension of individual and
world events. We become involved in a reorientation of our lives
which has immediate, concrete results. This is important because
many spiritual books imply that such changes cannot take place
without self-sacrifice, harsh discipline, travail and total renunciation. Perhaps the efforts of earlier spiritual seekers have opened a
door for us, through which with God's grace we can now pass
much more easily.

In the last 27 years, we at the Findhorn Community have developed an approach to spirituality which requires no more effort
than that needed for learning any complex skill. Yet this approach
is effective in developing a level of human consciousness that
could bring us through humanity's present crises to a higher stage
of human interaction. It could enable us to live in relative harmony with one another and in a much more positive connection

with the physical world around us. Such a transformation is available to all, *now*. It can give people a feeling of purpose and direction in their lives which, on a world scale, could do away with racial, social, religious and nationalist intolerance, and with gross economic exploitation. It creates awareness of common humanity, and leads to more fulfilled and happier lives for everyone. A big return for a relatively modest investment!

The sceptic may be hesitant. Is this not just hype, idealistic theorising, a self-delusion born of naiveté? How do we know that such things are possible? At one moment we proclaim dramatic changes in human identity and at the next talk of easy transitions!

The Findhorn Community is not an ideal, a vision, a high-sounding theory, or even a blueprint for transformation. We do not pretend to have a recipe for instant perfection, nor are we a community of recluses, living in retreat from the day-to-day world. We are an ongoing, practical working *example* of how a transformation can occur in relatively ordinary individuals within a short period of time. This transformation involves a lifestyle whose positive results can be assessed and measured by any social scientist or, more importantly, by any interested inhabitant of the planet. Furthermore, our origins and background are a clear and convincing demonstration of Divine intent—that something is being created here for a special purpose. One of the most widely read books about the Findhorn Community is called *The Magic of Findhorn*. Its journalistic style tends to emphasise the more extraordinary aspects of early community life, and the special characters who were initially drawn here, and this has created something of a reaction to the book among members. But there *is* a 'magic' in the community, a divine magic. It constantly stimulates us to perform the task for which we have been attracted here.

For the Findhorn Community was not founded as the result of a rational discussion among rational people about creating a new group of rational human beings. Our civilisation exalts rationality as the answer to world problems, but it is the 'age of reason' that has brought us to today's state of crisis. As bread needs the leaven of yeast, so, for positive change, rationality needs the leaven of intuitional inspiration. Perhaps there is a plan in place, of which our rational selves have no knowledge, a plan that is not, in a normal sense, human in origin and which has its own sense of timing.

Eileen Caddy heard an inner voice. Over a period of years, she

54

became used to the voice. Nothing happened in a hurry. Her auto-biography, *Flight into Freedom*, gives the distinct impression that a plan slowly unfolded. Guidance was given to *prepare* for events that later came to pass. The Caddy family found themselves, as predicted, apparently rejected, in a tiny caravan facing a rubbish dump in an uninspiring sandy caravan park in north-east Scotland. The voice began to provide instruction after instruction as to how to proceed. Because Peter Caddy followed the instructions and those heard by Dorothy Maclean, who learned to communicate with plants, the new garden started to produce enormous vegetables. This attracted international attention to the emerging community.

Even then things were not hurried. Only after David Spangler's arrival in 1970, and partly through his channelled writing, did the worldwide significance of the Findhorn Community become apparent to those outside esoteric circles. Spangler's inner teachers related the meaning of the developing community to the solution of world problems, and his impetus supported expansion. We began to redirect our main focus away from the relationship with the energy forces of nature towards spiritual education, the transformation of human beings. Often, at the beginning, the humans involved in these changes were uncertain of their direction. Eileen's guidance gave them the direction and understanding to help them to go forward. The story of the early days of the community is as exciting and inspiring as that of any of the romantic exploratory voyages in the physical world that have entranced generations of young people. We remain convinced that inner attunement through meditation, in conjunction with the signs the world is giving us, is a better means of making decisions than the application of reason alone. How this works today is described in the second part of this book.

As I was taking a guest around the Foundation recently, she exclaimed, "What luxury!" Yet there is no financial luxury here. We exist with very modest means, and there are many of us with visions which 'just a little more money' could bring into reality. Instead, we are held on a very tight financial rein. I am convinced that this is a question of responsibility and relevance. *We are being asked to demonstrate a lifestyle sustainable on a world scale.* My friend did not notice that the lounge carpet in Cluny Hill College, where she made the comment, was threadbare. She was actually responding to the love and care with which we maintain what we have, and to the energy which radiates from the building. Like so many people brought up with a materialistic *weltanschauung* she confused well-being, which we have, with the material luxury we don't have.

One of the great contributions a group of people can make to our society at the present time is to divorce the idea of happiness from that of material wealth. This is not done by pious theorising about the 'sanctity of poverty', but by demonstrating a way of living which, while not renouncing material things, is not dependent on them. Even though objects may not be new and expensive, if they are loved and cared for, they shine out those qualities for others to enjoy. We have no enthusiasm to retain things which are too old to be effective, but it is surprising how much more service a loved and cared-for machine will give than one that is not. The material achievements of the community, while modest, give an impression that is quite out of proportion to their scale and cost.

Turning within, as we see it, demands some kind of spiritual practice. To find it is the first hurdle to overcome as one seeks to change the 'frequency' of life. A few people who become members have maintained a strict discipline of meditation over several years, and it is surprising how such people tend to give up these habits once they live in the Findhorn Foundation—at least for a time. Our emphasis is on inner discipline, not one imposed from outside, even when one's own conscience is the imposer. Conscience may merely be the internalised voice of external authority. A sense of duty may help us through a difficult patch in our transformation, but if it remains the basis of our spirituality, our identity is still outer-directed. Truth is self-effulgent; it transcends conscience.

Others come seeking to turn inwards; but someone who has been prepared to spend hours mending a car or absently watching a television screen may find it a challenge to learn to spend even half an hour a day being still. Yet, relatively, attaining inward quiet requires such a small effort. Initially, a personal spiritual practice might not even involve much quiet meditation. It could centre on a movement discipline, like T'ai Chi, or even regular conscious appreciation of nature. We do encourage everyone to develop some practice which helps them to be inwardly still.

The nurturing and expression of love is another, very important kind of spiritual practice. When this involves people to whom we are attracted, it seems easy, but such love is very conditional. At the Findhorn Foundation, people are constantly coming and going. A loving feeling no sooner develops than the person towards whom it is directed leaves. Gradually, one learns to love in a less conditional way. Ultimately, everything centres around learning to love, for unconditional love expresses our Divine nature.

At the same time as encouraging individual spiritual practice, the community has developed its own small rituals of silence and inner connection. These, though imposing no heavy burden on the participants, both remind and enable us to change focus from 'normal'—outward directed—life. Attendance at the twice-daily collective meditations is encouraged but not obligatory. The members of each work department meditate together weekly, and community meetings always include a meditation. Work periods begin with a moment of silent awareness, in which hands are held in a circle. Many members bless the commencement and completion of special tasks with a meditation. These small rituals provide the basis of a life in the initial process of turning inwards, and require very small amounts of determination and perseverance. The immediate results of calmness and increased group harmony they bring give a stimulus to go further. They support—but do not force—inner development.

As we experience the divine in ourselves, we become aware that it exists in everyone else too. God is omnipresent. We realise that in order to express love, we must remove the barriers to doing so. We begin to see that those who do not express love are merely stuck behind barriers they themselves have erected for protection. We can regard them with more understanding and support them in finding the confidence they need to take the barriers down. Each person has to work at his or her own pace, for people who are under pressure usually feel threatened and tend to close up.

In this great spiritual adventure judgement is slowly replaced by comprehension. Judgement breeds punitiveness and gossip, as destructive of self-development as it is of the development of others. Comprehension, on the other hand, stimulates mutual support in change and transformation. Further, we gradually come to recognise that Divinity is as much the essence of the material world as of the human one. In the Findhorn Community we

57

symbolise this by giving names to the tools and machines with which we work.

All these practices are aspects of 'positive thinking'. Our positive thinking includes seeking to be aware of the reality underlying the apparent. It does not mean trying to run away from or deny that which is difficult, tedious or challenging. To try to pretend that things are good when they are difficult is merely a symptom of being controlled by fear.

The Findhorn Foundation lifestyle is not retreatist. We consistently aim to present the 'good news' of our Self-discovery and to maintain it in our daily practice as a working community. We are exploring a new, positive meaning in work—not only in what is done, but in how it is done and the way it is shared with others. We express this by the phrase 'Work is love in action!' To begin to experience work in this way is often very revealing for our guests, who discover that they can find satisfaction in tasks they previously regarded as menial and mundane. As currently dominant social desires to maximise material gain and output are superseded and people become used to working in an economy of sufficiency, our perspective on work, which includes discussion and mutual sharing, decentralisation and democratisation of authority, could gradually transform working life. Changed attitudes to work are not a means by which greedy employers can extract more output from individuals. The new approach we foster in our daily life at the Findhorn Community is part of a transformation of working situations and values. We seek to move in the direction of a world characterised by caring and mutual respect.

Cultural and Religious Integration
From its outset, the Findhorn Community has been an international one. Dorothy Maclean, a Canadian, shared the earliest years with Peter and Eileen, who were English, and with Lena who was Scottish. At present the community contains people from many countries and cultures but, up to now, almost exclusively from wealthy 'Western' societies—the heartland of materialistic civilisation. The challenge and stimulation of other cultures helps to expand our limited assumptions about reality. To our guests we demonstrate in practice that cultural difference can be transcended in everyday living. This shows how the world unification process that communications technology has created can be experienced

positively.

Our particular function in a worldwide movement of change is to work with people from the 'exporter' nations of materialism —those nations whose cultures emphasise material possession as the most desirable human value—rather than with people from the 'importer' nations—those whose spiritual heritage has been undermined by such values. This 'Westernness' has been a challenge for many of us. We are aware of the plight of the poor of the world, and of the dedicated and self-sacrificing efforts made by both religious and secular organisations to alleviate poverty and starvation. We have had to examine our consciences deeply to enable us to justify working with relatively wealthy people in a task of personal spiritual transformation, when there is so much material deprivation to be found. But we have had to come to the conclusion not only that every human being is inherently divine and worthy of transformation, but also that the real root of the problem of poverty lies in the destruction of a spiritual core to life in the so-called 'advanced industrial societies' themselves.

My visits to India have convinced me that spiritual richness and material richness represent alternative world value systems. While the 'advanced' societies may be the centre of material wealth, they are the backward nations of spiritual wealth. Many cultures are spiritually much richer than ours. From this perspective, the Findhorn Foundation's work could be described as missionary work. Without such efforts our societies will continue to export cultural destruction—and very possibly extinction itself—to the rest of humanity.

With the proper use of resources, the elimination of the grosser extremes of poverty in the world is no impossible task. In the end it is more crucial to transform the value systems of our societies, societies that have lost much of the vitality of their spiritual traditions. This is the social meaning and purpose of the Findhorn Community. It is a significant irony that spiritual teachers from the cultures that have been colonised, and sometimes almost extinguished, by our own—the Native Americans, the aboriginal peoples of Australia and, above all, the great Masters of India—have become the source of inspiration for an ever-increasing number of people in the 'rich' world, including many members of our community. In my view the export of spiritual wealth is a healthier trade than that of material wealth.

Another tenet of the Findhorn Foundation's existence is the acceptance of religious diversity. It must be abundantly clear that the practice of the great fundamental teaching of all religions —'God is Love', 'Love thy neighbour as thyself'—is not limited to believers in one religion alone, nor even to those who profess an organised religion at all. Feuding and rejection because of religious belief still remain prevalent all over the globe. *Once the meaning of the divine as the Indweller in all humanity has been discovered, it is inconceivable to believe that divine truth has been revealed in only one religion or creed.* When Jesus says, "I am the Way, the Truth and the Life," and, "Only through me shall you reach the Kingdom of Heaven," he is certainly talking about the *essence* of his teaching, which we in the Findhorn Community call the Christ Consciousness, rather than the particular form that the Christian church has made of it. We are sure that the 'Christ Consciousness' may be as present—or absent—in Hinduism, Buddhism, Islam, Judaism or even Humanism as in Christianity. Sai Baba affirms:

> *There is only one God—He is present everywhere! There is only one race—the race of mankind! There is only one religion—the religion of Love! There is only one language—the language of the heart!*

Our chosen religion is our personal way to help us towards that Essence underlying all different forms: our own true nature.

At the Findhorn Foundation we welcome people of any religious faith or none who are searching consciously for the love that is their inner truth. We are open to insights from all religious practices which promote this inner discovery. We have members professing Buddhism, Hinduism, Sufism, those who find inspiration from Native American spirituality, or from esoteric teachings of the so-called 'Western mystery school', as well as Christians. We find we can get along together, learn from each other, and benefit from the spiritual diversity. I came to the Findhorn Foundation as a humanist, became a devotee of Sai Baba, and through his teachings learned to appreciate the meaning of Christian tradition and ritual. This mutual recognition is not a weakening of faith, but a strengthening of it, for we are now citizens of one world. The wealth of each tradition becomes our own heritage as we learn that the essential truth of each religion is the same. Religious forms are like clothes, put on for an individual's personal comfort.

Bigots may cavil at this, but the experience of our community shows that where love is, all religious beliefs flourish.

The Generation of Hope
Reading the long catalogue of dangers that threaten humanity, it is easy to become despondent, even despairing. Many people share such feelings but suppress them with escapist and nihilistic lifestyles. By living superficially, they try to bypass an increasingly pessimistic underlying awareness which feeds their insecurity and anxieties. Sometimes even to bring these feelings to the surface generates great emotional distress, as we at the Foundation have discovered in workshops on ecology held here.

The experience of living in the Findhorn Community transforms this anxiety into hope and anticipation for the future. The discovery that the divine meaning of life is personally available to the seeker is empowering. An awareness grows that all is not moving in a negative direction—the tide can be turned and is being turned. Each person may be part of this force for change, a force of love that conquers without exercising any violence. By living and learning in this community, we generate hope and excitement, without losing sight of the disasters our civilisation creates. Even if we wanted to avoid awareness of the problems that beset our planet, the noise from the military airbase nearby constantly reminds us. It is no accident that the Findhorn Foundation is in such close proximity to the base.

Through our guest programmes this hope for change spreads to those who visit us. It is not an energy of protest or negation. Though we do not condemn people who take the path of protest, we do feel that it tends to entrench reaction, as tends to happen when two energies oppose each other. Little changes, except perhaps in situations which are anyway exceptionally volatile. There is a difference between demonstrating the existence of a problem to those who are not already aware of it—perhaps choosing dramatic means—and actually solving that problem. Often protest groups have confused the two and after a while their members become disillusioned and cynical, always in opposition to forces which appear overwhelmingly powerful. Ultimately, it is not what we strive against that counts, but what we strive for. We in the Findhorn Community seek to demonstrate another method, a practical and meaningful one that can be incorporated into the life of any individual—inner transformation. Our hopefulness expresses 27 years' experience in the practice of personal spiritual development.

As we become integrated as members into the Findhorn Foundation, we tend to take for granted what we do and achieve. Members often emphasise the long way each of us has to go towards the perfection we seek. The impact that our lifestyle has on our guests is a corrective to this feeling. The guests' excitement at what has been created here is a reminder of our purpose and of our success. In turn, we provide our visitors with a situation which supports and stimulates their own path of inner discovery.

An Ongoing Workshop

The Findhorn Foundation has often been compared to an ongoing workshop, a laboratory for spiritual change. This is partly because people constantly come and go. Guests stay here from a week to several months. Student members stay for 18 months and staff members may live here for several years. There are always new faces, always people starting out as guests or as members. Each newcomer experiences an equivalent process of self-transformation, finds similar blockages and difficulties, and overcomes them. The process of personal change never stops, no matter how long one stays. In the 1989 brochure Eileen Caddy wrote:

> *Changes are not always comfortable, but they are very necessary if we want to grow and expand. If we stopped going through changes, I would really become concerned because it would mean we were becoming static. That means stagnation, and stagnation means death.*

Sometimes the first period within the community is spent with quite a lot of personal drama. Old habits and ideas are exposed as redundant and the situation invites their release. Those who stay longer usually become more accepting and graceful about the process, but no one in the community is released from the challenge of personal transformation.

Since life at the Findhorn Foundation is not monastic, it differs from that in the surrounding world only in quality and orientation. Work, relationship and interaction with others occur as in everyday life. But here they are considered an arena for transformation. Situations have the habit of presenting themselves in

62

ways that are exquisitely appropriate to this end. It is useful to have a sense of humour to live here; it helps us to appreciate the delightful irony with which events seem to be 'set up'. It is pleasant, when one knows the community well, to stand back and observe the 'Angel of Findhorn' at work. It lovingly provides the circumstances in which ego is deflated, lifelong attachments are questioned, suppressed emotions are brought to the surface, evasions are countered, and escape from situations is thwarted. As you observe it all, you must smile wryly at the human capacity for self-deception and its transparency. Then you are drawn back once more to be subjected to the same process yourself.

Gradually, we learn to release the idea of the 'one right way', and we discover that what has been invaluable in assisting *our* personal transformation may be anathema to someone else. It is as if we were in a market place with many stalls offering goods. Some people go to one stall to buy, others go to another. We support each other constantly, but the path of inner transformation is ultimately a personal one. However much we may share with others, each of us has a unique path to the Self. The appreciation of this fosters a sense of awe, reverence and humility at the specificity of the Love that is available when we seek to discover it.

In Harmony With the Divine Plan

This small community in northern Scotland, with its special inspiration and apparent divine purpose, does not exist alone. There is a transformation going on all over the planet that is fuelled from many sources. With some of those sources we are directly connected, with others we are not. They have varying emphases and practices, but all are concerned with giving new primacy to inner exploration. We call them a 'network of light', a transformational matrix through which the energy developing the new human identity operates.

There are communities like Esalen and Sirius in the United States, or Auroville in South India. We have exchange relationships with some of them. There is the great river of spiritual renewal flowing out of India, with its tradition of the spiritual master—the guru—and devotees. We have, or have had, members following Rajneesh, Babaji, Muktananda (Gurumay), Yogananda, and especially Sathya Sai Baba, whose teachings parallel those of Eileen's guidance. We respect the spiritual energy expressing itself through Native American teachers, several of whom have visited us. It inspires many young people with a renewed awareness of the sacredness of our relationship with the earth. The Buddhist tradition, in its various forms, is widespread. Members sometimes visit Samye Ling, a Tibetan Buddhist monastery in the south of Scotland. Hatha Yoga and Ta'i Chi are found almost everywhere, and the best of the martial arts advocate a form of inner discipline and awakening. Sufism, Transcendental Meditation, and the entire Christian ecumenical movement exemplified by the Taizé community, are our brothers and sisters in the 'network of light', as are, in another way, the organic food movement and schools of massage and transpersonal psychology. The extraordinary book *A Course In Miracles*, channelled by an agnostic academic psychologist, has sold more than half a million copies.

In every city small groups have developed, seeking inner change as a means of a new relationship with the world of the senses. If we take them all together and imagine the energy they generate, it is not so difficult to visualise a network of light covering the planet, spreading a new level of human awareness.

Taken together, all this makes up what has been described as the 'new age' movement. We are now a little wary of this description, which was once eagerly embraced by the Findhorn Community, because in popular thought it has become connected with the sensation seekers joyously satirised in Doonesbury cartoons, whose interest lies less in seeking spiritual transformation than in dabbling in the occult, or in practising classical capitalist entrepreneurship on the naive. One cartoon shows a fortune teller gazing into a crystal ball and addressing a client: "You are gullible, and you give your money to charlatans!"

* * *

An act in the great drama of life is coming to an end. Humanity cannot go back to a religion of custom and tradition, where obedience to the law was simply 'what is done'. Attempts to provide human satisfaction by an appeal to the external senses and the accumulation of possessions have led to a crisis unparalleled in human history. The Divine will, the energy of creation itself, is steering us in a new direction, towards the discovery of Itself within. Before long, human beings with a new consciousness will become dominant across the globe, relegating *Homo sapiens* caringly and lovingly to the history books. The quicker it happens, the less damage will be done, and the less suffering will there be.

Why should it be so? Who can ask that question? Divine will has no commentator, and it cannot be criticised, for it is the criterion of all criticism. It is 'just so', as it is 'just so' that spring follows winter, as it 'just happened' that apes developed consciousness. It is an expression of That Which Is, in a new form.

To solve our human crisis, God has allowed us to discover that we are, indeed, Himself and we may not forget it again. He has allowed us the chance to capture Him in ourselves—we must never let Him go. He will make, through us, a new humanity.

Part Two

Park Garden
and Sanctuary

Chapter 5
The History of
the Findhorn Community

What have I done!
itself,
with giant strides
the sun
is coming at my call.
I try to cover up my fear,
retreating lobster-wise;
it's coming
it's already near,
I see its white hot eyes.
Through door and window,
chink
and crack
it crammed into the room.
Then stopped
to get its hot breath back,
and, blimey, did it boom!
"I'm changing my itin'rary
the first time since creation.
Now, poet, out with jam and tea,
else why this invitation?"
—Vladimir Mayakovsky

Introduction

A detailed history of the Findhorn Foundation requires its own book. Hopefully it will have one while the main participants can still be consulted. One of them is already dead. Some of our archives have been sent to Edinburgh where they can be properly preserved. Versions of the history of our earlier years are given in the *Magic of Findhorn* and especially in Eileen Caddy's autobiography, *Flight into Freedom*, which brings the story very much to life. In this chapter my task is to indicate trends in our history and to point out some of the challenges we have faced in developing a new lifestyle. Some significant themes of our collective history are also relevant to changes in individual consciousness as humanity is taught its new identity. 'Those who do not learn from history are condemned to repeat it.'

While the various trends in the history of the Findhorn Community may be viewed from different perspectives, there is one common underlying theme. A current of spiritual energy is present in the community which directs and governs what happens. If those who live here lose contact with this current, they either can't stay, or they reorient themselves. It is not that anyone tells them to leave; they just don't feel comfortable living here any longer. The energy that guides the Findhorn Community is not something material. It operates through circumstance and coincidence, which are felt as pressures in daily life. In the Findhorn Community we are learning to harmonise with divine will, to separate it from impulses deriving from the ego, and to find it within ourselves. If the community diverges from this current of energy, which we often call the 'Angel of Findhorn', our collective life becomes more and more uncomfortable until we return to it.

In 1984, I was a new member living at Cluny Hill College, a large former hotel now owned by the Foundation, which accommodates up to 150 people. Perhaps life had become over-structured; there was a feeling of formalism and living for routine. One day the sewers blocked, and the sub-basement area was flooded. Sewage rose through toilets and baths, but no one could find the source of the blockage. No plan of the sewer line was to be found. Attempts to flush the sewer with water failed. Attempts with rods failed even to find where the block was. The water board had no idea of where the sewer ran after it left the main, and their attempts to unblock it from the main road also failed. We went out with divining rods and pendulums to try to find the line of the sewer, without much success (the driveway is about 300 metres long), and frantically dug holes into the banks to try to locate it. As an emergency measure, the sewer outside the house was holed, and sewage began flowing into the garden. Meanwhile, it backed up into the other outlet line from the west of the building. After about two weeks, we were at our wits' end, afraid the health inspector would close us down. It became increasingly clear that the sewer blockage was a symbolic way of showing us something about our life.

A channelling was received. It told us we had become too concerned with outer forms, neglecting our spiritual connection. The sewage began to flood the garden. We organised a meeting and agreed that each member would make a personal commitment to their own spiritual development. In the afternoon we shared what we had individually decided. At 4 pm, when the meeting ended, the sewers were unblocked. They had unblocked themselves! We are not allowed to stray far from the work we are here to do.

In the Beginning—Preparing the Ground
The initial phase in the community's history was not its founding, but the preparation of the founders. They had to be spiritually strong enough to deal with the energies that the community was to embody. Even today some people prepare themselves before coming here, so they can receive the most benefit from their experience. A friend wrote to me: "Now it's once more the right time to come again to the Findhorn Community. For a long time I had very much fear in the face of so much love and acceptance. So first I'll go with a friend to a monastery and meditate for some days."

Eileen and Peter were put through exacting challenges in the years before 1962, when the community was founded. Peter had been initiated into the Rosicrucian order as a young man. He sums up the quintessence of his teaching in three basic principles:

—Eliminate the words 'if' and 'can't' from your language.
—Love where you are, love who you're with, and love what you're doing.
—Positive thinking is powerful.

A fourth one, almost as central, is:
—Only the perfect is good enough for God's work.

He avidly read books on esoterics and the Western mystery tradition. He then had a five-year spiritual training from his second wife, Sheena, a demanding teacher who played a significant role in the spiritual development of all three of the community's founding figures. They had a strong faith in her in these early stages, although Eileen found her to be irascible and exacting.

To be with Peter, Eileen left her marriage and children, a step that most around her interpreted as highly immoral and sinful.

Peter took both Eileen and Sheena to Glastonbury, and they went together into a sanctuary to meditate. Stricken with guilt and remorse, Eileen prayed with her whole heart, surrendering herself to God. Then, for the first time, an inner voice came. That first message contained the kernel of the whole:

> Be still and know that I am God. You have taken a very big step in your life. But if you follow My voice, all will be well. I have brought you and Peter together for a very special purpose, to do a specific work for Me. You will work as one, and you will realise this more fully as time goes on. There are few who have been brought together in this way. Don't be afraid, for I am with you.
>
> (Flight into Freedom, p. 28)

Eileen thought she was going crazy, but Peter and Sheena supported her. Sheena insisted that Eileen listen to and write down the words of the voice, which she began to hear regularly in her three daily meditations. She went through a very hard and challenging period of her life, during which she struggled to resist surrender to Divine will. She writes:

> (I was not) . . . searching consciously for the meaning of God in my life. I wasn't even sure it was God's Voice I continued to hear. Least of all did I believe that the vivid visions I was beginning to have were divinely inspired. For all I knew they may have been the work of the devil or caused by my emotional distress. The only reason I was there was Peter.
>
> (Flight, p. 31)

Finally, she endured six months alone with her and Peter's second baby in a cottage on the west coast of the Isle of Mull without electricity and running water. Her older child had been taken away by Sheena, and Peter had apparently deserted her. She became depressed and contemplated suicide, but instead at last surrendered to God once more. On Christmas day, Peter, who had been trying to get work in the south, reappeared at her door carrying a chicken under his arm for Christmas dinner. Eileen's inner voice commented:

> To achieve absolute freedom, you must live fully those words, 'Let go, let God.' When you do, all strain and resistance goes and you are no longer clinging on to anything of the self . . . . Strain comes when you are trying to

*cling on to something which you feel is being taken from you. Everything
you have is a gift from Me . . . . When you do this with everything, with the
family, with Peter, your home, every material possession, then every spiritual gift, you will find true freedom and release from all strain . . . . You have
begun to understand the greatest secret in life, that we are One.*

(*Flight*, p. 49-50)

The phrase 'Let go, let God' is also often used by Sai Baba, of
whom Eileen was not to hear for many years.

In the second world war Peter had been Air Force Catering Officer for the whole of the Burma front. His confidence and determination persuaded the representatives of a Scottish hotel company
to give him the job of manager of Cluny Hill Hotel in Forres, even
when he declared straightforwardly that the establishment would
be run under divine guidance. The hotel was certainly run down
and it was not easy to find a competent manager, but perhaps a
divine hand was at work in this appointment . . . .

Running a large commercial hotel is very good preparation for
organising a community. You have to provide continuous service
for transient guests and maintain an effective and courteous staff.
Peter based his efforts firmly on the principles of his Rosicrucian
training. He was convinced that Eileen's voice had a divine origin,
and used its advice in managing the business. Dorothy Maclean,
the third co-founder of the Findhorn Community, came to Cluny
Hill as Peter's secretary. After two years Lena Lamont, another ex-
member of Sheena's group of disciples, also joined them as a
housemaid for the staff. Whatever qualms the hotel company may
have had were calmed by good commercial sense—Cluny Hill
Hotel flourished. For five years God, one might say, via Eileen's
voice and Peter's administration, became a hotel manager. Lena
provided information about the situation among the employees.
How to deal with staff, who to employ and to release, hotel policy
—Eileen was told all and Peter carried it out. Earnings went up
three-fold. The little group was being trained to have trust in
Divine will, and to develop skills appropriate to running a
community.

The divinely inspired team were so successful that the hotel
company transferred them with 25 staff to a large, ailing hotel in
the Trossachs to repeat the performance. But they were not
destined for a career reviving derelict hotels. Things changed

73

dramatically. The hotel was built in an inappropriate location and had a bad reputation. Eileen's inner voice informed the group that this was their final period of testing. For all their efforts the season was unsuccessful. On the eve of a meeting with the General Manager, the voice said to Eileen:

My child, I want you to keep very, very positive about everything tomorrow. If you are in touch with Me, you can change quickly in midstream, without it throwing you out. You must be ready to do this. Be prepared to change your plans at a moment's notice.

(*Flight*, p. 72)

On the next day, they were stunned to receive their dismissal notices. They had practically no money, and all they owned was a caravan on a summer site near the village of Findhorn. From this dramatic lesson in the need for faith and flexibility, the Findhorn Community began.

The First Years of the Community: Anchoring—and 'Patriarchy'
In the absence of any other home, Peter, Eileen and their three children found a permanent site at the Findhorn Bay Caravan Park. They moved in in mid-November 1962, and Lena and her three children came to live in a caravan close to them shortly afterwards. The community had begun! Eileen comments about the caravan park rather unkindly:

I was reminded of the many times we had passed it on the way to the beach and commented, "Who would want to live in a dump like that?" The area we were offered really was like a dump, with rubble and litter all over the place. There was an old garage standing in one corner, its windows broken and weeds and brambles all around it.

(*Flight*, p. 75)

Today, custodians of the whole caravan park, we proudly show our guests around the extensive organic flower and vegetable gardens which surround this original site, now sheltered with beautiful hedges and trees. The old caravan is still there, a midget as caravans go, and the current community 'focaliser' has his office in it. It is interesting to see this caravan, with its tiny extension, and to realise that for seven years it was the home of Eileen, Dorothy, Peter and the three children—the years in which the community took form. God provides, but not always according to the standards of the materialistic lifestyle we in the West take for granted. In terms of housing the founders of the Findhorn Community lived in conditions more typical of an Indian village home. They also lived on £8 a week social security money. At present, Eileen, now 72, still lives in a small caravan near the original one. We plan to build a house for her in 1990.

Dorothy had enough money to build a small annexe to the original caravan and she moved in. Peter started a small vegetable garden, which is still lovingly cultivated today. Eileen's inner voice commented:

Time is not what matters but unity, cooperation and positive thinking. Know that every time you put the spade into the soil, you are putting in radiations. Love that vegetable garden, use all My gifts and be grateful for them. Let it be a joyous time for you all as you create a place of harmony and beauty. You can be sure that something is wrong if there is no harmony amongst you. It would be far better to stop and do nothing than to do something which causes discord.

(*Flight*, p. 78-9)

After 1965 this garden became the source of the publicity which made the Findhorn Community famous. In these early days the aim was to live simply, as an expression of God's will, and to meditate together to try to make inner contact with other like-minded souls. It was in this period that the phrase 'network of light' came into use. Eileen had visions of varied groups meditating in different parts of the world. Much later there was confirmation that at least one of these groups did indeed exist—a group of businessmen in Turkey who eventually found out about the Findhorn Community and made contact. In 1972, Eileen and Peter visited Istanbul and Ephesus, of which one of the group was Mayor, and there Eileen had a powerful vision of the Virgin Mary.

In 1953 Peter had visited the Philippines, where he met an American woman called Naomi Stephens who introduced him to the network of meditating groups. He wrote regularly to her about what was happening in the infant community. She was doing similar meditation work in the United States. In 1964 she came to live with the group at Findhorn, adding another caravan. Eileen's inner voice commented that the four foundations of the community

75

were now present. Peter started a series of visits to esoteric circles in other parts of Britain and engaged in a voluminous correspondence with people he met. From 1965 on, increasing numbers of people began to be drawn to the community.

Attention shifted to the garden. Dorothy Maclean also received guidance and she began to make contact with the natural energies controlling the growth of plants, which she called devas. They gave her very precise instruction as to how to treat each kind of plant in the garden. Some beautiful examples of the more general messages from these energies, linking nature and humanity, appear in Dorothy's autobiography, *To Hear the Angels Sing*, and we still use the deva communications in our nature calendars.

Peter put Dorothy's instructions into practice with remarkable results. The exquisite vibrancy of the flower gardens can be seen even in the old photographs. Although no chemical fertilisers or pesticides were used, huge vegetables began to grow—the forty-pound cabbages for which we became famous. Peter met, and was excited by, a man called R. Ogilvie Crombie ('Roc'), from Edinburgh. Roc had had experiences of nature beings, which took the form of elves and fauns, and finally met Pan himself. An account of Roc's extraordinary abilities is given in *The Magic of Findhorn*. Over the following years Roc, although never living in the community, became an adviser to Peter, not merely in regard to the gardens. They made several trips together with the aim of re-energising ancient natural power centres.

Roc continued to visit us until his death. He is remembered in our weekly guest outing to Randolph's Leap, a local beauty spot. Roc identified this spot as a place where it might be especially easy to make a connection with the energies of plants and natural forces in meditation. There are many such spots in the relatively unspoiled countryside of the southern Moray Firth.

Peter's journeys to groups around Britain, and the publication in mimeographed form of the first volume of Eileen's guidance —*God Spoke to Me*—as well as the publicity surrounding the gardens, began to draw visitors to the small community that was forming in the Caravan Park at Findhorn. Some stayed. In this period there was much interest in the esoteric and the paranormal, for it was in circles with such ideas that the idea of a 'new age' first became accepted. Attempts were made to contact UFOs and 'space beings', but they remained marginal to the main development of the community.

Peter's firm belief in Eileen's guidance, which he put into practice using his organising and executive abilities, led to the creation of the physical form of the community, still recognisable today.

In the first eight years, the community was anchored by Eileen's inner work, and by Peter's work in the gardens. Eileen went through a period of powerful spiritual development. Seeking a quiet place to meditate in the overcrowded living conditions, she asked within and the voice, in a joyous piece of guidance, replied: "Why don't you go down to the public toilets? You will find perfect peace there." (*Flight*, p. 78)

The little toilet block referred to has been preserved and is now a herbal apothecary and wholefood cafe.

At first Eileen meditated for about two hours daily, apart from collective meditations with the others, but as she became more and more inspired, she would snatch a couple of hours' sleep and meditate from midnight till 5 am, then return to look after the children and spend the day caring for the guests and new arrivals. This remarkable intensity rooted the spiritual energy which we maintain here. Eileen appears a very ordinary and unpretentious person. In her seventies, she continues to share our own processes of release and development. She remains an anchor of the community and has always been instructed to remain here, although the other founders have moved on.

If Eileen provided the divine link, Peter was tirelessly active in giving it form. In the earliest days he created the garden. As the community developed, he organised the work, maintained the appropriate spiritual style of members and guests, and was a ceaseless publicist, visiting many English esoteric circles while continuing to run the garden. If Eileen's energy for the home and her inner connection with the Divine was limitless, so was Peter's for the community's growth. His background as a military officer led him to favour a disciplined lifestyle, with a clear chain of command. Reminiscences of the early days tell us of a compulsory morning sanctuary. If members did not attend for a few days, they would receive a 'visit' from Peter. In sanctuary, Peter read out Eileen's current guidance after meditation and then allocated members and guests to their work. His authority was virtually absolute, and this period of community life has often been described as patriarchal. However, his type of leadership enabled a lot to be achieved in a short time on the material level, and Peter proved himself relatively flexible later, as changing conditions required other methods. As well as relying on Eileen's guidance, he had a sharp intuition of his own, making him a very commanding figure.

The community grew slowly during the first eight years. In 1968 it became a charitable trust, and trustees were appointed. The publicity connected with the remarkable plants attracted an increasing number of guests. Eileen recalls that there were 600 visitors in 1969. In faith a sanctuary was built and, indeed, enough funds were forthcoming. Six prefabricated mobile holiday bungalows were assembled; these are still used as guest accommodation. The real significance of this period is that the vision began to be grounded in form, the spiritual energies which are expressed through the community were anchored. In the next period, the 'parents', Eileen and Peter, were gradually required to release control, and a new educational impulse developed.

From Plants to People; From Patriarchy to Oligarchy
The end of the first period in our history and the beginning of the second are bridged by David Spangler's stay in the community. He and his partner, Myrtle Glines, first visited in 1970 and returned in 1971 to live here for three years. He was the last of the Findhorn Community's founding figures. By the time he left, the Findhorn Foundation was as large as it is now, had oriented itself towards spiritual education, and had a much more youthful personnel. Peter's authority had been supplemented by a leadership group.

When David arrived he was 23 years old, but since childhood he had had contact with an inner wisdom. Eileen saw him on the one hand as a young man who loved chocolate cake, but in her inner vision ". . . he as a person seemed to disappear and in his place was a huge and very wonderful being" (*Flight*, p. 144). Peter adopted him instantly, taking him into sanctuary to speak, an unprecedented step. David began to lecture regularly, material which gave inspiration and direction to many young people visiting the community. He emphasised the creation of a new human identity appropriate to a new age, for which modern civilisation had prepared the ground. He was able to channel guidance from inwardly experienced entities. Sometimes these were 'masters' known in the Western mystery tradition. He received material from sources which named themselves 'John' and 'Limitless Love and Truth'. Eileen recently passed me a piece of channelling from 'Limitless Love and Truth' which I have not been able to locate in the published books. It gives an indication of both message and style:

The New Dispensation
On Christmas Eve 1967, Earth entered a new Cosmic Frequency, and the Spirit of Man merged with the Cosmic Christ. As a budding Christ about to blossom forth, man is now a twofold being. The true and real estate of man is spiritual. The outer manifestation is but a chalice for the use of the Spirit Man.

. . . True religion for the New Dispensation is to express the Christ from within oneself. The hidden splendour, buried deep within the heart, is bursting to be free. Look within, O Sons of God, and BE the light that all might see. God's kingdom upon Earth can only come about through Man, and the New Earth emerges from out of the chaos of the old. The crumbling world is past. Be not concerned with what must be, but build for the future with the vision within. Only the new man can build the new world, so rise up, O Sons of God, and exercise your birthright. Each tiny soul upon this planet is a cell in the body of Christ. No matter what his state of being, or what his function is, each has a part to play.

The essential information conveyed here is that a new human identity is indeed possible and necessary, one which gives priority to spirit over matter, and that this change is a divinely ordained phase in human development. It is what we have been exploring at the Findhorn Foundation ever since.

Between 1972 and 1978 we published much of David's writing (a list of his books appears at the end of the chapter). More recently, David himself asked us not to re-publish these works. About his most popular book, *Laws of Manifestation*, he writes:

. . . I became dissatisfied with this book. I felt that it did not express as well as it could have the essence of what I wished to say, and it did not represent the further evolution of my own thinking on this topic. So in 1981 I withdrew it from print.

He is at present working on some new books, including one about manifestation and another dealing with the concepts and philosophy underlying the Findhorn Community.

David Spangler was a great intellectual influence on the community's development in the seventies. To him we owe the idea of the community as a College or University of Light. Our first residential conference for guests was held in 1972. Directly or indirectly, David drew to us many young people, who brought with them guitars, long hair and a lifestyle with a definite Californian flavour of casual manners and sun shorts. They drank in the wine of early Findhorn Community esoterics and began to build. The majority did not stay very long. In the early seventies the average length of membership seems to have been only about six months. But others took their place, and many were practically minded. The flavour of the community began to change—cramped living conditions, sing-songs, artistic groups, collective projects and a gentle resistance to authority are characteristic of this 'middle-period' Findhorn Community. Words like 'democracy' were occasionally breathed. Paul Hawken reports that Myrtle Glines was very effective at helping these younger people to reconcile themselves to Peter's style of leadership. It was she who introduced counselling techniques to the community (*Magic of Findhorn*, p. 189-90).

In this period an area called Pineridge in the north-east of the Caravan Park was 'colonised' and transformed, the community centre was extended to accommodate the many new members and guests, the craft studios went up and the present publications building was completed. The community started to produce audio tapes, and there was a strong emphasis on the performing arts. The mood was one of dynamism and expansion. A member who was here at the time recollects that the most valued type of person was the 'mover'—someone who got things done. By 1974 the physical layout of the Park was much as it is today. There were 180 members, and an education programme was in place.

Over a seven-year period, Peter and Eileen released their control over the community. In 1972 Eileen was directed to cease sharing her guidance with everyone else:

> Let go, stand back and allow all those in the community to live a life guided and directed by Me. Let them learn from experience to live positively, demonstrating the laws of manifestation in their own lives. If this means that the work is held up for the time being, let it be held up. Until life is lived, lessons are not learned, and these lessons are far more important than expanding without learning, living on what others have learned.

80

In Eileen's view, Peter had become rather dependent on her guidance; its withdrawal was a challenge for him. But without sharing her guidance, Eileen herself became unsure of her role in the community. An examination of copies of *Findhorn News*, circulated to supporters of the community in this period, shows how important the guidance was. Up to 1971 practically every item of information is backed by a piece of guidance. By August 1971 David Spangler's work begins to fill the magazine, which Peter edited at this period. The withdrawal of guidance increased the strain in Peter's relationship with Eileen, for her guidance-receiving ability was, for him, one of the ties between them (cf. *Flight*, p. 170-174). He began to turn to others for support, and also formed a 'core' group of seven, the nucleus of a management group, which soon grew to 12 members. But often the delegation of responsibility did not provide results that met his standards. Eileen's inner voice said:

... Peter's work has been to establish this centre of light. The time will come when he will be free to move into the universal work. Tell him to let go of the reins more and more and allow the community to learn and make mistakes if necessary, but learn they must.
(From 'View from the Centre', by Peter Caddy, *Findhorn News*, April, 1974.)

Peter continues:

To prepare for my leaving the community for short periods of time, we have decided to form a Core Group of seven members who would be responsible for the community while I was away . . . . During the past few months I have been sharing all that has been happening with the Core Group, and am now gradually withdrawing to enable them to take on the running of the community.

(ibid.)

Peter also set up a 'focalisers' group of those responsible for departments in the diversifying community (March, 1974). Key decisions were discussed in community meetings. In addition, in 1973, not only David Spangler but also Dorothy Maclean left the community—soon to organise the Lorian Association in the United States. The era of the 'big authorities' was coming to an end.

Peter's heart opened to a young Swedish woman to whom he

81

had given responsibility in the community. Although there was no sexual relationship, Eileen reacted sharply. The community was thrown into a period of uncertainty but there was no challenge to Peter's overall authority. An editorial in the February 1975 *Open Letter*—which replaced the *Findhorn News*—reports:

> We at [the] Findhorn [Community] are embarking on the first lap of a new cycle in our development; the phase of building the foundation of the community is reaching completion and now we are involving ourselves in a deeper and more conscious commitment to the New Age through training and education. Individual wholeness comes first, and the changes that Peter and Eileen Caddy are experiencing within their own relationship are reflected in the changes in the whole community.

Early in this transition period, in 1973, the decision to build our 'Universal Hall' (originally the 'University Hall') was made. Eileen's guidance for the Hall was clear. A functional hall was to be put up fast, with the emphasis then turning to proper housing for members, who had to live in very cramped conditions in caravans. But although this guidance was shared, the Core Group were now receiving advice and ideas from many sources. The divine inspiration of the Findhorn Community required the development of inner attunement by the membership, so that each could individually harmonise with higher truth. But the community had in the past relied on others for its decision-making process, and was not experienced at this level of inner work. It was much more exciting to embark on the building of a major monument, a project which kindled the collective enthusiasm of the young members, rather than on the construction of a utilitarian hall, and this more superficially attractive view prevailed.

Ten years later we had the monument, a superb building in stone, beautifully furnished and decorated, with magnificent mural paintings. It also contributed greatly, however, to a very large debt, and the collective energy of the community for construction was exhausted.

The Hall remains a very expensive building to maintain, and requires considerable subsidy. Nor is it a spiritual symbol in the way that the great Matrimandir of the Auroville Community is. We are still living in even more dilapidated caravans. Perhaps the lesson of all this is: in periods of transition when your connection with spirit is being developed, don't embark on major projects, but test yourself out on minor matters! Having said all this, the community has a superb building as a result of its decision. We have not been judged too harshly.

In the period up to 1979, when he left, Peter delegated more authority to the Core Group. This group still used meditation and attunement as a basis for its decision-making, but without Eileen's guidance a current of more ordinary, administrative decision-making became stronger. The Core Group was self-selective; as someone dropped out, so someone else would be attuned to by the group, which functioned as a kind of spiritual politburo, managing the community under Peter's overall leadership. In an article in the *Open Letter* of December 1975 Nick Rose commented:

> *During the first year of the Core Group's life, Peter shared his vision with its members and continued to make all the decisions. Now, nearly two years later, the Core Group numbers 12 and it has administrative, financial, communication and personnel groups to assist it in its work. Some feel that little has changed, that Peter still dominates the decision-making process. Others sense that a real evolution of government is taking place, and that the concept of a 'theocratic democracy' is a meaningful one.*
>
> *Like the rest of [the] Findhorn [Community] the Core Group is divinely ordinary. It is prey to the lures of glamour and illusion like any other group. It is striving to improve its communication with the community. It is trying not to impose a vision in such a wilful and purposeful manner that it inhibits the growth of personal vision.*

In the Findhorn Community, Divine will unfolds itself unhurriedly, without the stress and impatience which our cultures regard as the norm. We have to relearn patience and right timing. The Core Group provided stability during a time when membership turnover was high and individuals had a shorter period in the community for spiritual development. Only in the later part of the 1980s did a new trend in management emerge.

Expansion—and Glamour
From the earliest days to the present time, even though personalities were changing and settings and phases came and went, members and guests continued to learn to live together with love, awakening their connection with their inner truth, and thus transforming themselves. On whatever level that transformation had occurred, most people left to share it in their home environment.

83

Throughout the seventies thousands of guests visited the Find-horn Foundation, were inspired and returned to spread their inspiration in changed lives. *This is the true and simple history of the Findhorn Foundation, and it continues today.* The more detailed events and dramas are the stage settings within which this process of transformation and development of love occurs.

Peter and Eileen were not exempt from change. They had had a rather traditional relationship, but new human identity requires personal wholeness. Eileen had been the passive receiver and good housewife, Peter the authoritative actor in the world. The 'Angel of Findhorn' set about transforming these stereotyped roles, for in some ways the couple remained a model for the rest of the membership. Peter's relationship with Eileen became steadily more distanced. His priorities were changing, and he left the community in 1979 to develop himself by means of a new series of relationships. He remarried in 1982, and his new wife demanded from him a large share in the physical upbringing of their child. Peter was, in his seventies, required to learn the more mundane aspects of fatherhood—washing the nappies and taking real responsibility for his young son, whom to our pleasure he some-times brings back to the community. Through a further marriage he has been experiencing the more devotional aspects of religion so familiar to Eileen in her moments of inner surrender.

Eileen, on the other hand, has gradually conquered her shyness to become a lecturer and spiritual guide, unafraid before mass audiences of thousands. In this respect Peter and Eileen's example, which has demanded great readjustment relatively late in life when others are thinking of 'taking it easy', has been inspirational to us.

While they were still together, Eileen and Peter were given the gift of returning to Cluny Hill, as promised in Eileen's guidance many years earlier. In the intervening period the hotel had become very run down, and the community purchased it for the ridicu-lously small sum of £60,000. At the time, though, it was a huge step to take. It was a relatively collective community decision, although the then community treasurer resigned over it. So Cluny Hill Hotel became Cluny Hill College ('Cluny').

With more than eighty bedrooms, extensive grounds, tennis court and swimming pool, Cluny is an imposing establishment. It is a very expensive building to maintain, and we have recently had to spend more than the original purchase price to renovate the central heating system alone. But it is also a place of great energy and has become our major guest centre. It is a pleasure to lead workshops in its main rooms, to feel the love and care with which the building is maintained, and to be supported by the work and consideration of its members.

The purchase of Cluny set loose an impulse for property acquisition which turned out to be a double-edged sword for the community. Eileen's guidance spoke of the development of a 'Planetary Village', eventually growing into a 'City of Light'. Members began to feel that God was guiding the process, so all we had to do was acquire, and He would make sure of the funds. The key year was 1978. We were given Drumduan House, a beautiful Georgian mansion in a very run-down condition, on the north side of Cluny Hill, overlooking Findhorn Bay. Perhaps it would be a creative arts' centre. It and its garden were lovingly renovated at great expense. It was finally occupied by the Moray Steiner School in 1987. Station House, the old railway building in Findhorn village was bought as members' accommodation and refurbished. In a more controversial decision Core Group decided to buy Cullerne House and grounds, situated a little to the north of the Caravan Park. As the financial backing for this decision did not materialise, a group of members raised loans to cover the cost. In spite of the miserable soil, it was to become our major garden centre. A team led by Dick Barton, an ex-RAF officer, put a tremendous amount of work into the gardens, but the property remained a financial liability. Cullerne was not really integrated into the community until the mid-1980s.

A group of members borrowed money to purchase another old house, Newbold, a half mile south of Cluny Hill. It adopted donation financing and is independent and flourishing. We accepted the custodianship of an island called Erraid, on the west coast of Scotland, off the island of Mull. Erraid is owned by two Dutch families, but we were offered its use for a small community for ten months of the year. We were getting big and over-extended and the debts were mounting up. At the end of the 1970s we were far out-spending our income, and owed more than £400,000 to private individuals and to the bank.

With hindsight it is clear that a superficial interpretation of divine protection led to irresponsibility and carelessness, a kind of collective materialism similar to that evident in the Soviet Union, where no one has felt responsible for property that belongs to the abstract 'State'. Even in 1985 after a new, strict financial policy had long been in place, I arrived in Drumduan garden, which had not been properly worked for two years, to find four lawn mowers in the garden shed, none of them functional. With a little attention we managed to get three in working order!

* * *

The attraction and glamour of esoterica also reached their peak in the late 1970s. David Spangler had warned the community about glamour in an open letter written from America in 1975:

Glamour is the greatest challenge facing us today. It causes us to step off the balanced track and wander in culs de sac. It is a form of entrancement, bewitchment, hypnotism. It generates illusion (and is a product of it, as well) and it hinders communication. In fact, that is its greatest danger and characteristic. Glamour distorts communication and communion by altering the perspective of a single quality so that other qualities can no longer relate to it. It is like loud music playing when you are trying to quietly think or to converse with others; it is like over-inflating a tyre on your automobile so that the vehicle tilts and cannot run on a level. It fosters the creation of private worlds in which our attention is trapped and others cannot truly communicate with us.

. . . The Christ is found in life's processes, high and low, and not just in special events or people who may satisfy certain needs for stimulation and glamour. Building for the New Age is not tripping from charismatic happening to charismatic happening, like a junkie looking for his daily 'fix'. The Christ, the New Age, planetary transformation are not meant to be addictions; our work is not really expressed in terms of visions, lights, sounds, seizures of energy, and hallelujas. . . . Being the Christ is an everyday commitment to life as it is and as it is unfolding to become in revelation of its Divine Essence, a life seen beyond frills or glamour, lived in recognition of the uniqueness of each day and of the Divinity that is the fabric from which that uniqueness is woven.

(Reflections on the Christ, p. 102, 113)

In spite of David's warnings, the community had to learn its lesson about glamour. The problem came to a head with the 'crystal incident' in 1978. A small group of people began visiting the community, and some became members, who felt that only with certain kinds of decoration and design, and particularly through the use of crystals, could the appropriate energy be properly channelled here. Indeed, it was not so much divine energy, but the energy of the fabled past civilisation of Atlantis which was to be incorporated into our almost completed Universal Hall through a special configuration of crystals and wires. The whole conception was not properly communicated to the membership, and Peter's authority was still such that there was considerable acceptance of the new idea.

A specially cut quartz crystal, about the size of a grapefruit, was prepared and suspended on gold wires in the centre of the Hall. The gold wires led to the supporting pillars, from which silver wires led down into the foundations. In the basement, a smaller crystal was embedded in the floor, and a piece of meteoritic iron sat above it. A third crystal was fixed to a light in the centre of the ceiling. The Hall was closed for some time before this occult arrangement was finished and then, around Christmas 1978, a special ceremony of invocation was held to inaugurate the energy transfer. Craig Gibsone, the present focaliser of the Foundation, remembers walking out of the ceremony and leaving the community, so great was his disgust. He returned only in 1983.

A year and a half later, during a presentation by a visitor from the Edgar Cayce Foundation, the wires snapped and the crystal fell, smashing a two-inch-thick glass panel in the floor and narrowly missing the speaker, who had 'providentially' not chosen to stand in the centre of the Hall. The crystal shattered into many pieces, to almost everyone's great relief. Eileen was not present at the talk, but her comment when informed of the event was: "Thank God." She collected the crystal fragments and, following her guidance, they were returned to the earth from which they came. This curious incident ended a period which taught the community some hard lessons.

'Psychic glamour' is widespread in the 'new age' movement nowadays. It caters for people who are dissatisfied with the cruder aspects of materialism, but who still retain a desire to purchase personal transformation quickly for a fee. Such demands are fulfilled by a large coterie of 'psychic entrepreneurs' who advertise their wares in the host of 'new age' magazines. Many people still visit us expounding their 'visions' or new techniques, trying to set us to rights. We enjoy them and thank them, and they pass on elsewhere. We are becoming more and more conscious of the simplicity and directness of the divine message—*that our purpose is to find the divine within, the criterion for which is the practice and experience of unconditional love.* Our work is too important to be sidetracked.

The Early 1980s: Caution and Retrenchment
As a result of the controversies surrounding the acquisition of property and the distortion of glamour, a number of members left the community. We entered a phase of caution and uncertainty, like a child who has been disciplined. Strict accounting became the watchword, and the attempt to take responsibility for our debts and reduce them a primary goal. Instead of a warm welcome for anyone who claimed paranormal abilities, the community became very cautious about psychics. Peter, who had tended to welcome such people, left the community in 1979 to remarry and has not lived here since, although he frequently visits us.

When I arrived at the Findhorn Foundation in 1983, my practice of what I then called 'psychic healing' and clairvoyance was regarded with considerable caution, and I was advised to give it up for a few years while I adjusted to the community. In 1984 when I started an intensive organic vegetable garden at Cullerne, I noticed a beautiful rose quartz crystal in an out-of-the-way corner of the Park, and thought it would be a lovely decoration for the centre of the garden. Not knowing about the 'crystal incident', I was taken aback by the hornets' nest this proposal stirred up, and had to release the idea. We were still in reaction against crystals, which are in themselves harmless enough things. But when the rose quartz crystal was finally put in one of the Cullerne gardens a couple of years later, guests started doing rituals around it and it had to be removed once more.

When Peter left, he handed on the focalisation of the community to François Duquesne. It was a critical time. François's cautious and rational approach to finance and organisation was essential for this period of retrenchment. The community needed to reconnect with a coherent vision. François deeply felt the need for the 'village' of Eileen's guidance to be made into a reality. He strongly supported expansion beyond the Educational Foundation of the Trust Deed into a spiritually based community, embracing business activity.

The great opportunity in this direction was the purchase of the Caravan Park, which François negotiated. The Park, where the community was founded, came up for sale in 1983. It was obvious that we should become custodians of this land. Furthermore, the maintenance of the commercial side of the business for some years could give us a source of income, which we sorely needed in our indebted state. The owner, knowing that we were the only likely customer, drove a hard bargain. A sustained campaign was launched, in which each member took responsibility for manifesting funds for the cost of a particular area of the Park. This gave individuals a direct stake in fund-raising. Appeals were sent to previous community members and visitors; auctions and fund-raising events followed each other in quick succession. We were able to raise what we considered an appropriate price for the land but the owner held out for another £80,000. We had to go further into debt, with the affirmation that we would pay this new debt off within a year, which we did. The Park was purchased in November 1983, the high point of François's time as focaliser. He describes his feelings about this period in an interview later in the book.

As a new arrival I witnessed this process and observed the determination of the Core Group to purchase the Park. I also noticed the hesitation of some of the members, who nevertheless had great anxiety about voicing it in the series of community meetings called to confirm the steps in the purchase negotiations. We were not yet mature, but participation was increasing, and the process was a very responsible one.

Current Trends

The purchase of the Caravan Park marked a positive turning point. A programme for steady debt reduction was in place, the membership was smaller and its average age began to go up. Members stayed longer. Some independent businesses started to form. People began to come here to live their lives with and around us without being members of the Foundation. For the first time a real distinction between the Community and Foundation emerged. There has been a move towards the decentralisation of responsibility, which means that individual members become less dependent on a centralised leadership. It halts a trend towards bureaucratisation that develops frighteningly easily. Our experience suggests that future human societies will require dramatic decentralisation so that everyone can really enjoy social involvement.

Another challenge is that of personal attachment. When someone is really inspired by their work, their achievements tend to become involved with their ego, instead of being dedicated to the divine Self. Such people become possessive and clinging when the time for change has come. This problem brings us back to the central theme. If one is in contact with the loving Divine essence within, and sees 'reality' as its outer manifestation, one can be responsive to the messages it gives. The result is happiness and non-attachment; but it requires steady practice in deepening spiritual attunement.

The main contemporary trends are described later in the book. In 1988, Foundation members were involved in a long period of collective and individual attunement to create a new spiritual Core Group. This process represents the most determined attempt yet to move towards a spiritual democracy, based not merely on simple voting, but on contact with inner vision.

Although our financial crisis is by no means over, within very limited means the Foundation is beginning to build permanent accommodation for members.

Finally, a Community of people is growing who want their lives to have a spiritual centre and who find support in the Findhorn Foundation ambience.

In all histories, the real heroes are the ordinary people around whom the dramas are played. The Findhorn Community is no exception. Our purpose is to act as a laboratory of transformation; to create new identities and wholesome ways of living together appropriate to a world technologically transformed into a global culture. In their day-to-day work and interaction, in their expression of love and mutual support, in their attempts to face their blockages and remove them, ordinary Findhorn Community members have steadily fulfilled this aim.

People come and go; ideas are in vogue and pass away; but the practice of putting love at the centre of human interaction does not pass, but spreads everywhere across the planet. This task, simple to describe, complex to live effectively, is our service, our contribution to planetary development. In undertaking it and sharing it with our guests, we are fulfilling the divine purpose for which Eileen's inner voice originally spoke to her. We are very ordinary people, but that is the great significance of our community. Our practice is not beyond the reach of ordinary people, and our challenges are not strange to them.

Early books by David Spangler
Links with Space (1971). *Revelation—The Birth of a New Age* (1972). *New Age Rhythms* (1972). *Festivals in the New Age* (1976). *Laws of Manifestation* (1976). *Towards a Planetary Vision* (1977). *Vision of Findhorn Anthology* (1977). *Relationship and Identity* (1978). *Reflections on the Christ* (1978). *Explorations* (1980). All published in Great Britain by Findhorn Press and now out of print.

Books by Dorothy Maclean
Wisdoms (1971). *The Living Silence* (1971). Both Findhorn Press and out of print. *To Hear the Angels Sing* (1980), now published by Morningtown Press, USA.

The Community Centre

Chapter 6
The Management & Organisation
of the Findhorn Foundation

The really helpful things will not be done from the centre; they cannot be done by big organisations; but they can be done by the people themselves. If we can recover the sense that it is the most natural thing for every person born into this world to use their hands in a productive way and that it is not beyond the wit of man to make this possible, then I think the problem of unemployment will disappear and we shall soon be asking ourselves how we can get all the work done that needs to be done.
—Ernst Schumacher *Small is Beautiful*, p. 184

Spiritual Management

Although our community is small, the way we relate to each other is complex. Yet there is a basic assumption: daily tasks are organised to express inner wisdom. In our outer structures and practices we are trying to manifest an inner purpose, meaningful for each member as an individual, and also for the future development of humanity on the planet. We do not, therefore, merely attempt to come to simple, rational decisions, based on the perceived interests of the parties involved. We seek to find 'what wants to happen', by inner attunement. This practice we call spiritual management.

There are two grounds for the belief in spiritual management. In the first place, the history of our community shows that divine guidance founded it and was responsible for the manner of its development. We maintain the contact originally demonstrated to us. Who would wish to substitute a lesser for a greater source of inspiration? Secondly, we are here to practise love in action—a manifestation of inner reality in the sense-observable world—so that each individual can find security and confidence in their journey towards truth. Following Eileen's guidance, we want to look within for our decisions. It is very tempting to avoid this process, in order to 'speed things up', but we always come back to it. We feel its lack when we neglect inner consultation and, without fail, things start going wrong when we omit it. Of course, almost every member or guest who comes to us is learning this process anew, so rather than rapidly getting better and better at managing our daily life, the community as a whole changes very slowly.

Individual self-confidence in inner guidance and support varies widely. This is only to be expected in a school of transformation. We are wary of 'glamour channelling' by individuals who claim to be in touch with complete knowledge, particularly when their ordinary day-to-day behaviour belies it. Our job is to make available the practice of inner guidance to ordinary people, so that they can live their lives in wiser, more inspired and more harmonious ways. The Findhorn Foundation consists not of realised beings but of stimulating people who have found something of the truth and are demonstrating what follows when they live what they have found. Immediate changes are available for ordinary people now, changes which could help to transform the quality of life and interaction in the wider world.

Visitors who come to the Findhorn Foundation full of notions of business efficiency and 'modern management methods' are often taken aback by the slowness, complexity and apparent vagueness of our decision-making processes. If they stay with us for a while, however, and try to find an inner understanding of what is going on, they 'mellow'. The pace of life here raises questions about the wider civilisation of which management techniques are a part. Does a society organised for the maximisation of production create relaxed, harmonious and holistically developed human beings? All the evidence says no. On the contrary, stress levels in such societies run high and stress-related disease is endemic. Individuals are alienated from their jobs, working rather for their pay packets than because what they do satisfies them. There is widespread disillusion and purposelessness.

Many of the Findhorn Foundation's guests have already taken steps—whether in the form of individual therapy or spiritual discipline—to mitigate these features in their personal lives; but they still feel dependent on the 'system' for their income, and the pace of that system itself is much too stressful for balanced human development.

Although we do not confront or fight the lifestyles prevalent in

94

wider society, our living practice itself is a recommendation for a new way of living. It puts in question the presuppositions of both capitalism and socialism about social priorities. If we didn't need so many material things, we wouldn't have to produce so many of them. If we tune in to the divine order, we are more leisurely in our activities, take longer over them, and put more love and care into them. People who can find joy in life without the purchase of material objects will not need so much money, and will therefore be able to work less to provide what they need. Economic life can become moderate and self-sustaining, allowing people to develop holistic and varied lifestyles. It sounds rather utopian, but the community actually lives in this way. I find it a preferable way of being.

A student of mine, a director of a large research institute for nuclear physics, who also practises spiritual healing, spent a month here as a guest. He worked in one of our kitchens. At first he told me: "How inefficient it all is! I like X because he's really in charge, but when Y and Z are there, they don't really seem to have authority." He was still relating to the models he knew in the outside world. At the end of a month, he was relaxed and gentler. "I don't know about my work any more," he said. "I don't want to go on working like that, but I'm not confident enough to change." He had begun to question the unspoken values that ruled his life outside.

In the community he worked about 15 hours a week in the kitchen, his main department, and another 15 hours in one of the gardens. He spent three of these hours in a sharing with his work group and three hours in a sharing with the other guests who were living in the community. He had time to do some spiritual healing with guests and for a workshop, and participated in a group preparing our 'Beauty of Surprise' conference, which aimed to explore the relationship between science and mystery. During his stay there were films, plays and events like a Solstice celebration for him to enjoy, as well as contact with nature and lots of interesting conversation. With a reorientation of human values, I believe a comparable lifestyle could be available to every inhabitant of this planet. This man and others who visit us start to question the quality of their lives, reassessing the standards by which they make judgements about such things as efficiency and effectiveness.

Meetings within the Findhorn Foundation are also personal learning situations. We are interested in such questions as:

—How do we improve our inner attunement?
—What is the quality of our interaction?
—How do different individuals blend and conflict in a group context?

Such meetings are complex processes. It is as if we were in a dance in which action, inner learning and mutual understanding take the floor together. They all need to be in balance.

In the year I served on our Finance Committee I hoped to sort out our relations with the British income tax system, which has a hard time with communities such as ours, where most people earn less than the tax thresholds. I never succeeded, but I began to appreciate our Finance Officer, to whose personality I had previously had a great deal of resistance. As we got to know each other in the long meetings, where many of us were often out of our depth amongst the issues we had to solve, I realised his spiritual integrity and learned to love him—not in any sexual way or even as an intimate friend, but just for who he is. Such a gem of comprehension is worth a lot of meeting time. We also managed, more or less, to get through the business, laughing a lot in the process. It made a pleasant contrast to the university faculty boards I once served on.

Wherever you go in the Findhorn Foundation, you will start your meeting, your work or your leisure with an 'attunement'. Usually this means holding hands in a circle, closing your eyes and becoming calm. Maybe a focaliser will say a few words; sometimes it is just silent time together. The hands holding yours feel supportive. After several attunements, you start letting go to them, forgetting that someone else is feeling the same about *your* grip. Once this mutual inner moment is over there is a time for sharing what you are feeling. There is little point in trying to express love in your work if you feel so preoccupied with other things that you are not really able to be present.

If you happen to be in one of the many committee meetings that proliferate in the Foundation like mushrooms after rain, you will start with a meditation lasting up to half an hour. This might provide inspiration. At the least it calms the mind and harmonises the energy of the group, a good basis for the meeting to follow. Then you will talk about last week's unsolved problems, who has forgotten to do what they were supposed to do, and all the new things that have come up for solution. If a significant decision is to be made, the group will meditate in order to make the decision from a place of inner focus.

I remember a Finance Committee decision about our staff allowances (which members begin receiving after two years in the Foundation). We had been paying ourselves £50 a month, and there appeared to be money for a little more. Various sums were suggested. I thought £55 would be a sensible, modest increase. We meditated. As I asked inwardly what would be right for the members, the staggering sum of £75 a month came insistently through, a 50% increase! I understood that we were to value ourselves materially without becoming materialist, so a significant increase was appropriate. We shared what we had received. To my astonishment, the other cautious members of the group had received the same information. We have managed to maintain this allowance ever since!

At the end of the meetings there is another 'attunement', holding hands again, to release the energy and each other inwardly. It usually feels pleasant and complete to leave with this harmony and mutual support.

All these simple practices change the way we regard things and people. Through them we pause, listen inwardly and remind ourselves that the experience of love and its expression are the truth behind all our seeming significances and momentary excitements. Without the intention to find love, no ritual, however complicated, will have any effect. Our practices are not efficient in a business sense. They take time, they make one aware of a much broader picture than the issue at hand, and they tend to take away a sense of immediate urgency. In order really to understand what goes on in the Findhorn Foundation, one has to stop and ask what life is about and why things are done anyway, questions which get forgotten in the stress-filled rush of materialistic living.

The 'Focaliser'
Wherever you go in the Findhorn Foundation, to a department, group or meeting, you will find at least one 'focaliser'. This is not new age jargon. We use the term to indicate that our leadership

here is different from that of normal managers, directors and bosses. Fundamentally, focalisers have responsibility without authority over others in their working groups. They should be aware of the overall context of whatever is being done, seek to balance different demands for time, energy and finance, make sure people's states and situations are considered, stimulate effective group interaction and act as a link with other groups. Focalisers are also responsible for what we call 'holding the energy'—connecting with, and making sure that others connect with, an inner, spiritual significance of situations, so that things can happen 'from the inside out'.

When I became focaliser of Drumduan House (before it was taken over by the school), the previous focaliser and I meditated together in the sanctuary, to allow the transfer of the energy of focalisation to take place. I actually felt a kind of movement, as if a featherlight bird had settled on my shoulders. I began to notice all sorts of things I hadn't bothered with before. I encouraged people to attend the Saturday morning sanctuary, during which, using guided meditation, we refilled the building and gardens with light. I became conscious how bare the floors were, and used some of our meagre funds to buy carpets for rooms and hallways from the local auction. I made curtains for the windows. It was important to remind the members of our Monday evening meal together, and make sure someone was cooking, or getting the food from Cluny, seven minutes' walk away. At the meal we would share how we were feeling, and discuss any business to do with the house. Nobody obeyed me because I was focaliser, or treated me like a boss, but there was an awareness of the particular responsibility I held. Such is the focaliser's role.

The focaliser of the whole community has the greatest responsibility. When the community was still very small, Peter Caddy was very much a powerful father figure. He had a great deal of real authority. But gradually, over the years, the role changed. The last two focalisers, Jay Jerman and Craig Gibsone, have been dealing with such a complex organism that they could not hold an external authority over all that goes on. Their main focus has been to stimulate inner responsibility among the members, moving us towards our fledgling spiritual democracy, and busying themselves with the link with divine inspiration of our activities. Gradually we moved towards the setting up of a spiritual inner group, the new 'Core Group'. This group does not concern itself with day-to-day management. It attunes through meditation to the expression within the community of the Divine purpose. The new Core Group meets weekly for a long meditation, after which images and visions received are shared. Major issues of community policy are meditated upon, but without the long, detailed discussions which still take place in other management bodies. I was supported to write this book after a meditation by the Core Group.

Setting up the new Core Group involved a number of community meetings in the Universal Hall. The general idea of separating the Management Group (the old Core Group) from a meditation group (new Core Group) was discussed, and eventually agreed upon. The idea had begun to take form two years previously, in vision meetings of the old Core Group. Bringing these ideas, which are often stimulated by collective meditations, into real form usually takes quite a long time. It is as if we are held back until our consciousness is sufficiently developed to make a new vision workable; only then can it move ahead. Nothing which polarises the community is acceptable, for our job is to demonstrate a harmonious lifestyle, not to be fighting amongst ourselves.

Once the decision to accept the new Core Group had been made, we concerned ourselves in community meetings with the method of selecting it. Previous leadership groups had been largely self-selecting, meditating on applicants who felt that they were 'drawn' to join. This excluded the majority of the members from any say in the choice of their leaders. This time we agreed to try to have a 'spiritual election' in which members meditated individually on how large the group should be, and who should be in it. The results of these individual meditations were used to create a list of those who were most widely supported.

How far inner attunement actually decided the issue is uncertain. Members undoubtedly meditated on the questions, but there was much discussion of the merits of different individuals, which certainly influenced the process. Most people felt that a relatively small group of five or six people would be most appropriate.

All those who had received a considerable measure of support sat in front of the membership during a series of community meetings. There were several meditations about individuals and the composition of the group. Those who had received support expressed their own views about participating; others shared their hesitations and doubts. One member who had been selected dropped out because of time commitments outside the community. Another, who had not been selected, joined because during a meditation he felt it was appropriate to do so. In the end a final meditation was held, which indicated considerable reservation about three of the candidates. Instead of trying to exclude them —in a small community it is much more difficult to say 'no' to someone than 'yes'—the group was sent off for a week to our retreat house on Iona. There they became used to interacting with each other. At the moment of writing, the group of eight remains the same and meets weekly to meditate.

In this way one of the most important steps in our history was taken—the choice of spiritual leadership involving the attunement of the whole membership. The account illustrates the sometimes labyrinthine complexity of our decision-making mechanisms. Such a process can work only in a situation where the priority is not immediate action. At the Findhorn Foundation, we allow few situations to demand immediate action because we are seeking to develop a less pressured, less stress-filled lifestyle which gives us time to consider all the ramifications of a situation. We savour our decision-making, taste its flavours, enjoy its composition and relish the eventual denouement. On a decentralised planet, with transformed human priorities, a spiritual basis to life and a new level of consciousness among individuals, such practices could be very wholesome for all. These changes may not be as far off as they seem, but they will involve a global 'rebalancing' of humanity.

The Organisational Structure of the Findhorn Community

Our community is constantly changing. Organisational forms are being questioned, dissolved, re-formed. A new community outside the Foundation itself is forming, the 'village' spoken of in Eileen's guidance of 1968:

> I want you to see this centre of light as an ever-growing cell of light. It started as a family group; it is now a community; it will grow into a village, then a town and finally into a vast city of light.
>
> (Foundations of Findhorn, p. 152)

Attempts to create an organisation for this wider community have not yet succeeded. An interesting newsletter, 'Open Forum', was not well enough supported to continue. At present the Find-horn Foundation is still too dominant for any wider community structure to feel balanced, but this will slowly change as we decentralise.

A series of diagrams may help to make our present organisational structures clearer for the reader. What is important about the Findhorn Community is, however, not so much the form of its structures, but how things are done in them.

Level 1—The Emerging Community

i. The Findhorn Foundation.
ii. New Findhorn Directions.
(Businesses working to support the Foundation.
See Chapter 7)
iii. Independent businesses associated with the Findhorn Foundation.
(See Chapter 7)
iv. Independent caring or charitable organisations associated with the Findhorn Foundation.
(Chapter 7)
v. Associates.
(Individuals spiritually drawn to the area who support the Foundation in some way or other. Chapter 7)
vi. Organisations very closely associated with the Foundation and working in related spiritual education.
(Newbold, Chapter 7; Erraid, Chapter 6)
vii. Independent communities in other countries with exchange or other relationships with the Findhorn Foundation.
viii. A Development Wing to support projects associated with the community.
(e.g. the wind generator, Chapter 6)

The Findhorn Foundation, though the major body, is now only part of a much larger whole. The size of the Foundation has halved in the last ten years. There were over 300 members in the late 1970s, about 160 in 1989. Everything else is growing. In 1989 two former Foundation departments joined New Findhorn Directions, a trading company owned by the Foundation which runs the commercial caravan park we acquired with the purchase of the land in 1983. They are our mail order business and the Phoenix shop. Other departments may join them in the near future. Some ex-members have started small businesses, and are running them with varying success from the Caravan Park. Other ex-members offer a variety of counselling and therapy services to provide them with enough money to live here. There is a growing interest in opening businesses in the area using spiritual management methods. The Moray Steiner School, which has been strongly supported and subsidised by the Foundation; Meadowlark, a very beautiful nursing home owned by a Canadian doctor and his wife; and Minton House, a therapy and retreat centre—all seek to bring spirit into their activities. A growing number of individuals have been attracted to live here after making a connection with the Foundation. There are already more of them than members of the Foundation itself. They often support community work activities and other projects.

Newbold and Erraid are smaller, sister organisations. They maintain their own programmes, are financially independent and recruit their own membership, but there is much interchange between us. The Foundation maintains a costly weekly bus service to the Erraid community, which challenges and has once or twice defeated the skill of our drivers. We also have looser relationships, mainly small-scale exchange programmes, with other communities in several countries. They provide our members with experience of parallel ways of doing things.

Level 2—Locations

i. The Caravan Park
(Findhorn Foundation, New Findhorn Directions,
independent businesses, some associates.)
ii. Cullerne House. North of the Caravan Park.
(Findhorn Foundation gardens, see Chapter 6)
iii. Station House, in Findhorn Village.
(Foundation members' accommodation.)
*iv. Drumduan House, Forres. At present owned by
the Findhorn Foundation.*
(Some members' accommodation. Moray Steiner School—see
Chapter 7)

v. Cluny Hill College, Forres.
(Major guest centre)
vi. Newbold House, Forres.
(Closely linked spiritual centre)
vii. Traigh Bhan, Iona.
(Retreat house. Open for guests in summer and members in
winter. Mentioned in Chapter 5.)
viii. Erraid, an island south of Iona.
(Small, self-governing spiritual community living
in harmony with nature)
*ix. Minton House, an independent retreat centre adjacent to
Cullerne House. Meadowlark, an independent nursing home in
Forres—Chapter 7*

The physical diversity of the community supports a decentralised structure. In the same way as we encourage individuals
with different religious and cultural backgrounds to learn to live
harmoniously together, so I believe we are being asked to work
with different kinds of institutions, with different approaches to
organisation, developing different kinds of mutually stimulating
relationships in harmony together. We are linked by the shared
belief in the discovery and expression of love as our common reality. At present the trend is for more autonomy and self-sufficiency
for Cluny Hill College. The significant change in this respect will
be when Cluny retains a proportion of the funds it earns for guest
programmes, so it can become financially independent.

Very small communities like Erraid and Newbold can be managed collectively, while at the Park so many different things are
going on that a more complex organisation is needed. The Core
Group's inner work underpins the variety of forms and structures
in the different parts of the community.

Level 3—Findhorn Foundation Organisation

i. Trustees
(The Foundation is a registered charity)
ii. The Core Group (described above)
iii. Community Meetings
iv. Community-wide management:
a) Management Committee. b) Finance Committee.

c) Education Branch. d) Personnel.
(Chapter 4)
v. Location Meetings:
a) Park Family meetings. b) Cluny Family meetings.
(Members' meetings)
vi. Area Management:
Park Department Focalisers' meetings.
Cluny Department Focalisers' meetings.
vii. Park departments:
Kitchen (+ Food Shed), Home Care, Stewardship, Park Garden, Cullerne Garden, Health & Wholeness, Audio, Visuals, Accounts, Communications (+ Reception), Universal Hall (+ Visitors' Centre, Green Room Cafe), One Earth Magazine, Findhorn Press, Game of Transformation.
(Chapter 3)
viii. Cluny departments:
Kitchen, Home Care, Maintenance, Garden, Dining Room, Accommodations, Youth Project, Garage.

At present, the Findhorn Foundation is the dominant feature of the Findhorn Community. Because of the immigration laws, it provides the only way that non-EEC citizens can stay here for extended periods of time—we have an agreement with the Home Office that bona fide members can live here and work with us for the duration of their membership. Because of its history, people often identify the Foundation with the Community. They still tend to think that to be here means to be a member of the Foundation. But the trend is to decentralisation, moving towards a community with varied types of association between independent individuals and groups.

In the Foundation, regular meetings for all members allow us to attune to and discuss the major decisions that have to be made. Political debate or conflict between opposing factions with different philosophies is rare here. The attunement process reduces tendencies to outright opposition. The emphasis given to personal development reduces egoism—a dominant feature of most political institutions—in our discussions. A polarisation of view did happen at Newbold recently. Some members felt that the direction of that community should resemble a family style of living. Others felt it should emphasise retreats and inner work. The second

104

approach prevailed, and about half the membership left. One solution suggested by Newbold's Trustees in this situation was to purchase another old house, so that each group could develop its ideas separately, but this has not happened up to now.

As has been stressed earlier, it would be inappropriate to regard the various management organisations within the Findhorn Community merely as decision-making bodies. In them people are learning a new level of responsibility. The way personalities blend and interact is an integral part of collective life. We call this 'group process'. Through it, members become sensitive to others, practise how to listen, and realise how others hear their attempts to communicate. They become aware of what in others or in a situation stimulates an emotional response in themselves, and how to deal with such a reaction. In meetings these aspects of the interaction could be suppressed in order to save time. But when this is done, the 'psychological component' enters the decision-making process itself, leading to factionalism. That would turn us away from inner, spiritual awareness to superficiality. Our kind of decision-making takes a long time. Sometimes we complain about the disease of 'meetingitis', which is chronic in the community, but in a reorganised world where time pressure was not the deciding criterion everyone could learn psychological awareness from meeting situations as we do. More humane identities would result.

Dedicating Work to God
Attachment is a very common psychological distortion of responsibility. As a person accepts attunement to a position or function in the community and commits him- or herself to it, they find their own style of performing the job. They come to see 'their' way as the 'right' way. Possessiveness confuses attunement. This is a common problem among personally insecure people. They tend to find validation through what they do. People with such personalities are frequently attracted to the Findhorn Foundation, as they define this orientation to outer performance as service. They are in fact serving their insecurities rather than other people, but learning this is often a hard lesson. Problems come up when it is time to release a job to someone else.

It is necessary to work with much patience and caring on these issues, for such people will ignore inner indications and outer signs that it is time to release and move on. Then they find themselves in a situation which is painful for all concerned. As is usual in the Findhorn Community, if the lesson is not learned, it comes up again and again. We are expected to work on our insecurities until being, not doing, is the source of our self-confidence, and our actions become an expression of a degree of inner realisation. Then we are no longer attached to the results of our work or to the position it gives us. The exercise of responsibility is a teaching situation here, an exercise in spiritual development.

Finance and the Material World
Ever since the late seventies, community financing has been one of our greatest challenges. The big debts incurred through the building of the Hall and the purchase and renovation of other buildings have loomed large in our thinking. Finance policy up to 1988 was very cautious. Our aim was to pay off £50,000 of our debt every year. By the beginning of 1988 we had reached a position where three more years would probably have eliminated it. But in the last two years the debt has risen once more to over £300,000, as we have paid for a new community centre and for the replacement of Cluny central heating. In 1989 there was no provision for debt repayment. Our smaller sister community, Newbold, which has based its financing on donations rather than fixed payments, has cleared its debts. Erraid is self-financing. Is this a matter of size and scale? Have we found an appropriate relationship to money? Are our attitudes rooted in anxiety and insecurity? How does a community operating from inner attunement relate to financial matters?

Perhaps the very variety of views on these issues in the Foundation demonstrates that we have not yet found maturity in relation to our finances. Some members favour borrowing up to the limit of our security to improve our material situation. Others are unhappy at any debt at all. It is another aspect of the training process that the Findhorn Community represents. For we are, in microcosm, working with the issues that challenge the wider world as well. In that world, material standards are still the main criteria of prestige and power. Ever-increasing consumption fuels the industrial machine which returns profits to the investors and owners, and taxes to the government. To finance this, indebtedness has become a global pattern. Third world countries live in permanent debt. The majority of consumers in the West are also in debt to pay for material goods and services.

Materialism has not provided happiness for humanity. Those who don't 'have' are unhappy about that. Those who do either want more or feel frustrated that it hasn't given what was promised—personal fulfilment. So what should we do? In the United States, the Old Order Amish have retreated into an 18th-century civilisation, rejecting almost all modern technology. At the Findhorn Foundation our general position is that we should cautiously accept modern technology, examine its value to us from a spiritual perspective (i.e. we should not be accumulating technology for its own sake) and use it wisely, trying to be good custodians of what we have. Even this view, however, gives no clear guidelines.

This book, for instance, has been written directly on to a computer. The thought of writing it on a typewriter and manually correcting it, as I did my last book, now seems daunting. But Shakespeare and Goethe did not even have fountain pens, and it did not affect the quality of their genius. If we come to think we cannot exist without material goods, they have taken us over. When we have developed a strong spiritual connection, material things can be used as a means in the expression of love.

"First seek ye the Kingdom of Heaven," said Jesus, "and all else will be added to you." The more we find that Kingdom, the less we need, for insecurities around self-worth, status and happiness are resolved and material possessions can become means, not ends. The only 'end' that really makes life worthwhile is the discovery of the Divine within and its expression. The tools so easily become the masters.

I came to the Findhorn Foundation in 1983 without any money, having spent all I had in three fascinating years in California. It felt right for me to be here. My mother's sister had just died and left her a small legacy. This sister had, many years earlier, been the nurse of Sir George Trevelyan, one of the Foundation's trustees when I joined, and a supporter of the community from its early days. Because of this 'coincidence', my mother sent me most of the money for the membership fees; the community waived the rest. My first visit to Sai Baba also cost a lot. An old friend, whom I had helped when I was in work, gave me £500. Members and guests of the Foundation gave me the rest within four weeks, in astonishing gestures of generosity. My personal experience is that I am supported to receive what is appropriate for me in material terms. But can this trust be adopted for the financing of a large community?

And how should such issues be dealt with? Working with them can be fraught with anxiety, or it can be fun. The community alternates between these feelings, as I did in my year on our Finance Committee. Sometimes we lost ourselves in our financial problems and left meetings frustrated and snappy. Mostly, however, the level of inner trust brought us through. Often the greatest confusion was over the smallest things—whether a member could default on an obligation, or whether someone could exceed their budget to buy an 'essential' computer program. In such cases we found ourselves acting as moral as well as financial arbiters. The Finance Committee gave me some of the most intense training in human relations and in detachment I have had in our community.

At present we are caught between the level of our debt and our programme for community expansion. Is it right for members to live in old caravans, which are dreadfully wasteful of fuel in our cool climate, while guests in the Park are accommodated in temporary chalets that have become 'permanent'? We rejected a proposal for permanent guest accommodation, on the grounds that the chalets are, at present, still habitable. We would have had to go deeply into debt to build it. As for members' accommodation, which has been an issue ever since the decision to build the large and expensive Universal Hall, an interim solution has presented itself. Some members have private funds. Using them, we are planning to start building some acceptable housing in 1990. This will free up some caravans, perhaps allowing us to scrap the very worst of them. One or two of the people who can afford larger houses have offered to share them with other members. At least here is a beginning. The present size of our building department does not allow for more. But should the community support private building with all its complications of ownership and future sale?

In comparison with the budget of our neighbour, the air base, our financial problems seem small beer indeed. The base has just spent many millions of pounds modernising installations for their reconnaissance planes. The Foundation has not received, so far, large sums in donations. Many visions for development remain visions. We would like to have an organic farm. We would like to consolidate the land around the Universal Hall, so that the Community can use it as its natural centre. We would like an area of the dunes to be preserved as a nature reserve. We would like to build permanent office space to accommodate all our administrative activities. We would like modern telephone exchange facilities; and so on. Perhaps the lure of money is still too great and we are externally constrained—to demonstrate that our undoubted happiness is not dependent on material well-being, our potential desires still need to be curbed!

It is not that nothing has been done on the material level. At the end of 1989 we have a beautiful new extension to our community centre, which was hopelessly cramped; a wonderful nature sanctuary sits like a gem in the heart of the community; the expiring central heating system in Cluny has been replaced. Two new houses are under construction.

So the dilemmas continue. We dance between dreams and restraint, wondering whether we should increase the price of our guest programmes, and by how much, while Eileen's guidance is now telling us we should switch to donation financing. The purpose of this section is not to provide answers, but to engage the reader in the kinds of questions which emerge in trying to re-balance the relationship between spirit and matter. The paradox is that, in a spiritually oriented world, the more one feels a need to have things, the less one is guided by spirit; hence the less one gets the 'needed' things.

As soon as the need for something is released and spiritual values are predominant, then material things become available. I would like to see us pay off our debts, because I see indebtedness as part of the crisis of the world we have to leave behind. I think it would be nice to set an example of living within our means; but it is also nice to have good dining facilities and warmth for our guests and members. The dilemmas continue and the 'Angel of Findhorn' guides us through!

Cullerne Gardens

Chapter 7
Educating the World

"Here's the thing," say Shug. 'The Thing I believe. God is inside you and inside everybody else. You come into the world with God. But only them that search for it inside find it. And sometimes it just manifest itself even if you not looking, or don't know what you looking for. Trouble do it for most folks, I think. Sorrow, lord. Feeling like shit."

"It?" I ast.

"Yeah, It. God ain't a he or a she, but a It."

"But what do it look like?" I ast.

"Don't look like nothing," she say. "It ain't a picture show. It ain't something you can look at apart from anything else, including yourself. I believe God is everything," say Shug. "Everything that is or ever was or ever will be. And when you can feel that, and be happy to feel that, you've found it."

Shug a beautiful something, let me tell you.

—Alice Walker. The Colour Purple.

Introduction to a Workshop

It is June 1989. A Saturday morning at 8.30. Christa and I have arrived for the beginning of our workshop. We want to meditate in the room we have been allocated, the Beech Tree Room—best workshop space in Cluny—to clear out the old energy and make everything fresh. However, the focalisers of the previous week's Experience programme are vacuuming it. We can't get in, so we wait.

Experience week is the 'way in' for guests at the Findhorn Foundation. There is now a version at the Park as well, called 'Living the Life We Choose'. Once you have done Experience week, you can go on to the other programmes or into workshops. Only as a conference guest or short-term visitor can you come without doing an Experience week. Even then you have to do it if you want to stay on. Christa and I have focalised Experience weeks together, the German language ones. There are always two focalisers for programmes in the Foundation, to give mutual support. It reduces projections from guests with 'authority stuff'.

This time we aren't doing an Experience week, but starting a two-week workshop. We meet Dianne, Guest Department focaliser at Cluny. "Didn't you know, we have registration on Saturday morning in the Beech Tree Room now. You'll have to wait till lunch time for your meditation. Your registration will be up there too." "We Parkies don't know what you're doing here, changing things around!" There's time to snatch a quick cup of tea. Soon we're up in the Beech Tree Room with all the others. As always when I first go in, I notice Harley Miller's beautiful picture of the grandad beech tree in front of the building. How many of us have sat under that tree and asked for a healing, or surreptitiously hugged it when no one was looking. We are never refused.

I have to go a couple of times to the toilet. Why do I still get nervous at the beginning of a workshop? I'm supposed to be experienced now. God is running this show, not my personality! At one side of the Beech Tree Room is Susan, the 'finance person', with her money box. We'll send our guests to her as they arrive so payment is out of the way. Some people will pay less than the full amount for the workshop, making use of our bursary scheme. We don't have anything to do with that, though; the Accommodations Department organises it. At the other side are Anne and Sandy. They're focalising an Experience week, so the real newcomers will go to them. They'll be in the Sycamore Room, the second largest room for programmes. For the kind of work I do it only takes 15 comfortably, but if you're sitting in a circle it'll take twenty. Christa and I sit down at our coffee table, already set up for us with chairs by Guest Department members. Several of our workshop guests are waiting. We look at each other. Maybe we should have speeded up the tea break a bit!

At present our guests come mainly from northern Europe, the United States and Australia, with a sprinkling from other areas. Most are white and middle class. We have never done a survey, but my sociologically trained eye reads that the majority are between 30 and 45, in various kinds of caring professions, already concerned with the environment and their own identity. Many will have explored some kind of therapy as a means of self-development. For their age groups, there are more than average single and divorced people. People who want to come are asked to write a letter of application. This screens out a small number who would not benefit from being here. The energy can be too strong for mentally unstable people. Three or four times a year we have to help visitors who are not ready to be here to get back home.

Accommodations has prepared lists of guests, using their computer. Computerising Accommodations took quite a time. Our Accommodations focaliser didn't think it was necessary; she had her own wall chart system and did a very efficient job on her typewriter. But her understudy, a logical-minded Frenchman, couldn't type well. He was excited by the idea of creating a system model for the computer. There was something of a clash of wills. At one point, a guest let water overflow in the bathroom upstairs, and the ceiling fell on the computer. Was this a divine message? Anyway, the previous focaliser has now moved to Reception, and Accommodations has moved to a room without a bathroom above it. Now there is talk of putting a new, computerised switchboard in Reception!

Accommodations allocates everyone to a bedroom shared by three or four people. Sexes are segregated, of course, and smokers put together where possible—otherwise they can't smoke in their rooms. Some people are surprised that we don't ban smoking, but prohibitions don't really help people to give it up. There is even a cigarette machine. But there's only one public room in the building where you can smoke. It is the old bar of the hotel, with no windows, furnished in deep red. You really know you're going into hell when you go in there to smoke! However, it is rumoured that the best conversations take place in the bar. I wouldn't know. We don't ban alcohol either, but are rather aware that it is incompatible with advanced spiritual development (it suppresses higher brain function).

We ask our workshop members their names and tell them their room numbers. These people are all 'old hands'—they've done an Experience week some time or other. We don't have to show them round the building, as Sandy and Anne at the next table must—a survival tour, so the new arrivals know where the sanctuary is, where to eat and where to find the toilets. Everything else they can discover later. Our guests are a little more confident. They have all gone through it before. They know where things are. We even know some of them already, or rather they know us. If you see a guest once or twice during their first week, they soon become a face in the crowd. There are always crowds at the Findhorn

113

Foundation. Cluny has two special guest-free weeks a year, so that members can take a breath and experience the building to themselves. It always seems very empty and large.

"You came in and talked to my Experience week in 1985. That's why I signed up for your workshop." "Oh, yes, I remember your face but not your name." Actually it's not a lie; there is a faint familiarity about the face. After two weeks' intense work together, we will be very close, like old friends.

Of course, some people can't stand sharing a room. They are lucky—Cluny is not quite full this week, as it will certainly be during July and August. One of us goes and pleads with Accommodations. "You have to talk to Terry in Homecare," says Ian. "They don't like having to clean rooms for one person. If it's all right with him it's all right with me." Where's Terry? Everywhere. It's his busy morning. He's the star of the building, organising, directing. Every room has to be cleaned between 8.45 when the old guests are supposed to leave, and 12.00, when all the new ones should be safely 'at home'. He is coming out of the little-room-under-the-stairs, where Homecare lives. Yes, it's OK with him. He sighs. It's always the same. Who can say no when there are empty rooms? And the guests always have the best of reasons.

During the morning our 18 guests arrive, sit and chat and go off to settle in. For this workshop we have set a limit of 18, because that's a very comfortable number to work with and get to know well. Since they have all arrived, from the 'States, Canada, Australia, England, France, Holland, Switzerland, Israel and Germany, we have to ring Newbold and tell a man there he can't do the workshop after all. The building is the usual Saturday morning hive of activity. Homecarers, members and guests who are staying on scuttle everywhere, dangling vacuums, old laundry, tooth glasses and vinegar sprays for cleaning mirrors. 'Work is love in action.' Saturday morning tests it out! In the kitchen, the lunch shift is preparing a soup and salad meal. The dining room crew are cleaning up after breakfast. Lucia is doing a superb job on Reception, handling phone calls and six enquiries at the same time. The entry hall is full of cases and rucksacks. One of our buses comes back from the railway station, disgorging a new group of wide-eyed newcomers. Taxis come and go. There is a faint flavour of an Indian railway station in Cluny on a Saturday morning in summer. You can let yourself go to it, riding on the energy. Or, if you have somehow escaped homecare, you can run away up to your room and hide.

Christa and I at last clear the tables away and close the door. We have the big room to ourselves. We make a circle of twenty chairs and put the candle in the centre, ringed with flowers from the garden—only the gardeners can pick them. I put Sai Baba's picture on the mantelpiece. Since I am focalising the workshop and He is my teacher, He has a right to be there for the two weeks. We light the candle, close our eyes. The bustle and business of the morning fade away into beautiful silence. I ask for blessing on the workshop; that everything should come from the highest; that the qualities of love and joy should be with us for the two weeks. Then we are silent together for a quarter of an hour. It is all going to be fine; I love to work with Christa .... There is still some lunch left when we go down. Saturday morning is over and another workshop has begun.

Learning What the Findhorn Foundation is About—
The Experience Week

The summer 1989 brochure, running from April to November, lists Experience weeks for all except four weeks, two of them during conferences when everything else stops. In the summer there are often three Experience weeks at a time, two at Cluny and one at the Park. There are Experience weeks in Dutch, German, French and Italian. There are Family Experience weeks, organised for parents and children. In addition 48 different workshops are listed, with another 17 or so at Newbold. As well as workshops there are the Departmental Guest programmes and the Living in Community programme for those who want to experience our life on a longer-term basis, while for guests who want to be quieter there are four Retreat weeks. Each Experience week and workshop needs two focalisers. Accommodation has to be organised, letters answered, meals cooked, cleaning and renovation done, vegetables and flowers grown ... and ... and ... and! When I write it all out, it really seems a little miracle that everything works. *And* we are a spiritual community. Or rather that is the secret. Guests come here to share what we do. What we do, largely, is to look after them. They learn to care for themselves in a new way. It is a divine economy!

Part of the function of Experience week is to introduce people to the community. But that doesn't merely mean showing people around. The best way for people to understand what is going on at the Findhorn Foundation is to experience it in their own group. Guests begin the Experience programme with varying degrees of caution, shyness and defensiveness, but by the end of the week a group has formed, characterised by mutual trust, acceptance and love; it almost always works. My friend Anna was just invited for a holiday in Greece for the third reunion of an Experience week she focalised. It is this transformation that is important, not learning who lives where and who does what, for, as hopefully I have already made clear, learning to find love in ourselves and express it in our daily actions is the community's raison d'être.

Experience week is quite intense. Typically, the guests and the focalisers meet on Saturday afternoon, introduce themselves and learn how to attune. They have the evening free to get used to the place. On Sunday morning the group starts with Sacred Dance. I love Sacred Dance, although my head and my feet have not yet found bliss together. In circles, usually holding hands, we learn simple adaptations of folk dances from all over the world, each expressing some different quality appropriate to a fulfilling life. It is innocent and joyful. Jesus pointed out that the development of childlike qualities is a key to the kingdom of heaven. That kingdom is available on earth, now, if you have the keys to get in.

On Sunday afternoon, there is the chance to get to know the 'other side' of the community through a tour of either Cluny or the Park, and then, in the evening, there is a time for sharing feelings and experiences with one another, a process that is repeated every evening of the week, with a final, long session of completion on Friday afternoon. Each evening there is also a presentation by members about various aspects of community life, but sometimes, if the sharing becomes intense, the presentation is dropped. All the members who are due to come in to the group know that they may, as they wait in the lounge, be visited by one of the focalisers saying, "I'm afraid we really can't stop at this point." Wednesday, the evening when members share about their personal experiences, is most often 'crisis' night as guests begin to trust each other enough to go a little deeper into what they are really feeling. In these sharings, and at the other times when the group is interacting, the guests begin to learn the difference between relating to someone with love rather than with judgement, with support

116

rather than criticism. How the same process unfolds in the community the guests experience through their focalisers and in the departments where they work for four mornings of the week.

Each week, departments send in a note of how many guests they can work with the following week; then the Experience week group meditates to attune to which person goes to which job, another practical example of how we do things. In work departments guests experience a new attitude to work. They sample how members and longer-term guests deal with day-to-day problems as they arise. We can call it 'learning love on the job'.

The rest of the time—apart from a Thursday afternoon off, to gasp for breath—is spent with the group in new age cooperative games, a group work project and a nature outing. It is an intense, but not pressured, programme. The focalisers are there to support everyone through the week, deal with their problems, if need be, and to take responsibility for the energy of the 'Angel of Findhorn' as it works with the group. The Friday afternoon sharing is special. We start with a guided meditation, recalling the events of the week. There is a largish stone in the middle of the circle, next to the candle. Following the meditation, in a practice based on a Native American tradition, someone takes the stone and begins to speak. While they have it, everyone else gives them total attention. No one must interrupt until that person has finished their sharing. Often people are moved by the experience of love and attention they have received during the week, and even more by the way their own hearts have opened. They have begun to see people and work in a new light. After the completion session the group stays together for the evening meal, often sharing a bottle of wine (or two) to celebrate the week.

We do sell wine and beer for the Friday night dinner, which is also the one meal when fish is available as well as vegetarian food. In Cluny the proceeds from the sale of drinks have gone to renovate the lounge.

The Experience week is just that, an experience of our life in microcosm. The guests represent Foundation members, and the time spent together represents the way we live and discover how to get in touch with some of the unconditional love that is humanity's real essence. Just like members, guests can choose whether to go to the sanctuary for the various daily meditations or to meditate alone. It is a week spent saying hallo to spirit in very practical ways. Although the time is short, for many it is very moving and for some it may be life-changing. On Saturday morning, the majority of the guests return home to see how they can integrate what they have discovered into the lives from which they came. Sometimes they may return to the Foundation years later. Other guests stay on, deepening their connection with spirit by living longer with us or going into one of the many and varied workshops offered by members.

Not everyone who visits us registers for an Experience week. In the summer, particularly, many people drop in just for a day, or wish to stay just a night or two in caravans in the Park. Through the Short-Term Guest Programme they can learn a little about the community. There are guided tours and an audio-visual in the Visitors' Centre in the Hall, and it is even possible to spend a morning or afternoon working with us in the gardens. But this is still really just observing the community. To explore the transformation of identity that so many visitors undergo requires the closer contact given by the Experience week.

Living and Working with the Findhorn Community
Undoubtedly the best way of experiencing what the Findhorn Community has to offer is to live with us over a period of time, working and attuning with a work department, sharing the ups and downs, the discoveries and resistances of a contemporary Western spiritual lifestyle. If you say you are going to spend a month or more working at the Findhorn Foundation, people may raise their eyebrows, particularly if you are in a well-paid job. "How can you pay money to go and work?" they say. "You must be crazy." Actually, the amount we ask for the programme, which provides full board and lodging, is less than the weekly cost of bed and breakfast plus evening meal locally, but your friends have a point. Why should anyone pay money to work?

For us, it is because the cost of maintaining and developing everything we are doing is very high. Guests are prepared to pay because spending time in the Findhorn Community is deeply transformative. It challenges you in your relationship to work, companionship, leisure and, above all, to yourself. Through day-to-day practical experiences the question 'Who am I?' and its companion 'Why do I live my life the way I do?' come alive. It is very hard to leave the same as you arrived. Sometimes the greatest

118

challenges come afterwards, when from a new perspective the world you return to seems artificial and meaningless. You have become, just a little bit, a creator. Can you change things? A former Living in Community guest ('LCG') telephoned me. His wife had fallen in love with someone else, but couldn't decide whether to leave. "It's a hard time," he said ruefully, "but I'm learning a lot—about myself. We've decided to split for six months, and then see if we can come together again. I can't imagine how I'd have got through it without the inner work I've done."

The structure of the programme is simple. An 'LCG' works in a department like members, joins them in their attunement and has the opportunity to take part in almost all community activities except a few members' meetings. The LCG group also has a focaliser and meets once a week—on Tuesday morning—for a sharing. It also spends Thursday evenings together. Perhaps one of the members presents his or her views; perhaps one of the LCGs with a creative skill shares it with the group. The LCG programme lasts a minimum of a month.

I remember my own days as an LCG, in 1983, with great affection. I knew inwardly that the Findhorn Foundation was the right place for me, and that I should become a member. But it was June and there was no Orientation programme to train for membership till November. After my Experience week, my Departmental Guest week, 'cooling down' before joining the LCG programme, was in Cluny garden. I had heard of the community through *The Findhorn Garden* and was fresh from an intensive course in herbalism at the California School of Herbal Studies, where we also meditated with plants and learned to communicate with them. Cluny garden was perfect for me. I worked, full of enthusiasm, with Brian, the vegetable garden focaliser. At last the weather turned hot; the summer promised to be gorgeous and the garden was beautiful, with curving rows of vegetable beds around a central point. Brian was full of energy, but seemed to be making an effort to concentrate. At the end of the week he said to me, "Carol, my inner guidance is telling me to go down to London to fundraise for the purchase of the caravan park. I've been waiting for God to send me a replacement, and I think you're it!"

In my work in America I had learned never to look a spiritual gift horse in the mouth. "OK," I said, "but I don't really know anything about gardening. I'll have to learn as I go." Brian seemed to find that acceptable—perhaps he had no alternative. We went to the garden group attunement that afternoon, and I was properly introduced to the other members. Brian had made a six-month commitment, which he was breaking right in the middle of the season. In one sense, he was really letting everyone down; not only that, he was asking them to accept me, in my second week at the Foundation, with virtually no gardening experience, as his replacement. I would have to take responsibility for guests straight away, as there was much too much work for me alone.

The group's response was a huge lesson for me. Instead of the furious reaction that I expected, everyone respected Brian's attunement. He was leaving to do higher work for the community, not because of some personal evasion. They looked quizzically at me, brash and a little self-important, but when we meditated, the 'Angel of Findhorn' didn't say 'no'—and who else was there? I spent the weekend really getting to know the garden, and frantically reading up on organic vegetable gardening. Basically, I had quite a lot of confidence. I was supposed to be here. The events were an outer confirmation of that. Alan, who now focalised the whole garden and had looked after the vegetable garden for several previous seasons, promised his advice and support. On Monday morning, my first work day as an LCG, the last piece of the jigsaw fell into place: Olive wanted to work with me. Olive had just started Essence, a twelve-week workshop. She would be working half-time. She had been growing an organic garden in New Zealand for eight years and really knew her stuff. But she wasn't confident with people. From my training in California, I knew how to lead meditations and to connect spiritually with the plant devas. We made a perfect team.

The next eight weeks were blissful. The sun shone. I made friends with my room-mate, an American woman called Tera who lived on an island military base somewhere west of Hawaii. I had a romantic friendship with someone else in the Essence programme. I went watering the plants at six in the morning—the only time the water pressure was reasonable—and late in the evening. Olive and I meditated a lot in the vegetable garden with the plants. The other guests loved it—it was like the old Findhorn Community. I began to respect Alan, of whom I was a little afraid. His photographs of nature, particularly of trees, seemed to me to be deva messages in another form.

120

I was also rather afraid of Angela, who focalised Cluny dining room. So that I could get to know the community better, I was asked to do two shifts in the dining room. Angela seemed unsmiling, severe. Everything had to be done exactly right. This perfectionism I had read about, but I had difficulty with it, because I tended to be slightly disorderly. I felt she considered me hopeless and incompetent. After a few weeks, however, she was the first member of the Foundation to trust me enough to ask me to do a clairvoyant reading for her. I had projected my own insecurities onto her. Instead of criticising *her* identity I learned how to examine my reaction to it. That helped me to work with aspects of myself that held *me* back. This was a new way of thinking about people.

I took a two-week holiday at the beginning of August, and then the going got tough. I was asked to share a room with Gisela, a member. Gisela, a German, had had the room to herself for five months. She was really upset to have to share with someone else. I found her crying and resentful at the invasion of her space. The room was spotless, in perfect order. The next three months were hard work. Gisela complained constantly of my untidiness; I found her sullen and unhappy. Very slowly we learned to tolerate, and then actually to like, each other, in a fragile, shy sort of way. I learned to be tidy and to clean up after me, German style. I had some reggae tapes with me, and discovered that under the stimulus of this music, Gisela became vital and vivacious. She was having a hard time in Homecare, where she worked. I supported her through it. Gradually I realised that through these situations and experiences I was being changed little by little, learning to love unconditionally.

Bert, the LCG focaliser, was a Canadian who lived at Drumduan House, where LCG meetings were held. He was a great David Spangler fan. The meetings consisted of interminable readings from and discussions of Spangler's works. Influenced by my years as a radical feminist, I found Spangler's rather authoritarian guidance irritating. I went to very few of the meetings. This was cheeky, as I was hoping to become a member. I expected a reaction from Bert, yet he did not seem to hold it against me. It was another Findhorn Community lesson: there was I, all squared up, prepared for a fight—actually reproducing my relationship with my parents—but there was no one to fight me. Again I was forced to examine my own reactions, to notice the times I created conflicts without realising it, by acting out old, unresolved frustrations.

For me, the path from the LCG programme led to membership. For others there is a return to the life back home. Everyone has their own experience, their own gentle or more dramatic story. People leave calmer, more self-aware, more distanced from their problems, better equipped for a more positive life in the world. There is no guru. We teach each other, through situations provided for us by 'coincidence' which is no coincidence. The wonder of God's love unfolding in us starts to melt the 'objective world'. Through the lessons we learn we are prepared to embrace more love; it is an ascending spiral.

Giving Workshops

Many members come to the community with skills or talents. Others learn new skills while they are here. As members gain an inward self-confidence through their life in the community, they want to blend it with these skills and share the result with guests. Professional 'new age' workshop leaders frequently visit us, but they come more for love than money, as they can usually command much higher prices outside than we can pay. It is not the Findhorn Foundation's role to become a professional workshop centre. Nor can we be a therapy centre, concentrating on workshops in therapeutically oriented personal growth. Other places, less remote from the major urban areas are better located and organised to do such work. The high costs of travelling to the Foundation and the need for residential accommodation make such ideas unrealistic in any case. *Our job is to share a lifestyle with people.* It is a more important job, though we do not see it as being in conflict with therapeutic work.

Our workshops, therefore, are really ways of relating to our lifestyle in a thematic way. The best-attended workshops are those directly concerned with spiritual development. Typical titles are: 'Bringing more love into your life', 'In search for the God within', 'Wholeness—our challenge', 'Healing the cause', 'Breaking in—to the Divine self within'. But even workshops with more specialised themes—such as Sacred Dance, primal painting and 'Fool of spirit' (a clowning workshop)—have a spiritual emphasis. They link guests to our lifestyle and approach. Visitors find here a unique blend of theme and spirituality. Up to now, Newbold's workshops, with some exceptions such as the Meditation Intensives, have been slightly more personal-growth centred. Yet in Newbold also there is a special spiritual flavour, which has given that centre an individual style. Many guests return there again and again. The current trend in Newbold is to increase the amount of meditation-centred work.

There are two workshops at the Findhorn Foundation which are worthy of special mention. One of them is Essence, a 12-week experience of the community in workshop form. Its sharing of community life is much more structured than that of the LCG programme and it involves participants in an intense relationship with the same group over a long period of time. For me, Essence is like an extended Experience week. Often I am invited to talk in the 'Personal and Planetary Transformation' sessions of the Experience week. Working with the Essence group I have a chance to develop similar work over a day or two, with practical exercises.

The other experience—it is hard to call it a workshop—which has been very special to the Findhorn Community is the Game of Transformation. The Game, as we call it, was the inspiration of community member Joy Drake in the seventies. She and her friend, Kathy Tyler, developed it into an extremely sophisticated tool for spiritual self-discovery, which continually provides powerful experiences for both members and guests. In the 'classical' version, five players meet with a game guide and a scribe, whose job is to chronicle the progress of play. They seek through meditation and discussion to find individual purposes for the game. These involve both what the players want to receive and what they are able to give—the latter usually in terms of qualities. Then, with these purposes in mind, they begin a complicated board game lasting for a day and a half. In it they may re-examine patterns in their lives that block them, strengths which they can develop, and their relationship to intuition, inner attunement and spiritual empowerment. Finally there is a summing up session in which all the players, the game guide and the scribe offer each other insight and feedback. Each player is given a tape recording to take away of feedback relevant to them.

There is a gigantic version of this game, the 'Planetary Game', which can be played with up to a hundred people. A couple of years ago the whole community played it to gain collective insight into our situation. At the other extreme, Joy and Kathy, now living in Washington State, have developed a self-guided version of the Game, 'The Transformation Game' or, as we have nicknamed it, the 'Game in the Box', a way of blending fun and personal spiritual awareness that can take something of the Findhorn Community spirit out to many thousands in their own homes. Whoever wants to improve their 'game of life' has an excellent teacher in the 'Game of Transformation'.

Conference Time

It has become our ritual to hold conferences twice a year, in the spring and autumn. For conferences everything stops. Normal working rhythms are suspended. Everyone goes on rotas for 20-24 hours during the week to make sure that the conference guests are provided for. The rotas allow members and LCGs to participate in what's going on. During the conference there are no other workshops and no Experience week. We become totally focused on the event.

At least a year before the conference, somebody will have an idea for a theme. Management Committee will attune to it. If the idea feels appropriate, it is put out at a community meeting to see if there is support. A co-focaliser emerges. Gradually, a conference group forms. Their job is to do all the organising and to invite speakers. Every now and again they report at community meetings for further feedback and support. As the conference approaches, pressure and excitement mounts in the conference group. Will the speakers show up? Are guests registering to come? What have we forgotten? How could so-and-so get ill just now! Over the years, a detailed manual has been developed, a checklist of things that need to be done to ensure everything works smoothly. The actual structure of the conference is up to the conference group. Sometimes we have been so full that guests have stayed in local hotels. We run extra Experience weeks prior to a conference so that guests can understand us better, but anyone can come to a conference without having done a week first. Whatever we actually call our conferences, their implicit title begins: 'The relationship of Spirit with . . . .'

I must confess that I am not a conference fan. Often at present I am doing workshop tours at conference time. Otherwise I bury myself in my beloved Phoenix shop, where I can meet the guests in small numbers, and eat at home to avoid the buzzy atmosphere of the community centre. I peep out shyly to attend some particularly interesting session. But I am the exception; most of us really enjoy the adrenalin-provoking atmosphere of our conferences, with discussions going on late into the night, and baggy-eyed participants dragging themselves to morning sessions. It is a change of routine, a chance to demonstrate how efficient we are at providing a stimulating and supportive conference atmosphere. We have quite a number of regular conference attenders, who come as much for the high experience as for the theme itself. There are main speakers, mini-workshops and small sharing groups led by members, so everyone gets a chance to participate. Members introduce main sessions with dances or music. During the week some kind of concert or event also takes place.

In 1988 we explored the relationship between spirituality and politics in a conference entitled 'The Individual and the Collective'. The conference group invited a large number of speakers at great expense. But bookings were late. The community began to get nervous. Perhaps for the first time it wouldn't be a success. Gradually the numbers began to rise, passing the point at which we could cover our costs. The community relaxed, but in the conference group there was dissension. Were there too many speakers? There wouldn't be any time for small groups. It would be a talking shop! Somebody loaned us large quantities of video equipment. Stand-mounted cameras and cables took over the Hall. Would there be any room for seats? Every session would be videoed, and there would be tapes for sale within 24 hours. A daily conference newspaper was set up, so everybody could express themselves. A contingent came from the Soviet Union and a special fund was organised to support them, as they had no foreign currency.

As the week sped by, we excelled ourselves. Exhausted amateur camera crews forced themselves to film yet another session. At night they duplicated videos and sound cassettes into the small hours. A conference critique group set itself up and it began to publish statements criticising conference structure.

A superb Russian pop singer arrived. He began rehearsing frenetically with a new-age rock band from the south of England. On Wednesday night he opened the concert with a solo set of Russian folk songs, so beautifully performed that there was hardly a dry eye in the house! Then the band came on; the guitars roared. The whole Hall became a sea of dancers, tripping over cables and twisting among the musicians, chanting the refrain of his song: "This time it's real; this time it's now, this time, believe in Perestroika!"

Two experiences from the conference remain particularly in my mind—my nuclear physicist friend leading three hundred people to the far reaches of the universe and back in a guided meditation, and a wonderful Japanese speaker, a senior business executive who had changed his life and healed himself of cancer, introducing a very critical discussion of Japanese society by playing an exquisite Bach piece on his cello. We all called him Mr Shin and loved him unreservedly.

At the end of it all, we paused for breath. The post-mortem showed that the conference had only just broken even, and the conference group received much criticism for abandoning the usual small group structure. There were too many speakers, too much big talk. Yet the conference was a success. It woke us up, challenged us, brought the whole world and its problems into our community, gave us a mirror to see how relevant we are when the talking is finished. I still have a tape of the concert with Sasha Malenin, the Russian singer.

Beyond the Findhorn Community
The main way that the Findhorn Foundation reaches the 'world outside' is through the experiences of our guests, shared on their return home. We, and they, are part of the 'big change' that is taking place in humanity, quietly, 'from the inside out'. In the Communications Centre in the Park we keep a card index of our visitors, by country and town, and a computerised mailing list. The Communications Centre also connects with a network of 'Resource People' in many cities across the world. They support us in various ways, from meditating to organising workshops for touring members.

For many years Eileen Caddy has gone on extensive speaking tours, addressing large audiences. She personifies the energy of the Findhorn Community; she is a powerhouse of activity and love although she is in her seventies. As she gets older, she is having videos made, so even though she can't travel so much, her message can still reach people. More members are being invited to speak or give workshops abroad. To support this work an Outreach section of Education Branch has been started.

I have found it very valuable to travel outside the Foundation. It has given me confidence in what we are doing, in our significance in world transformation. Such an awareness can sometimes fade if one is always involved in the day-to-day activity and challenges of the small community. With only this latter perspective, it is tempting to measure one's spiritual progress against perfection and feel disheartened. By observing life outside it is easier to see what a radiant gem has been created here, how it shines through the gloom and stress of materialist civilisation. Members who go out take a little of the gem's lustre with them. The world badly needs the Findhorn Community.

The community was set up as a centre of demonstration. It demonstrates the working out of a new lifestyle, a new, divinely-inspired way of joy-filled living. We are truly 'God's children' and are glad so many people want to visit us. The numbers will grow still further. We are educated, too, by our guests, for everyone is inwardly a child of God. As that begins to become apparent, there is no one who is not inspiring.

Cluny Hill College

Eileen Caddy

Peter Caddy

The Findhorn Foundation's 25th birthday celebration

Craig Gibsone

François Duquesne performing a mime

David Spangler

Dorothy Maclean

Barbara Hellenschmidt

John Talbott

Elfreda Coy

Mari Hollander

Alec Whittam

Angela Morton

Anna Barton

Ian Sargent

Helen Martin

Shirley Barr

Michael Dawson

Barbara Swetina

Jean Prince

Kajedo Wanderer

Mary Inglis

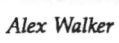

Alex Walker

Judith Bone

'Polar bear' swim on New Year's Day

Building ecological housing

In the Hall—'Partnership & Family' conference, 1990

Kinloss air base

Children performing

Findhorn Bay looking north-west

Chapter 8
Joining, Staying & Leaving

Perfect being is God. All else that is, is only half. It is imperfect and forever becoming, is mixed, and composed of possibilities. But God is whole. He is One, has no possibilities, but is all completion and reality. Men are transitory, we become, we are possibilities, and for us there is no perfection, no final being. But in all by which we pass on, from potentiality into action, from possibility to fulfilment, we have our share in this true being of God. That is what I mean when I say, 'to fulfil oneself'.
—Herman Hesse, *Narziss and Goldmund*

So You Want to Become a Member?
The Findhorn Community is an open one. To join it, all that is necessary is to come and live in the area and interact in some way with others who see themselves as part of this spiritual project. You have to find your own accommodation and make sure you are eligible to live in Britain. For a small sum to cover costs, you can become an Associate of the Findhorn Foundation, which entitles you to take some part in the life of the Foundation. But we recommend that everyone who contemplates coming into the wider community takes at least an Experience week first, so they have some practical idea of what is going on here. It is even better to spend time as an LCG, to explore the meaning of our lifestyle in more depth.

It is this wider community that is now developing fastest. From it will emerge a way of living that embodies the Foundation's guiding principles, without the fairly intense commitment and dedication that being a member of the Foundation requires. As the wider community evolves, there will be more possibility of employment in the small businesses that are slowly developing. At present, though, it is necessary to have some means of support if you are not a member of the Foundation and are non-British, i.e. not covered by the British welfare support system.

To join the Findhorn Foundation itself is a rather different matter. We are conscious of the spiritual purpose for which the Foundation was set up. In the Community, it should have an exemplary role. Foundation membership also requires dedication both to the guests who come here and to personal transformation. It doesn't matter to us if a person is intellectual or not. Their profession of religious belief is not important. Nor is their social class, nationality or skin colour. What *is* important is that they are prepared to go through the experiences which the 'Angel of Findhorn' will provide, to strip away the egocentric identity and begin to replace it with a God-centred one. Members must also be prepared to do this in a community in which work is seen as service, not something done for remuneration. They must be able to live with other people, and work out the problems they have with them. Furthermore, they need to be able to do this in the context of a modest standard of living, which takes into consideration the environmental consequences of one's material possessions. Beyond all these things, it must be spiritually appropriate for each person to be here. To be a member of the Findhorn Foundation is not quite so easy.

In 1988 the system for becoming a member was changed. One of the features of the Foundation is the frequent change of form of organisation, but the new system seems to be working well. It may still be in place when you read this! After the Experience week, you go on to the Departmental Guest week. In rare cases, the focalisers of the Experience week might have some objection to this; if so, an attunement with them would take place—all such attunements involve a meditation. To go on into the LCG programme you have an attunement with the focaliser of that programme. After three months you have another attunement with the LCG focaliser, who will recommend you to the Orientation focalisers for an in-depth interview centred on a guided meditation.

The Orientation programme lasts three calendar months, after which there is an interview with Personnel, with an Orientation focaliser present, again centred on a meditation. This complete, you become a student member for 18 months. As a student member, you are asked to pay a sum roughly covering the costs of your food and lodging and the use of Foundation facilities. We attune in the Personnel interview to how much that should be. After a year, there is an interview with Personnel to review how things are going and after 18 months, if you wish to stay on as a staff member, there is a further interview.

In the Findhorn Foundation there is normally no payment for work done. Work is love in action. Its reward is spiritual and personal development.

As a staff member you receive, if you wish, an allowance of £75 a month. Since many people, like myself, used all their resources during their student membership, this allowance is the 'pocket money' that enables one to have a holiday, a night out, some new clothes and so on. One or two wealthier members don't take it, as they don't need it. We do not pool financial resources at the Foundation, although we live an egalitarian lifestyle. One of the spiritual lessons to be learned here is how to get on with people of different class and financial backgrounds, for all of us are seeking our connection with the Divine within. An externally imposed uniformity has no relevance to this.

Being a member of the Findhorn Foundation requires sufficient maturity to enjoy the challenges it provides. We want, as far as possible, to be sure that everyone who becomes a member is ready for it—which does mean that the Personnel Department has to take the responsibility for saying no, sometimes. We are a laboratory for a human identity in development. What will one day become commonplace for all may at present be too much of a challenge for some. In the same way the spiritual disciplines of the mystics of the past would be too great a challenge for most members now. God is operating through humanity in appropriate ways to make and change our world.

Leaving the Foundation
Very few people make the Foundation their permanent home. Nor is it encouraged. We hope that more and more people will make the Findhorn *Community* their permanent home, developing themselves in the spiritual light that an association with the Foundation gives. Anyone in the wider community comes and goes as they please. In the Foundation, members are asked to make a commitment, usually of a year at a time. But we are not some sect trying to hold on to people. After a while, a member may feel a call to leave, either to develop themselves further somewhere else, or to train in some skill or profession, or for some other reason. Then they will have a 'completion' interview with the Personnel

Department, again with a meditation. We never try to hold someone back. It would be pointless to have members here who felt they were under some kind of duress. This is a community concerned with the discovery of love as the basis of life, not with externally imposed discipline.

Every now and again, a member loses their inspiration for living here and seeks merely to depend on the meagre living standard that we provide. Then the Personnel Department enters into a gentle process of negotiation, to see if the Foundation is really the place for that person to stay. Signs of inappropriateness might be an inability to find and enjoy one of the available work areas; a lack of vibrancy in day-to-day life; a lack of interest in further spiritual development; or a long-term withdrawal from community affairs. It is much easier to say 'yes' than to say 'no'; often members in such states are expressing that they want to leave but that they are afraid. It may mean that they have something more important to do in the outside world, which they are resisting for fear of change. It would be counterproductive just to say to them "Leave!" because resentment would be added to their confusion. We try to work with sensitivity and attunement so that members involved can come to self-awareness and leave in harmony. It is like trying to catch a large fish, except that we are trying to get one off the hook!

Who Comes?

In summer 1989 the Foundation had 153 members; there were 27 children and 126 adults; 49 of the adults were men, 77 were women. This sex imbalance is similar among our guests, and probably among all spiritual seekers nowadays. Perhaps while men are more open to material change and dominate technology, women are more interested in spiritual change and have less resistance to intuitive development. Among the adults 15 were over the age of 60. Only 8 were under the age of 30; 89 of us were between 30 and 50, a relatively mature group. We were all white-skinned, a large majority of middle-class origin, with the largest single group having a background in the so-called 'caring' professions. We came from 17 countries, with more than three quarters from the UK, the USA and West Germany. There was no one from the communist countries, although we have had Yugoslav and Czech members. In the atmosphere of 'Glasnost' we are enthusiastically developing links with the Soviet Union. In the early 1980s, Eileen's guidance indicated that it would enter a powerful phase of spiritual development; perhaps we will soon have Soviet members. The main problem is financial. People from Eastern European countries don't have any hard currency, so we must totally support every visitor from there, which is a strain on our resources.

In one sense it is sad that no members are from the Third World. It reduces our cultural diversity and our international complexity. The problem is partly financial. But our civilisation is largely responsible for the world situation. Change has to come from inside the juggernaut; one title I thought of for this book was 'Mission in the West'. We also form part of an international network of communities with similar aims. Seen in this context, the imbalance is not as significant as the statistics suggest. There are, as yet, no strong links with Japan, another rich, materialistic society. To build them will be a challenge to a major cultural divide.

Initially, some people come here seeking to change the world; they may not be aware that the modern method of doing this is by changing themselves. Others come seeking the therapy they need; they have to learn that we are a very special spiritual centre and not a therapeutic community. Yet others may 'hear voices' or 'have visions'; they must understand that we are not a centre for psychic development, nor are we overly impressed by such things. Another motivation for coming is a desire to serve; people with such motivation must be sure that it is not a cover for a feeling that they are only worthwhile when they are helping others, i.e. a sense of personal inadequacy. And yet others may be inwardly lonely and seek companionship in a community; they have to learn that a spiritual community can be a lonely place, for members are concerned to develop their relationship with God, and this may be a very private thing.

My definition of a 'model' member would be one whose heart is open to God, who dwells in it, and who derives their joy and inspiration for action from this reality. This opened, or opening, heart is sought in our members, for it is the inner connection that is required in the world today. A loving heart may be masked by personality, but the six-months' preparation period and the several attunement meditations reveal if a person is ready for further self-discovery as a member.

133

We have always had a dilemma about adults with children. On the one hand, we welcome children in the Foundation. On the other, with the kind of guest programme we run and the kind of transformation process that occurs, demands on time are large. This can be unfair to parents, children and the Foundation. So it is preferable that parents come to the wider community, perhaps sending their children to the Steiner school, whose education develops them more effectively for the changed human values we need. Of course, partners who are in the Foundation sometimes become parents and their children grow up in the Foundation itself.

One of our staff members recently became pregnant. After a meditation in a meeting of staff members, we agreed to continue to support her as a single mother through her pregnancy and when her child was born. Baby Elisabeth is now a delight to the community. But we have the means to give this support only on an exceptional basis.

There are, so far, no reliable statistics about the members of the wider community. From observation, their backgrounds and nationalities are similar to those of the Foundation, though less people come from non-EEC countries. There are also more families with children, as is appropriate for a developing spiritual community.

Working in 'Personnel'
I worked in the Personnel Department for 18 months, and for the last year co-focalised it with Cally Miller Simpson. Cally and her husband, Harley, who did the line illustrations for this book, are now part of the wider community, having gone 'independent'. They are running a small business selling Harley's pictures of local beauty spots, but Cally is still working with the community. She will co-focalise our Easter 1990 conference. During our time in Personnel we became good friends, developing a mutual respect. By the end of our time together we were so in harmony that even the images we would receive in meditations were similar.

Personnel is a very responsible job here. Decisions that are made affect people's lives, sometimes in major ways, so meditation is always the basis of the work. In these meditations there is a clear form. Everyone closes their eyes, and quietens down, releasing any previous discussion. They attune to the highest interests of the

Foundation and of the individual. Then they visualise a column of light or similar symbol representing the Foundation, or a particular job if it is a job interview. The aim is to see if the person concerned can enter and comfortably be in the column of light. If they cannot enter or have difficulty in staying in the column, this is an indication that membership, or a particular job, is not right for them, or that the timing is not appropriate. The person guiding the meditation asks for information relevant to the image that has been received. At the end of the meditation the results are shared. If one can let go of 'performance pictures', a sense of wanting to succeed, and 'ego-involvement', thinking of the results in terms of status, it is remarkable how effective this process is. It provides not merely 'yes' or 'no' decisions, but also much information on problems that arise, helping members to be aware of their challenges. Through such meditation techniques we have access to much more knowledge than 'reasonable discussion' provides.

Personnel is not only concerned with who comes and who goes. Members change jobs here frequently and Personnel supports them in finding a new place to work. If there is a problem among members of a department, to do with work or personal relations, Personnel may send in a mediator.

Housing is also an important concern of Personnel; there is something of a pecking order for available space. In the Park it is often about moving from a shared to an individual caravan. In Cluny it is about getting a sunny, south-facing room. Living conditions for members have improved, even in the six years I have been here. This is important, as it results in a tendency for members to stay longer and nothing is gained by having inadequate living space. The latest statistics show that nearly half the membership have been here for five years or more, and after such a time it is nice to have a reasonable, if modest, place to live.

* * *

It is a Wednesday morning in August, 1988. The Personnel department meets in the sanctuary at the Park for our Wednesday morning attunement. Michael and Margrit have already arrived, but Cally is a little late. She has taken her dog, Sheba, for a morning walk. It is tempting to stay out for extra moments, especially when it's fine. When she comes, Margrit leads us in a meditation.

135

Margrit is small, Swiss and a perfectionist. She had to be persuaded to come into Personnel. She used to grumble a lot about the way things were done; her challenge now is to be the one who gets the grumbles! Margrit has since left the community. It was hard to see her go. She married Jack, another ex-member, and they moved to Arkansas to send out light . . . .

Margrit says a few words to calm us down. She invokes the 'Angel of Findhorn' to be with us in our meditation. Half an hour later, she brings our focus back from the stillness to the outer world. This time the meditation is calm and quiet; sometimes someone will receive information relevant to the department or the community as a whole. We slowly get up and go up to the office in the Park building where the rest of the meeting will take place.

Our group celebrates the fact that we have all actually managed to meet together. We are such busy people. Michael and I both do a lot of workshops, and Cally has been doing some as well. It's two months since we were last all present. Cally enjoys some tea at this time in the morning. While she's making it, Michael lights a candle. He is as tall as Margrit is short, a soft-spoken, laid-back Englishman with an inner fire that never seems to get out of control. His detachment helps Cally and me cool down when we are excited about something.

Once Cally has made the tea, we start on the agenda. Margrit takes notes today. Management Group have accepted the idea that we have a few members whose full-time job is giving workshops. This is an innovation for the Foundation. We have been scared of creating a two-tier system of professional educators and 'servers'; but there are already one or two people who spend most of their time doing workshops. It seems sensible to recognise the fact, since their workshop commitments stop them from doing other jobs properly. Education Branch will work out the details of the new jobs. Michael is going to be in one of them. Who will replace him in Personnel in Cluny? Maybe Dianne? But she seems to want to stay in the Guest Department. At least Christa will take over as LCG focaliser there . . . . But the problem of Michael's replacement we have to leave without solution.

Next month, as usual, we won't be a full team any more. Michael is leaving the department, I go on a five-week workshop tour in Europe and Margrit is thinking of taking her holiday from mid-September. That leaves Cally. She groans, but she will do it. Anyway, Margrit may not go. She is preparing a file of all the guidelines the community has developed over the years for regulating our communal life. We call them 'guidelines', because there are so many exceptions in practice that it would be pretentious to call them rules. Margrit will code and index them all—a magnum opus. Margrit's departure from the community is looming. She really wants to finish the job before she goes and it won't be done by mid-September. Cally is safe. When Margrit's work is distributed, no one will have any excuse not to know community policy. But will anybody read it?

A former member is returning to the community. I am enthusiastic—I used to work with him in the garden at Drumduan. What will he do? He could go to Cullerne garden, but the Park garden needs a focaliser and so does Park Homecare. Cally, who does accommodation, will have to find him somewhere to live from Sunday. We'll need to have an attunement with him next week. Who's going to do that, and when?

So the business goes on—12 more items. We take a break for biscuits and more tea. We used to buy biscuits from our budget, but Finance Committee has stopped it. One of us runs down the road to the Phoenix shop to get the biscuits .... We haven't had a personal sharing again this week. It's been too long since we had one. If we don't know how the others are feeling, how can we work with real rapport? Also, we haven't shared our vision for the development of the community. If we don't have a common vision, how can we be sure we're working together? We agree to have a two-day meeting at Mansewood, a house in the country owned by a member. It is quiet there, away from the bustle and distraction of the community. We make plans to stay overnight, have a real personal sharing the first day and invite some members of Management Group to discuss vision on the second day. I agree to draft a vision statement so we will have something to discuss.

It is already noon—time to end our meeting before the 12.15 meditation in sanctuary. We hold hands together. In the quiet, with our eyes closed, we feel loving and loved. It is good to be alive. Later, at lunch, people descend on Cally and me like wasps on jam—business, business . . . buzz, buzz. No wonder my stomach plays up.

As I write, I can hear laughter from the group at the Maintenance shed, across the way from my caravan. They have stopped work to share a joke. Is the way we work efficient enough to be a model? As I look back over the minutes of the meeting I have just described, I can see that we covered 16 items of business in three hours, including a half-hour meditation and a 15-minute tea break. There was much warmth in the meeting, little sense of pressure, and above all a feeling that we knew each other very well. It is not only an outer knowing, but an inner knowing. No ambition is involved in the work; no concern about financial return; we do not have to demonstrate our abilities. We are God-centred people —imperfect, of course, but being together and doing our work together joyfully. Energy and enthusiasm for our community bubble up inside me.

Yes, I believe we are visionaries—visionaries for a human existence in which ordinary, everyday life takes on this inner, relaxed, caring quality. We are here to support each other with an abundance of love. The kingdom of heaven is going to rule on earth, yet most of us will not even know that it has happened. It will, however, feel a lot better. As I write, the news tells me that the Stealth bomber has just taken its first flight. It cost more than $500 million. The world still talks of peace and prepares for war. *The little meeting just described, and the many others like it, are the quiet events which are making real human history now. I look forward to an era when humanity both talks of peace and lives it.* Perhaps historians will scour the archives of the Findhorn Foundation and read the terse, sometimes frivolous minutes of our meetings to see how it came about.

Dining Room Attunement
Cluny Hill

Chapter 9
Getting On Together in
the Findhorn Community

You can hold me only
as close as your
expectations allow.

Reach for me for what
I may be, and come away
with empty hands.

Wait for me for signs
of change, and grow old
in your impatience.

Listen to me for answers
to your dreams, your ears
will sting in silence.

Hope for me for happily
ever after, and your loneliness
will complete the tale.

Expect me to be anything you wish
me to be, and distance between
becomes a canyon.

Come to me only
as close us your open
heart can bear, and I will sing
for the gift of you,
or quietly turn the other way.

—Guy Thorvaldsen

The Spiritual Context

The Findhorn Community's aim is not just communal living. Varying ways of life already coexist within its structure. In Cluny and Newbold, which are large houses, people live more collectively than in the Park, with its separate caravans. What is demonstrated is community living as a training ground in the discovery of the Self and as an expression of that discovery. Each individual experiences life here as a challenge and an opportunity. Through meeting the challenges, opportunities arise for more loving behaviour. The joy of becoming more loving provides motivation to accept even more challenges. As this upward cycle continues, the feeling that personal change is painful gives way to an awareness that, while it is not immediately pleasant, such change is the way to more joy. As a result, resistance lessens. Each individual experiences what has to happen on a global scale—the gradual substitution of the Divine Self for the ego-self. From the point of view of the ego-self, this is a process of surrender. In general, the more resistance there is to surrendering, the more painful the process.

The surrender refers ultimately to the very existence of the ego-self. It is not a tactical game, in which part of the self can be released to make the remainder more tenacious. Sometimes people whose energy remains centred in the ego-self delude themselves into thinking that they have made all the necessary changes. They re-consolidate resistance in other aspects of their personality. If such people stay at the Findhorn Foundation for long, they may receive very hard lessons. Eileen's inner voice comments:

Every soul along the spiritual path comes to a time when he is stripped of everything and stands before Me naked and in true humility. When that time comes, he finds that it is the end, for he has nothing. Yet it is when he has reached that point of complete nothingness that he becomes everything. That is when he finds Me, the Lord his God . . . . That is the turning point in his life. It may be a hard uphill struggle, but never will he want to turn back or choose the easy path . . . . He never gives up. His feet have been firmly planted on the path. He knows that he is no longer alone, that he can always seek Me and find Me. Together we will face the seemingly insurmountable and reach the heights. I am his ever present help. All he has to do is to ask. He is never refused help by Me. The more he turns to Me, finds Me, does everything with Me, the more aware he becomes of our Oneness. I never separate Myself from him.

(*God Spoke to Me*, p. 63)

Once it is understood that this transformation of identity is the purpose of the Findhorn Community, the reason for the life-experiences one receives, it becomes much easier to help and support others, even if personal surrender is not complete. The problems that others are going through are so much easier to understand than one's own! But in helping others, aspects of ourselves may be gently mirrored back to us. We may summarise all this as follows:

1. The Findhorn Community is a place where the Divine Self is being substituted for the ego-self.
2. The more resistance the ego-self makes, the more painful is the process.

3. The more the ego-self surrenders, the more joyful life becomes.
4. Surrender provides more joy, stimulating further release, and:
5. The joy of surrendering is expressed in service.
6. Through service, the opportunities arise for further surrender.

This is an abstraction of what is happening at the Findhorn Community. When you are living it, it is not always easy to keep such a model in mind. The drama of transformation is not always played out consciously, for increased consciousness of what is going on is a part of the upward cycle—you gain it little by little. It is like climbing up a mountain; from a distance you can get an idea of the lie of the land, representing the rational picture of what happens. Then, as you climb, through your successes you begin to get to know the mountain; you develop a practical sense of what the next part of the climb will involve and how to deal with it.

One aspect of surrendering is a reduction in forward planning. The main emphasis is on the ongoing present rather than on the long-term future. As you surrender to the Divine Self anxieties about the future are reduced. Instead, life begins to unfold.

It is hard to accept this way of experiencing life when one thinks of the injustice and poverty in the world. Nevertheless, on a personal basis it works. You are the agent of transformation. Without your transformation, nothing can change. You are the key to the log jam. Even in the face of oppression, inner change comes first. Then you can be clear about how to act against it. Gandhi taught this lesson.

In the Findhorn Community we learn a view of life that is both simple and sophisticated. It is simple because we become less and less concerned with the common anxieties of old-fashioned living. After a long decision-making process, Brenda became a member. She sold her house, but bought a smaller one and rented it out, to have somewhere to go back to, 'just in case'. Now she is no longer worried. She knows that she will never go back to her old life; if the time comes to leave the Foundation, a new path will open up.

Ursula left Newbold for the States. After a series of adventures, she arrived almost penniless in Santa Fe, knowing that she needed some therapy to free her for her next steps. 'By chance' she found an extremely low-rent room in a beautiful part of town. She came into contact with a therapist who took a liking to her and offered her therapy sessions in exchange for help in the house. She was able to make some money babysitting. Recently, when her visa ran out, she returned here. "I don't know why I came," she said, "but my time at Newbold is finished." Nevertheless, she returned. At that moment two old friends who had also left arrived from Germany. 'By chance' Newbold was short of members and desperately needed help over the summer. In spite of her assertion, she accepted that for the time being she was supposed to be in Newbold again.

The 'Language of Levels'

A Findhorn Community view of life is sophisticated because, from a spiritual perspective, everything seems to exist on several levels at once. Christopher, a Sai Baba devotee, prayed to 'come home' to God in the shortest possible time. He planned to go to an intensive past-life regression course in New Mexico. Instead, he had a major heart attack. 'By chance' his doctor was in the house at the time so he could immediately have appropriate treatment. He was rushed to hospital. Several months later, after three major operations, he emerged, a physical wreck. He regretted nothing. "I was so judgemental of people at the Findhorn Foundation," he said, "always judging their spiritual efforts as inadequate, thinking that they weren't working hard enough, and so on. Now I understand that they are all finding God in their own way, as best they can. Everything has its own beauty, its own logic." Through his pain he had been granted the new level of awareness he wanted above all else. Slowly, his physical body recovered.

In the community we tend to ask, "What does it mean?" "Why has it happened *now*?" rather than accept things at their face value. From a spiritual perspective, the 'face value' of a situation may be its most superficial aspect. As the spiritual path unfolds, our view of reality changes:

It happens.
What a strange coincidence that it happens right now!
From the level of my higher self I am creating the situations I need for the realisation of my Divine Self, at just the right pace.
Everything that happens is perfectly appropriate.

Each of these four statements is true, but they refer to different

144

ways of seeing an event. As it is a trick of dramatists to observe the same situation through the eyes of different characters, so in spiritual development we observe the same situation from different perspectives. As one slowly climbs the mountain of the divine view, one begins to see harmony behind the apparent discordance of scenery.

In our development different perspectives on life may coexist; at one moment we are calm and detached, understanding all; at another we feel hapless victims of inexplicable events. Part of the spiritual path involves learning to react appropriately to the levels of perception with which others are working. It doesn't do to tell a person who has just cut their finger in the kitchen that it is a lesson to teach the value of calmness under pressure. You need to get a bandage or give healing. One young man I knew tried to manipulate these different levels of explanation when he saw a woman who attracted him. "I'm sure we had a relationship in a past life," he would say. "You are certainly my soul mate!"

Nevertheless, it is often helpful to people who are struggling with problems to introduce them to a new perspective. Perhaps an observer can intuitively see a connection between spiritual growth and the meaning of particular events, more easily than the person involved. I use the method of viewing from a higher perspective very often, and very successfully, in counselling. The closer one comes to the Divine Self, the more appropriately one can respond, for it is the source of all knowledge.

The language of 'levels', of being able to view one's own personal experience as well as that of others from different—appropriate—perspectives, is one that has to be learnt. Ordinary means of communication are not sufficiently sophisticated for it. Sometimes visitors to the Findhorn Community are frustrated that a spade rarely seems to be called a spade. In apparent contradiction, we often seem childlike to outsiders. They are being introduced to an altered way of living.

As each new generation of members enters the Foundation, they experience a collective crisis of identity. Altered perceptions begin to impinge on old, established ways of thinking. This is often projected onto the community. "Why am I here? It's all too much!" becomes: "It's badly organised! Why don't we do things differently?" Members who have been here longer see this as a phase through which they too have been, and tend not to take it at face value. This view, in turn, makes it difficult to change things. Sometimes it feels as if one is dealing with cotton wool. The community absorbs your ideas and they disappear. Nothing seems to change. A few months later someone else will have the same idea and suddenly it is accepted. This is a lesson in releasing personal identification with things and also a test in patience. Our civilisation is very impatient. God, however, is not.

Meditating Together

The Findhorn Foundation's main focus is more on collective work than on collective meditation. Yet collective spiritual discipline is as valuable as personal discipline for the well-being of the community, as Eileen often stresses. In the early days collective meditation was obligatory, but this is no longer the case. Daily twenty-minute community meditations are held in the morning and at lunch time. In Cluny there is also an evening meditation, before dinner. They are well attended by guests, not so well by members. It is easy to find a good reason for not going, but the well-being of the community is supported by these moments of calm togetherness. At the end of the lunch-time meditation we visualise the energy we have generated together spreading to calm the world. Somewhere it will be felt.

Community meditations take place in weekly work department attunements, in fortnightly family meetings at the Park and Cluny, and at monthly community meetings. Every administrative meeting commences with a meditation.

It is beautiful to watch the community meditating together in the Hall. Of course, you can only do so if you arrive late and have to go into the viewing gallery! In these quiet moments comes a sense of our collective identity and of the dedication that each person, in their own way, brings.

Tools for Problem-Solving

Since we are not perfected people but people seeking perfection, and the Findhorn Community is a laboratory for change for the planet, life here brings up plenty of problems. A new humanity is not one without problems, but one with a different perspective on solving them. In the community we have developed and made use of many different ways of dealing with problems as they arise, drawing from the repertoire of both spiritual and personal growth movements.

The first requirement is: talk about it! People who don't have sufficient belief in their own self-worth to share their problems, or are too proud—another kind of insecurity—express them indirectly, undermining activities and relationships with others. On the other hand, some people with low self-esteem feel they can communicate with others only if they have problems, so they manufacture spurious ones constantly. At the Findhorn Foundation, there is always someone to listen to you. At first when I came I had a circle of 'special friends' who patiently bore my catalogue of woes. Now, although I am not particularly sociable and rarely seek an intimate exchange of confidences, I feel a great love for, and considerable trust in, all the members of the community. I can ask anyone for support in need, and I myself give it when asked. I do not always get the advice I want to hear, but if I knew what I needed to hear I would already have solved my problems.

When the problem is with someone else, mediation is often very helpful. It is always available. Jane's relationship with Tom was ending, but she was unwilling to recognise it. While she was away, Tom started a new relationship with Alice. Jane became furiously angry with Alice. She felt she should have consulted her before taking such a step. A couple of times she demonstrated her anger publicly. This upset Alice, who was a little afraid of her and felt defensive, although she was prepared to talk. Karen and Christine agreed to hear the problems and try to soothe wounded feelings. Finally, a meeting was arranged. Christine would 'hold the ring', assisted by Karen.

After an attunement, Jane had the chance to speak as long as she liked, uninterrupted. She shared her feelings and her own psychological background in relationships with considerable personal insight. Colouring all was her anger at the situation. Then Alice shared, cautiously, not wanting to get involved in Jane's feelings. Christine and Karen made sure each one had the space to speak and be heard. Although the mutual mistrust was not resolved, the face-to-face contact in a supportive environment enabled life together in the community to continue.

For Jane, the end of the relationship dramatised old patterns which she knew she had to deal with, while Alice in her new relationship learned much about the need to express her feelings. Living in a small community demands that we find some way of

147

dealing with difficult situations. You can't run away from them for long, when you are bound to see each other every day.

* * *

When we really transcend a difficulty, it ceases to be one. To do so requires changing the level of energy on which one lives. Spiritual counselling may help to give insight on what that looks like, and personal inner work, such as meditation, stabilises a new way of seeing things. The main danger in this is self-deception. A wish to be different may be substituted for actual change, with the result that unwanted behaviour is suppressed rather than transcended. One particular kind of tight, fragile identity bottles up a lot of psychological problems under a veneer of concepts of the good. In my spiritual counselling I often refer people to therapists to help them get in touch with similar psychological blockages.

At present there are people qualified in Reichian, Gestalt and Bioenergetic therapies in the community, as well as co-counsellors and art therapists. Several members have some training in Psychosynthesis. We learn not to be afraid of using these techniques to help us break through blocks, but we also discourage dependence on a weekly therapeutic 'fix'. More unusual therapeutic and transformation techniques are also available, such as clairvoyance, rebirthing and past-life regression. These can be described as 'changed awareness' techniques. In every case the quality of the support person, their ability to give total attention and their own degree of self-discovery are as important as the technique in providing support in change.

Living in the community provides access to a considerable amount of alternative medicine, from spiritual healing to herbalism, from acupuncture to foot reflexology. And, when all else fails, we have an allopathic doctor. However, it is remarkable how much of the sickness in the community relates to two states of spiritual development: release and resistance. Examples of 'release illnesses' might be colds, stomach upsets, skin eruptions. Resistance often manifests as back problems, exhaustion or constipation. Our array of healers and masseurs soothes and supports . . . .

Personalities in transformation need a lot of love and support on all levels. We talk of preventive and corrective medicine, but the greatest growth area for new humanity may be 'supportive medicine'—people trained and spiritually developed enough to support others in the transition from outer-identified to inner-identified states. Each supporter also needs support, in a chain of mutual assistance. This has nothing to do with selfishness or self-indulgence. Buildings need scaffolding as they are being erected. Every human being learning to discover and express something of their divine reality needs an effective support system as the process unfolds. The meaning of new community is not living together communally; that has no intrinsic merit, although it may be valuable as an experience. It is the provision of an effective and practical mutual support system, for the 'building' of human self-discovery is never complete. We advise guests who visit us to try to build such a system when they return home.

A 'Findhorn-Community-Style' Support System

Personal spiritual practice

Friendship & personal support

Alternative healing

Spiritual counselling & advice

Individual

Massage

Individual or group therapy

Allopathic medicine

'Change-of-awareness techniques'

Working Together
As far as possible, everyone in the community is in some sort of working group—book writing is one of the exceptions. The working group is not merely a means to accomplish tasks efficiently. Work is an opportunity to express one's inner divinity, and a teaching situation that often shows what further changes we have to make to become more in touch with that divinity. Relations with others are part of the work experience and the work group is a significant part of the support system. Occasionally big

challenges arise in work departments, for example if something has been going on that the department members together haven't been able to solve. Usually such a situation is the result of attachment; someone who needs to let go has become ego-identified with the work and their personality defence systems blend with their motivation. A person in such a state often uses any kind of justification possible to try to hold on. It is a form of obsession. Personnel Department will then try to intervene, sending in someone to 'hold the ring', to help the department work it out.

In normal circumstances we change jobs quite frequently. It provides a new arena for experience, a new working group to get close to. Two years is perhaps the average length of time in a work group, but it is often less in service departments—kitchens, homecare, maintenance and gardens— and rather longer in some of the others. New members usually go into the service departments, while it is rare for members to work in the Guest Department or Personnel till they have been in the community at least two years.

* * *

At nine o'clock on Monday morning, I cycle down to the Phoenix shop—crafts, books and wholefoods. By five past all of us are there: Anna, who looks after the wholefood section; Ienek, who is learning to take over the crafts from Ingrid; Michael, who focalises and looks after the tapes; Katherine, who deals with mail order. Ian has also come. He is an LCG who works in the kitchen, but has a few shifts with us. There are a couple of Departmental Guests, Marianne and Paula. My job is to look after the books.

"Good morning; let's attune."

We stand at the back of the shop in a circle, hands held, eyes closed.

"Let's bless the shop, and invoke the angels of joy and efficiency for our work this morning," says Ienek. Everyone leads attunements in their own style. Anna and Ienek bring in the angels. I like to talk about the God within. Ingrid does it silently. Michael loves the inner contact of an attunement, and he holds hands longest of all. When he's in a good mood, he's never in a hurry; it calms us down.

We sit down for a little while to welcome the new arrivals. Marianne is from Germany—she's an art teacher, who wants a time away from the shop to paint in the art studio. Paula is young, English and enthusiastic. What do we seem like in their eyes? Confident, joking, relaxed perhaps. On another day it can be very different. Anna and I could be quarrelling, Ienek and Ingrid arguing over the crafts, Michael getting irritated trying to make the cash balance, and Katherine behind with the mail orders. Then we'll know the weekly attunement will be 'heavy'.

The weekly attunement takes place on Tuesday morning. The shop is closed and we have time for personal sharing and a meditation, as well as larger issues of shop business. We always sort things out by the end of the attunement.

This morning everyone is in a good mood, so our short introductions are cheery. Ian vacuums the shop, and Ienek washes the floor after him. Katherine is getting rid of cardboard boxes, while Michael empties the waste-paper bins. The guests are tidying up the bookshelves after the weekend's sales. It leaves Anna free to start making up the week's food orders, and I check off book cards from books sold in the last two days. Ingrid is looking over some greetings cards that have arrived from Germany. By 10 o'clock, when we open, everything 'out front' is tidy and clean.

We light a candle and put some music on. Everyone has a different taste in music. I get fed up with the folksy, Scottish dance music Ienek puts on. She can't stand the way-out meditation music that I like; the bass notes do something to her stomach. I only play it when she's not on shift. Michael noticed that each person sells tapes of the music that they like; it doesn't seem to be so much to do with customer demand as with salesperson's pleasure!

Katherine's head is bent over her desk now. She is older than the rest of us. Sometimes she is like mother, and we are the squabbling kids; at other times, when there are a lot of orders and she is behind, she can be short and irritable, too. I use her as a reference. If I'm trying to hide something or not be quite honest, I have the feeling she'll see it. So she scares me a little, but is very helpful for my integrity . . . .

Anna has taken over the till. It's a nice job because, except in the high summer months when we're very busy, there are periods when only members are using the shop. You can have a little chat and hear what's going on. It's fun to watch the guests, too, what they head for, how their eyes light up at certain things. There are the jewelry people, who can't resist little silver Goddess earrings;

151

the 'inspirationals', who proudly demonstrate the special spiritual books they've sorted out; and the 'diet junkies', who raid our shelves for vitamins A, B, C and K, fortified with magnesium salts. People in a shop are simple and lovable. Behind their adult sophistication, the little child saying, "Mummy, I want . . . !" is very close to the surface. Maybe there's a very serious 'spiritual' person, conscious of his image, who can be humanised by being tempted with a bar of our famous chocolate. Or a bangle-hunter who walks out with a book on personal growth. Such are the little triumphs of running a spiritual shop.

In no time at all the lunch break has come. We close at 12 noon, so those who want to can go to the community meditation at 12.15. Lights go out, the last customer leaves, and the 'open' sign turns to 'closed'. We come into the circle again for a short attunement, this time at the front of the shop. As I close my eyes, I am suddenly overwhelmed by a sense of gratitude for being able to spend my time with such wonderful people. Ian, quiet and precise, will take over from me one day. Once he came in overflowing with restrained joy, to tell us he had started a relationship; the pleasure, pain and vibrancy of being in love. Ienek, slowly opening the creaky door of her exquisite self. Anna, symbol for me of perfect femininity, with whom I identified much too closely for our friendship to be comfortable. Michael, thoughtful and punctilious, holding the reins of our unruly group without ever being a boss . . . . Each person mirroring me, holding me back, supporting me in the complex enterprise of self-unfolding.

"Don't be romantic! Stop weeping!" says my inner, reasonable self. But, as usual, involuntary tears come trickling down. Such moments of revelation are infinitely precious. When we are next having our dramas together, they will be the reality that brings us through. Time to go off to sanctuary and give thanks.

Learning Together
Summer is guest time. From the end of June till the middle of September, the community is normally totally full, with hardly an empty bed. Everyone except Foundation members has their holidays during these months but, sadly, the weather is not at its best in high summer. May to June, when the gorse and rhododendrons are out, and September to October, with the russets of autumn, are magical seasons. In winter the northern days are short, and we

turn inward, with fewer Experience weeks and a smaller number of workshops. Then is the time for 'Members' Education', which is usually open also to our Living in Community guests. Everyone who wants to put on a new workshop tries it out on the members first, giving a sample of their wares over a weekend. Some favourite personalities from outside come to work with us. We always seem to have special favourites, who fit well into the community, and who enjoy visiting us. After a few years one star will wane and another will rise.

Winter is also the time of our internal conference, when the whole membership comes together and shares. We discuss our vision, our next steps, our collective challenges. In 1988, the year the new Core Group was formed, we agreed to experiment with special spiritual groups, which would meet regularly, developing our understanding of the meaning of inner work. Some of the groups are still meeting and *A Course In Miracles* is a popular work book.

The main function of the internal conference is to bring us all together after the hectic summer period and the conference for guests. This time always seems to me too short. The community is full of 'characters' and at conference time we are all 'on display'. Standard stars will get up and say their piece; maybe some new attraction will catch collective interest. We know each other and smile together knowingly. Human beings in spiritual development do not become uniform 'masks of God', with saintly smiles. On the contrary, as the common element of love unfolds itself in each of us, endless permutations of individual expression develop. Interested and lively people are varied people.

Twice a year, in recent years, we have been welcoming the 'Mastery' workshop to the community. Whenever it takes place, it is full. Many LCGs also take part. The Mastery is a workshop originally developed for actors. All community members have constantly to interact with guests, to focalise them in the various work departments, to talk with them, assist them, answer their requests. One has to have a degree of self-confidence and the Mastery helps provide this. Participants give a performance in front of forty or fifty others. Over an exhausting weekend, long hours, late nights, the experience develops, helping people to express, and not suppress, feelings and identities.

The Game of Transformation is played at all seasons of the year, though there is more time for it in the winter. Little groups of earnest-faced people appear at lunch, ostentatiously separating themselves from the rest of us—during the game you are not supposed to mix with the hoi polloi.

It is in winter, basically, that we get our annual ration of therapy, group consciousness and spiritual development workshops, emerging reinforced and clear for the summer influx.

We are activists, even in our inward times, and quietness is relative. But I like to get away for a week, to Traigh Bhan, our retreat house on Iona, or to Erraid, where the Erraid family also gives us a chance to retreat. There you can spend time in meditation; take long walks across the wild rock and moor of the Scottish west coast; or curl up in front of a fire on the long evenings reading a spiritual classic or a detective story—according to your taste. On one such retreat, alone over Christmas at Traigh Bhan, fasting for a week, I learned the real wonder of meditation—that it is not a time of passivity, but one of shining stillness. All the senses are sharpened, peacefulness enters like a swan and a quiet joy can become so intense that the heart feels it will burst. Many people are afraid of such times, for they do not like to be alone, but the companionship of God is incomparable.

The Findhorn Community way of life has a great deal to offer to a confused world . . . .

Relating to One Another
For the Findhorn Community to happen, Eileen and Peter had to come together. Eileen had to leave her husband and children by her first marriage and it was Peter's third marriage. In this respect, our origins seem to contradict the strictures of all religious belief about fidelity in marriage. Yet there is also another principle involved. If the perceived world is a means of self-discovery, relationships may be one of the means by which the discovery takes place. When the Bible speaks of not separating those whom God has brought together, what does that mean? Is a formal church ceremony between two people who may lack self-awareness an indication that God has brought them together? Perhaps a divinely ordained union may tear apart people who have come together in ignorance and immaturity. And if humans may not separate marriage partners, may not divine guidance sometimes do it?

Can we be sure, in such emotionally charged realms, that we can

154

trust inner guidance to be anything more than self-justification? When I fell in love with another member of the community, I had clear guidance not to turn it into a sexual relationship—guidance which I wilfully ignored, causing both of us much pain. It is, frankly, a difficult area, made more complex by the Western ideal of romantic love as the basis of relationship. In countries such as India, where partnerships are arranged, marriage is a phase of life, to be learned from or endured. Over the years love may grow out of companionship; sexuality is not so strongly emphasised. In the West, we now resist strongly the idea that parents should have a major say in our choice of partner. We dream of an ideal relationship, usually with a strong sexual basis. But immature people with very high expectations and in an intense state of sexual arousal are rather unlikely to hear a soft inner 'yes' or 'no'. Many people experiment with several relationships and trial marriages.

Sociologists have long pointed out that the old, extended family system has been undermined in our geographically mobile society. Many children nowadays find themselves being brought up by a single parent, usually a woman. Even in a couple relationship, with family size so small the emotional intensity of the parent-child relationship is very great. It reproduces itself in needy adult identities. Children, while loved and welcomed, mean a marked reduction in family standard of living and tend to disrupt neat, status-satisfying environments. They demand love and affection above material things till they learn to express love through them. Everything is coloured by the miasma of commercialised sexuality.

All this gives a sense of instability and uncertainty in relationship. It simply no longer works to superimpose a classical image of moral fidelity. In this sphere also, a divinely connected human identity is a precondition for the development of more mature, less ephemeral relationships.

There is, however, yet another complication. As one opens to Self, there come intense experiences of the beauty of other people; divine moments of unconditional love. Our emotional identity, less developed, may try to translate these moments into sexual attraction. Because of this there is a clear rule at the Findhorn Foundation that focalisers may not enter into a sexual relationship with a member of a guest group with whom they are working. A focaliser who transgressed this rule recently was asked to leave the Guest Department. Members, like everyone else, come to the

Foundation with identities formed in our civilisation's maelstrom of sexual uncertainty. Relationships form and break up, just as everywhere else. It is one thing to affirm that each relationship is a learning experience for the partners involved, but unless there is some evidence of learning, such statements can be facile ego-justifications masquerading as wisdom. In no area is it more apparent that we are not realised human beings but explorers.

What is clear is that relationships based on hypocrisy or unresolved problems never go unchallenged in the community. The energy of transformation here will not allow it. At present a couple with a very long-standing marriage and grown up children are in crisis. They are having to work through a legacy of unresolved and evaded problems. Since almost all relationships have elements of such problems in them, challenge exists for everyone in this area. A number of our members have come here after, or on the verge of, divorce. A few find a sublimation of sexuality in their spirituality but, for most, relationship is still a major life area, either in the having or in the seeking. We ran a workshop called 'Towards Sexual Wholeness' in 1989. Members attended the trial run with excitement; for a few weeks afterwards there were little 'sexuality groups' around the community, discussing what it had brought up.

As everywhere else, changes in relationship bring about problems for children. But for children born here, or brought up here from a young age, the community provides a very powerful support system. Parents retain the primary responsibility for their children, but the children learn that they can ask for support from any adult. They grow up in a loving atmosphere. There are small child-care support groups run mainly by mothers, a summer programme for toddlers, a playgroup, and kindergartens in the Steiner school. The atmosphere is much more that of the old-fashioned extended family than of isolated nuclear family units. Awareness and psychological understanding are, however, much more developed than in traditional extended families. For instance, in cases of parental strain or separation, children observe both parents being supported, and neither condemned.

Members cannot walk away from difficulties in a small community. Help and love are withheld from no one in trouble. Because of this, crisis resolution and release proceed very quickly indeed, on the whole.

My personal view is that, as in other areas of life, in regard to relationship our civilisation has created transitional identities no longer bound by custom and currently pulled hither and thither by commercial, social and sexual demands and stimuli. Working towards responsibility in relationship involves a much more sophisticated understanding of the interaction of love, emotion and commitment than we are yet able to demonstrate. To learn this understanding in practice is not easy. I believe that humanity nowadays should not be judged too harshly in its confusions. Here in the Findhorn Community we are making immense efforts to bring awareness into all aspects of our lives. The emphasis at present is on personal integrity, expressed as 'I have to be true to my feelings'. Another kind of integrity, 'I am mature enough to be responsible for my actions', is a stage beyond this. But it is no use pretending that one has reached a point that one has not.

Whatever their future may be, we still love marriages at the Findhorn Community and celebrate them in the present, as joyful occasions. Couples design their own ceremonies; the Hall, the gardens, power points, sacred dancing and ritual connections are much used. Wedding dresses have not gone out of fashion. The ceremonies are mutually created by the couple, with no trace of imposed formality. On such occasions there is a collective outpouring of love and affection among us which is innocent rather than naive. Although the community is overwhelmingly heterosexual, we accept relationship between people of the same sex without hesitation, where there is a feeling that love rather than ideology or exhibitionism is the basis of the tie. We had a most moving blessing of a relationship between two women not long ago; their partnership over a number of years had been a model of commitment and awareness of personal freedom in a couple situation. During the appreciations of the couple at the ceremony a woman remarked, "Girls, what taste! Your hem lines are exactly equal!"

In this transitional time, the most crucial relationship of all is the one with the God within, the Divine Self. By giving priority to this relationship in the Findhorn Community, we are working towards a new human identity—loving, aware, humorous, humane. Children brought up by adults with such an identity grow up more stable, less needy, more self-confident. Their way of relating to each other will emerge as a more mature human practice. We are just at the beginning of this aspect of social reorganisation, experiencing the dilemmas of trying to bring spirituality into the demanding area of relationship.

Playing Together

Before I came to the Findhorn Foundation from California in 1983, I went to as many artistic performances as possible. In northern Scotland, I thought, there won't be much going on in that respect. Not so! Over the years I have been astonished at the opportunities we have in the community to enjoy artistic performances of the highest standard. By and large they take place in the Universal Hall and are brought to us by the energy of the group which runs the Hall.

The acoustics of the Hall are very good. Sometimes the BBC uses it to televise recitals, giving us the chance to hear the best of classical music. The Aberdeen Youth Festival annually sends us a choir and a dance group from somewhere in the world. Our own Hall group scouts around the theatre scene to find performances which make sure we don't stifle culturally. Recent examples include 'Antigone' by Sophocles and an evening of 'Tales from the Arabian Nights', read delightfully by a professional actor—supported by one of our own belly dancers. Dancers from Poland and California were here the other week. Kathakali, an extraordinary music and dance group from South India have visited us twice to give us a taste of the Mahabharata, and so on. A film club satisfies escapist wishes by providing old American movies once a week.

Findhorn Community audiences are famed for their enthusiasm. When the BBC brought up an a-capella black group, Sweet Honey in the Rock, for a concert, we ended up dancing all around the television cameras on the stage, a scene joyfully filmed by the BBC ' technicians and shown on the televised programme.

Two Sacred Dance groups also meet regularly in the Hall. In addition, there is a free dance group, an African dance group and, of course, Jane Fonda workouts. Our theatre group recently took a performance to the Edinburgh Fringe. The Ceilidh Band entertains at every opportunity. As far as the written word is concerned, our weekly internal newspaper, 'Rainbow Bridge', is full of poems, jokes, meeting minutes and more or less spiritual comment. For public circulation we produce a high-quality quarterly magazine, *One Earth*.

Sometimes, on a Friday night, we have a 'Sharing'. It is an informal occasion when members and guests can share their talents. Quality varies, but we guarantee to provide a supportive audience even for the most mediocre, if they're willing to try. Some of our own members and some of the guests give performances of high quality.

In the winter, Cluny's comfortable lounge comes into its own, with groups sitting round the fire to have a sing-song or tell stories. Similar events happen at Newbold, and from time to time Kajedo Wanderer, the Newbold focaliser, organises Native-American-style sweatlodges in the garden there. There is a hill-walking group and, on New Year's Day at noon, a polar bear swim in the North Sea, which I always watch!

As a community we do not emphasise ritual—performed by Westerners it is often derivative and forced. But we try to be aware of the changing seasons, with monthly full moon meditations and quarterly solstice celebrations.

In June this year, we gathered in Cullerne gardens for the Summer Solstice. The evening sun shone from a clear, brilliant sky, chiselling the finest details of the forested hills to the south. After a short wait, someone announced that the focaliser of the event wasn't coming. His father had been taken ill with cancer and he was meditating in the sanctuary. Instead, members from Newbold started the evening with Native American chanting. More and more people turned up, till there were more than 200 of us—members, guests, associates—holding hands in a great circle around a fire. Barbara Swetina brought her accordion and led some sacred dances. Then we each ceremonially threw a piece of wood on the fire, symbolically releasing the past and praying for the future.

The water of the bay shone azure and golden in the setting sun. In these perfect surroundings the simple ritual became magical for me, transcending its form. We opened the circle so the two fires —the great fire of the sun and the little bonfire—could merge in a blaze of golden light. So it is as God finds Himself in us . . . .

Another memorable ritual took place on the day of the Harmonic Convergence in August 1987. We planted more than a hundred 'peace poles' inscribed in different languages. On that day, for the first and only time, the dolphins who live in the Moray Firth entered the Findhorn Bay at high tide, an occurrence so unusual that it was on local radio and in the papers. Was it only a coincidence that they came on that day, never before or since? Such signs remind us that the community is still blessed.

* * *

Life at the Findhorn Community is challenging, stimulating, varied and vibrant. It is impossible to be bored unless you have momentarily lost your inspiration. I emphasise this in order to show that a relatively isolated community of between two and four hundred people does not need to sink into either rural apathy or urban despair.

If our small numbers can provide such a varied feast of living, what will a new world culture look like as humanity collectively gives first priority to the experience of God within? As gross materialism is made redundant and gross material poverty disappears, life centres itself on its true purpose. Humanity begins to live richly, adventurously, in harmony and joy. We at the Findhorn Community are witnesses that this is not merely a utopian vision. But there is still much to do.

Erraid Island .

Chapter 10
Nature & the Environment

Weave it in, secure it
entangling it till it can flow strong and brown
With iron from the earth,
dissolve in the green limestone lake,
Catch the sky's own blue in its eyes as it melts
cutting the path through.

And on the hillside, as I see down,
down into the valley mist,
For a moment we both pause
Breathless at the beauty.

—Netting a Soul

From Miracle Gardens to Environmental Perspective

Since *The Magic of Findhorn* and *The Findhorn Garden* were published, the Findhorn Foundation has been associated with extraordinary vegetables and communication with plant devas. Some of our guests expect nature miracles when they come. Actually the miracles still occur but they are not as obvious as before. Other guests, particularly those from Germany, expect to find the most advanced relationship with the environment. They are astonished that they have already surpassed us in this respect. Neither group has understood the great change that took place in the community during David Spangler's stay. As we have become an ongoing workshop for spiritual development, the main purpose for coming here is neither advanced communion with nature, nor to find perfect ecological awareness—although we have been satirised as 'the Green Party at prayer'.

The purpose of the community is the substitution of inner, divine inspiration for a materialistic philosophy of need. Our concern is not really with the politics of what ought to happen with the environment, but with the practice of developing a loving relationship with all things, the environment included. As with every other aspect of life, relating to nature and the environment is a

163

means of expression of love, and a source of inspiration and teaching. For each individual member and visitor, the relationship with the environment is one that grows and changes. As one interacts with others, discusses and absorbs their views and connects with the natural environment here, the idea of relating to 'Gaia'—Mother Earth—as a vibrant being takes on reality.

When I came to the Findhorn Foundation I was a meat eater. As I became more sensitive to energy, I realised the truth of many things that vegetarians tell us, such as that the way animals are slaughtered has a powerful impact on the energy of their meat, transferring a small dose of terror and despair every time it is consumed. I realised that meat eating encourages rheumatic and heart diseases. There are often chemical or hormonal residues in it that are bad for the body. I read that it takes vastly more land to produce meat protein than an equivalent amount of plant protein and in some areas cattle ranching is destroying vital rainforest. I accepted the Indian tradition that meat eating stimulates hyper-energy and angry emotions. Slowly, I reduced intake and took to eating wild meat, easily available here. After Chernobyl, even that was contaminated. Yet with all this knowledge, I still liked meat! Only very gradually did that liking turn to distaste. It took a long while, till having a meatless diet became a way of being, rather than an ideology imposed upon an unwilling appetite. Now the thought of eating meat is unpleasant.

But I still liked fish, and fish and chips in this area are very inviting. I know that the energy of fish has a depressive effect on the identity, yet again I wasn't ready to give it up. It was only in June 1989, during a workshop I was focalising, that I had an experience which changed my feelings much more dramatically than had happened with meat. In the second week of the workshop we went for an outing to the River Findhorn, to explore nature using Native American exercises. One of them involved finding a power spot and looking fixedly at a certain point for a long period.

I had no difficulty in finding a power spot quite close to our assembly point. The others had dispersed farther away. The branches of a wild rose bush in front of my spot made a small triangle through which I could see a patch of the river beyond, perhaps a square metre in size. The spot had a strong energy for me; I began to feel warm, comfortable and relaxed. I looked steadily through the triangle of twigs at the rippling river surface. Suddenly a large salmon jumped, exactly in the spot I was looking at. A few minutes later it jumped again. Nowhere else were the fish jumping, only in this tiny spot. It felt as if I had made a real connection with nature energies and an interaction had begun.

Then I began to receive a message, a mixture of inner voice and images. I was shown the open sea, with a school of fish swimming and diving close to the surface, flashing silver in the sun. The words were:

With your human consciousness, you can enter into our experience, learn to feel the movement, the beauty of our expression, still retaining your own awareness. Our lives are not fear-filled, as you may imagine. Of course, we are chased, but we are in balance and harmony with nature and accept our deaths as part of the maintenance of that balance, so we do not fear. But there is one kind of experience we would not wish to inflict on you. That is our relationship with man. Man is not in balance, in harmony. In his lust to catch and destroy us, he knows no limit; his greed only goes on increasing. He is out of balance, and our relationship with him is fearful. We are terrified of him, and our only experience of him is blind panic.

Yet we know that in his primitive consciousness, man is trying to make connection with us. The only way he knows to do it is to incorporate us, endlessly eating us. We are not part of nature to be greedily eaten by humans. You are capable of an entirely different relationship with us; you can enter into our consciousness with your own and dance the seas with us.

You, personally, yearn for us, identify with us. That is why you like to eat fish. Become aware of the glorious adventure we can have together. Humans alone of all created species can enter the consciousness of others with their own, and share their experiences. Stop eating us, learn to love us and enjoy us, then we will lose our terror of you, and you can begin to share the wonder of our being.

The message stopped, leaving me astonished. It was clear and precise. I continued to look, and twice more salmon jumped in the exact square metre of river that was within my vision. What is the nature of such an experience? The rationally minded may describe it as self-hallucination. But why did the fish jump just there? They hadn't jumped in the whole stretch of river for an hour before while we had our lunch, and there seemed nothing special about the particular spot I was watching. Reason tries to shut out that which won't be shut out. Reality is something much more wonderful than reason; sometimes it is altogether awesome, an incredible dance between consciousness, experience and form, in which all are plastic and malleable. One day I will swim with the fish through the sea, jumping and whirling, shining as I turn in the sun, and know it all with a human consciousness. But not while I frequent fish-shops. I haven't felt any desire to eat fish since that time by the river.

I have quoted this personal example at some length, because it illustrates a process of change typical of that which takes place in the Findhorn Community. Instead of turning a spiritually desirable goal into a stick with which to beat ourselves, setting ideal against practice, we rather expand our awareness, so that gradually we become a little more God-like and no longer have any wish to retain the habit in question. It is not as quick as adopting a new 'Green' morality overnight, but it is a valuable basis for the sharing of the energy of new ways of being. Its basis is 'It is so' rather than 'You ought to do'.

Collectively, our aim is to 'live lightly on the earth'. We seek to move in the direction of demonstrating a human-sustainable/earth-sustainable balance for humanity. What that means is hard to define exactly. We live in and are largely dependent on an economy which definitely does not sustain this balance. We cannot tell what our life would look like if it did, but the question is hypothetical. The only way the global economy will really change is as humanity adopts attunement to the Divine within as its motivation, rather than the stimulation of demand without. As this happens, the Findhorn Community will merge with the wider society and disappear. For now, we operate within the existing situation.

Our ecological consciousness has been partial so far. In common with the general trend, though, it is increasing rapidly at present and an ecology group is meeting regularly. We have never used chemicals on our gardens (with a slight exception in the early period at Cullerne). We have always enjoyed vegetarian cuisine —except for Friday evening fish meals and at Christmas, when turkey is served to those who want it. On the other hand, we do not use totally organic food, which is very difficult to obtain in this area, our own gardens apart; we haven't made a stand for free-range eggs; and we only recently started to use fully biodegradable detergents and cleaning fluids. Up to the present there has been no provision for recycling paper in northern Scotland outside Aberdeen, so we have driven a truckful over there every other month, which costs us more than we receive in payment for the paper. Bottle recycling is just beginning in the local town; we are eager for it.

The buildings we live in are extremely energy-wasteful. Cluny is an old, leaky building, but the cost of wall insulation and double glazing are quite beyond our means. As a start, we are putting modern heat exchangers into the boiler system, which should reduce energy consumption somewhat. A plan for £15,000-worth of solar panels on Cluny roof is on ice!

In the Park, our caravans are ecological nightmares, marginally insulated tin boxes that puff out polluting smoke all winter. Until we have the funds to build ecologically effective houses, we can't do very much about this. We have, however, installed a heating system in the central guest bungalows which operates off a single boiler, reducing pollution. Several years ago, two well-known American architects, Sim van der Ryn and James Hubbell, were commissioned to provide us with a concept for interesting, energy-efficient housing in a cluster design that would counteract the kind of suburban isolation created by normal houses. They came up with a remarkable design, which became known as the 'Hubbell Bubble'. But some members objected on aesthetic grounds, and there was unease about the response of the ferro-concrete shells to damp weather. The buildings would also be very expensive.

In the meantime, we are supporting a limited degree of private building—hedged around with restrictions—by members with some funds. We have pioneered house-building using old whisky vats, a supply of which we were able to obtain cheap. A cluster of the small circular buildings is planned; one is complete and two are being built as I write. They are cheap, innovative and very attractive for single people. A Park Environment Group (PEG) has had assistance from visiting landscape architects to draw up tentative land use plans. A simpler housing cluster than the Hubbell project, called Bag End (after Tolkien), for 11 private homes with a timber-frame design is planned to start in 1990.

Already we have had our own building school for several summers. We subsidise people with building skills and a spiritual inclination to work in the atmosphere of the Findhorn Foundation. They have built an extension to our community centre, a marked improvement to the existing, functional building. Accommodation appropriate to a more permanent community has been long in

167

coming and any modest progress is very welcome.

We also have our first 75 kilowatt windmill, 'Moya', for generating electric power. After a sojourn in pieces opposite the community centre while we wrestled with technological and financial problems of integrating her into the grid system, she now stands and turns. The windmill is an important symbolic step, a gesture towards self-sufficiency. At present it is not economic, as we must pay off the purchase price through higher energy costs; nor will it provide all our energy needs; nor has it been easy to find an appropriate location—it was too noisy to have close, and to site it in the best spot, 800 metres away, has required transformer equipment, adding enormously to the cost.

In none of these respects are we 'world leaders' in alternative technology or housing design, although the 'Hubbell Bubble' would be quite unique. Nor have we, at present, all the land we need to make the Hall the hub of a developing community, as it would naturally be. But the vision for such a community is slowly being integrated into the consciousness of our members. As it becomes 'part of us', so we will make it real. I believe it is important that we demonstrate Self-discovery in physical form as well as in group education. The Hall is certainly a work of art. On a smaller scale, the nature sanctuary and the barrel-houses give a foretaste of the potential that exists here for ecologically sound, user-friendly, aesthetically stimulating architecture. Everything else is, at present, plan and vision—the biological, non-toxic sewage reclamation system, the circular-field organic farm, the nature reserve—parts of a dream that will be realised when their time is ripe.

Spiritual Gardening

Dorothy Maclean had been receiving guidance for many years when in 1971 the Findhorn Foundation published two volumes of it under the pen name 'Divina'. In 1963 Dorothy had found she could make contact with the energy forces organising and maintaining plant growth, which she called devas. Through this contact she was able to give practical advice to Peter in cultivating the gardens, which facilitated the remarkable plant growth for which the community became famous. The whole story is told in detail in *The Findhorn Garden*.

Since then our gardening work has been a little overshadowed by Dorothy's special communication skills. Everyone thinks that in order to be a 'real' spiritual gardener, they ought to have the same connection; but no one else has been able to get the specific messages that the devas gave Dorothy in those early days. Because of this the real spiritual gardening tradition became somewhat weakened. Some gardeners were cynical about 'nature energies', product of a romantic past, and would not dream of meditating with a compost heap! Also many people, like myself, feel pulled to gardening as a counterbalance to years of intellectual or office work and just as we are becoming proficient in what is a skilled craft, we feel called to other jobs. Nevertheless, a spiritual connection with the cultivation of the gardens was never entirely lost. When it seemed to be in decline in one garden, it sprang up in another. At present, it is strengthening itself once more. It is important to remember that Dorothy's was only one of many ways of being in touch with the energies of nature.

'Spiritual gardening' differs from ordinary organic gardening in that it uses meditation techniques in the garden as an integrated part of the work. There is a lot of evidence that plants are sensitive to energy and sound: they grow towards classical music and away from rock music, for example, and show micro-energetic disturbances in the presence of people with angry or violent energies (cf. Tompkins & Bird, *The Secret Life of Plants*, 1989 ed.) Here in the Findhorn Community, in addition to ordinary attunement techniques, we use short meditations after planting, on completion of compost heaps, and with individual plants or beds of plants. This kind of gardening requires love and respect for the plants and attunement with them before harvesting or pruning. It helps to develop a sense of the garden as a whole being with its own character. Gradually you as gardener and the garden come into harmony. You begin to have an inner, intuitive sense of what the plants need, what they will accept and what they dislike. They, in their turn, respond to your inner state and your vision for the garden.

In my first year at the Findhorn Foundation I had the good fortune to work with Alan Watson, who was then focalising Cluny Garden. When during a garden workshop Alan presented a slide show of wonderful nature images, I realised that through his photography Alan had come as close to the plant spirits as Dorothy had. His work, exemplified in our annual nature calendars, brings out the energy presence of plants in a unique way. In a supplementary chapter Alan wrote for the second edition of *The Findhorn Garden* (1988) he describes a situation in which flies attracted his attention by buzzing around him till he realised that a guest was doing something wrong in the garden. It reminds me of a time when I was working with a guest group on a garden project at Cluny, with Alan and Karin Werner.

Karin chose to dig out a rockery in the hill garden to remove the couch grass that had spread under the stones. It was the hottest day of the year, not at all a day to lift plants. As we attuned we all, including some of the guests, had bad feelings about doing the project in the burning sunshine. But we went ahead—18 people thumping into the bed, lifting out all the old established rockery plants in quick succession. It was like tearing off skin. After about three quarters of an hour Karin put a fork through her leg. A prong went in one side of her calf and came out the other. Alan raced her down to the hospital for a tetanus injection, and the rest of us continued working, subdued. At tea break Alan, barefoot, stood on a spent matchstick which penetrated his foot. After the shift had finally finished and the poor plants, wilted and dried, were struggling for life in their bed again, I fell down the steps in front of Cluny and twisted my ankle. Nature spirits can be rough if you invoke them but don't pay attention. It was an excellent, if painful, lesson in attunement in the garden.

Maria Thun, the German anthroposophical gardener, produces an annual calendar showing appropriate seeding and transplanting times according to lunar and planetary influences. This method has been widely used at the Findhorn Foundation, but we have found that meditating with plants can counteract the effects of doing things at 'inauspicious' times. Plants sown on such days will germinate just as well. While it is rare for people to get clear devic messages as Dorothy did, anyone can meditate with plants. It soon brings results.

Our main problems in the gardens of the Findhorn Foundation are not so much connected with the plants themselves as with the high turnover of gardeners. Not only are new guests constantly coming to the garden and working for a few mornings or afternoons, but it is often their first experience of this work. In such a case, the gardens almost always give more than they receive.

We teach guests to slow down, to discriminate between cultivated plant and weed, and where to tread. In the process, of course, the wrong things get pulled up, and heavy feet sometimes crush. But the gardens understand their teaching function. It is very important that some of those who have grown up in a concrete landscape begin to reconnect with the earth that is their real support.

We also get some sentimentalists whose fingers tremble at the grasp of a weed. Nature herself is not at all sentimental. Co-creation with nature involves a clear vision, in harmony with local circumstances and in balance with ecological imperatives, and then the firmness to carry it out. This relationship was beautifully demonstrated by Peter Caddy's gardening in the early days of our community.

As our guests make an initial connection with the garden, the various processes of the work—seeding, raking, composting, harvesting, weeding and so on—often seem to mirror aspects of their own lives: changes they need to make, the weeds of old habits they need to get rid of. Spiritual gardening is a remarkable teaching agent, as well as a stress reducer. The educational function of our gardens explains why the great vegetables of the past are no longer evident.

Members rarely spend more than a year or two in the garden. From the garden's point of view it is a great pity, for natural harmonies do not operate to the speedy rhythm of impatient humans. The really exciting results in the early gardens of the Findhorn Community happened after about three seasons. Many of our current gardeners move on just before this, leaving the gardens with withdrawal symptoms. Nevertheless, when a spiritually centred team begins to operate for a modest time period with coherent focalisation, the nature spirits respond.

At present this is happening in the beautiful Cullerne gardens. It can be seen not so much in outsize or unusual plants but in an overall vibrancy, noticeable even to the insensitive. I worked in these gardens for a season in 1984, when they were just beginning to recover from a very disharmonious time among the previous gardeners, who had been trying unsuccessfully to recover the cost of buying the house and land. A group of us began to do healing meditations in the garden every lunchtime instead of going to the sanctuary. We started the first intensive vegetable garden as an alternative to the maximum-production vegetable fields. It was designed like a butterfly's wings with a circular bed of thyme in

171

the centre.

There was considerable opposition to this project from more experienced gardeners, who declared that it couldn't work in the poor soil. The first indication that our approach was succeeding was when an oyster catcher presented us with a beautiful egg, exactly in the centre of the central bed in the new garden. For me it was a clear message of approval from the garden spirits. Then we were provided with an inexhaustible supply of free horse manure from a local equestrian centre. At the end of that year a deer-proof fence was built around the garden, a major job which had a symbolic function in defining the garden boundaries, which I believe to be as valuable for the nature spirits as for us.

The most delightful times I have spent in the Findhorn Foundation gardens were the two years in Drumduan garden working with Ian Sargent. When we started, the garden was very overgrown and neglected. We felt it was crying out for action. We put up a list of 19 major projects that needed doing, and gulped in guests. We tore out old dead broom, planted beech and rhododendron hedges, completely renovated the vegetable garden and expanded the herbaceous border. We lifted five hundred irises from the ornamental iris bed, weeded it and replanted them, created a new herb garden and, by realigning the paths, opened up a superb annual bed, Ian's pride and joy.

This time it was not the nature spirits who were angry at our pace; they thoroughly approved. Several of the house residents, however, felt we were disturbing the atmosphere of genteel decay that had settled over the place. The community environment group was summoned. Luckily such things take a long time to ripen in the Foundation and by the time the group arrived most of the projects were nearly complete. They were scathing. "The place looks like a building site," said someone. They threatened to remove me from focalisation. But now I was able to promise to slow down and tidy up, as the main work had been done. I knew that the garden needed and wanted the kind of energy we had given it, but I had to learn the lesson of the need for proper communication with humans, even when the attunement with nature was right.

In the winter we thinned about seventy trees from the forests surrounding the gardens. We cut almost all of them by hand. A man kindly offered to help with his power saw, but the garden screamed at the way he did it. Cutting seventy trees with bow saws nearly killed us, but it was worth it. The devas were happy, we talked to each tree before we felled it, and the remaining trees could breathe and expand. Finally, in the early spring, we got agreement to go ahead with the one project that had been denied us the year before—the removal of an old swimming pool filled with rubbish, an eyesore in the centre of the garden. There was just time before the planting season. With a small army of workshop guests we tore it out and installed a sunken garden with a pool and a sheltered sitting area for workshop groups, all surrounded by a rockery. We found beautiful yellow sandstone from a demolished house nearby for the rockery.

It was the finishing touch. That summer some of the guests began to see nature spirits in the grounds of Drumduan. The foxgloves grew over two metres tall and it was bliss to go out each morning. The old vibrancy of the early Findhorn Community gardens had returned.That season we started to harvest the snap peas at the end of July. They normally last for about three weeks. In December, we were still harvesting them. With an inch of snow on the ground they continued to flower!

Drumduan House is now the home of the Moray Steiner School. They need a functional garden, with plenty of grass. Our beautiful ornamental gardens have gone, a memory only. One has to learn to let go in the Findhorn Community

With the release of Drumduan garden, we are now maintaining three major garden areas in the Foundation—the grounds of Cluny College, the complex of gardens in the Park, where everything started, and the seven-acre smallholding at Cullerne. Each garden is tended with equal love by its gardeners and has its own character, but perhaps the Park deserves special mention as the originating garden. There is no single Park garden, but several small ones flanking paths between bungalows. Every time you turn a corner or pass a building, a new aspect of the garden opens up—the original vegetable patch, the flower beds outside the sanctuary, the herb garden hidden away between caravans behind the community centre, the rockeries, ponds and shrubs beside the guest bungalows. In front of the Hall is another garden, with ponds and a daffodil lawn set amongst mature trees. In Pineridge hides yet another area, honouring the nature sanctuary with quiet circular lawns set around with ornamental broom, and there is even a second small vegetable plot, formerly a nursery for young trees. The Park gardens are an intricate lacework of different aspects. To appreciate them one needs to wander around and afterwards visualise the whole, otherwise you may take each part for granted as we often do. Cluny garden lies around its house; the whole of Cullerne garden spreads out before you; but the Park garden only shyly shows you faces of itself—you cannot view it as a whole, except in your mind's eye.

In the wider community are the large grounds of Minton House and Newbold with its old, walled vegetable garden, and the new garden of the Meadowlark nursing home. Erraid, on the west coast, grows vegetables on a large scale too.

Back in the middle of the Park, by the old green caravan that was Eileen, Peter and Dorothy's home, is the original garden, flowers mingling with vegetables in different patterns of colour and setting. Standing there after wandering through the mature gardens of the Park, one can remember that in 1962 Peter Caddy put the first spade into the sandy rubbish tip where the family caravan had come to rest. From that spadeful everything else has grown.

To the north of the vegetable garden is a wild area. No one sets foot in it. Each of our gardens has such a place, a symbolic sanctuary for devic retreat when humans become too insufferable. The nature spirits have never been far away from humanity. As we supplement our rationalistic realism with inner consciousness and stop to look, they shyly emerge again:

We have met before. Whenever anyone contributes attention or feeling to a plant, part of that person's being mingles with part of our being, and the one world is fostered. You humans are therefore all very linked to us, but until you give recognition to these links, they are as nothing and remain undeveloped. Plants contribute to human food and give of themselves in this way, thus building tangible links. Although of the past, these links can be brought into the present, by recalling them. One great use of memory is to recall the Oneness of life.
(Rhubarb Deva, 20th October, 1963. From *To Hear the Angels Sing,* p. 200)

The Natural Setting
The introduction to Paul Hawken's book, *The Magic of Findhorn,* gives an extraordinarily misleading impression of the natural set-

ting of our community. He writes:

> *As the train moved north, the plants became more miniaturised, drawing*
> *back from the surface, hesitant and understated; shrunken trees, bracing*
> *themselves for the blast soon to come, were twisted into unseemly contor-*
> *tions, their strange and submissive shapes bearing witness to their master*
> *like stumpy oak-leaved dwarves kneeling to a king. Nowhere were there*
> *flowers, fruits and flowering trees, but supposedly Findhorn was growing*
> *them all and more.* (p. 11)

There is a disclaimer to this in the afterword, but the implication
that this description refers to the Findhorn area is quite an insult
to the local neighbourhood. Forres has won the Scottish Municipal
Garden Trophy and the Britain in Bloom award several times, and
is almost always placed. Beautiful, mature trees grow everywhere
and local people are justly proud of their gardens. The coasts of
the Moray Firth have been good farming land for centuries, and
the region grows the northernmost wheat in the British Isles. Rainfall is low and hours of sunshine are many, with delightful
autumn and winter weather. We certainly have a fair amount of
wind, with occasional gales, but nowhere near as much as the
west coast of Wales or the English Lake District. A rich flora and
fauna inhabit the charming river valleys of the Spey and Findhorn
rivers.

Perhaps Paul Hawken was trying to make the achievements of
the early gardeners of the Findhorn Foundation seem more
impressive. They do not need such dubious bolstering. Although
the Park garden began with very poor soil, the local area as a
whole has a quiet richness in which natural energies are very easily perceived. Roc pointed this out back in the sixties, directing us
to the special glades and corners of the Findhorn river valley, from
Dulsie Bridge and Ardclach to Randolph's Leap and Sluie Walk,
places where we take our guests to learn contact with the energies
behind the forms of natural life. At Randolph's Leap the ancient
beech trees reach magnanimously down to the visitors, encouraging small humans to give up their pretentions and abandon themselves to hug the thoughtful grey bark (as long as no one's looking, of course), while the water continues to shape the rocks to its
own forms in sensuous cascades.

Even in the commercial pine plantations there is an abundance

175

of mosses and heathers, blaeberries and fungi, the latter a rich harvest for the connoisseur, since local people tend to be suspicious of any but the supermarket variety of mushrooms! Just south of us, across the dunes, is an eight-mile-long sandy beach, with water luckily cold enough to inhibit commercial development, while further along the coast are miles of beautiful natural rock formations. Everywhere, nature calls to be recognised; part of our work is not merely to honour it in its beauty, but to make use of the gift of our location to help ourselves and our visitors to reharmonise with the energies of a living planet. *This kind of experience is the deepest ecological training one can have.* Many of our programmes include an element of nature experience. Our civilisation has strayed far from a loving appreciation of nature; it is high time to return. The remnants of the 'earth peoples', the Native Americans and the Australian aboriginals, have been able to share some of their gifts just in time. For most of us in the Findhorn Community 'living lightly on the earth' first involves the personal discovery of the earth and its energies by seeking, in quietness, to resonate with the moods and expressions of nature in the countryside around Findhorn.

Turning Outwards
The major contribution the community makes towards the solution of the ecological crisis is by the demonstration of a successful and fulfilling lifestyle at a low economic standard of living. A second contribution is made by helping people, through our gardening methods and nature connections, to re-experience their earth in a spiritual way and cherish her. Two other projects turn us outwards.

In 1978, two Dutch families who owned an island off the west coast of Mull in the Inner Hebrides offered us its custodianship for ten months of the year. Since then a small community of about ten members has flourished there, living in cottages originally built for lighthousemen and their families in the 1860s. The group is self-financing and, like all of us, its members share their lives with guests. On Erraid visitors experience a way of living much closer to self-sufficiency than the rest of the community can provide. Candles and stained glass are made. The large organic gardens, fertilised largely by seaweed, produce almost enough vegetables for all, and cows and hens provide milk and eggs. Some fish are caught in the summer. Other provisions are sent from the Find-

176

horn Foundation on our weekly bus run, an 11-hour round trip through some of the finest scenery in Scotland, including two ferry crossings each way.

The Erraid family, as we call them, have established their own rhythm of life, adapted to the demanding natural conditions on the island. The climate is quite severe and the island is subject to ferocious gales. The owners have been keen that the natural character of the island should be retained, a view that we heartily share. But what is that natural character? Until recently sheep have roamed and grazed Erraid freely. What would the island look like if the sheep did not strip its vegetation cover so efficiently year after year?

The owners agreed first to the planting of a small area of fenced forest in one of the few more sheltered spots. This small forest, mainly of pine, with young birch and oak, is growing bravely amidst the storms. Now the owners have supported the fencing of the entire north-west corner of the island, some 14% of the land area, for an ecological reconstitution project. The fencing was completed in 1989. After just six sheepless weeks the wild, mountainous area blossomed with abundant wildflowers released from the cycle of annual culling. The next step is the planting of 4,000 native trees—rowans, willows, oaks and birches—to provide the basis for natural regeneration. This is a practical project in reconnection with nature; humans and nature are acting as co-creators in the regeneration of a natural wilderness.

For our Erraid family, life is demanding. The one new building, a small sanctuary set on a hill overlooking the old Abbey on the nearby Isle of Iona, gives a spiritual focus to the hard-working life of the island. For those who want to explore a relatively simple lifestyle and who appreciate wild country, spacious mountain-fringed skies and island-studded seas, Erraid is sheer romance. The re-creation of a natural landscape, for its own sake and for human visitors, is a symbolic healing of the planet we have so mishandled.

Alan Watson was central in inspiring the regeneration project on Erraid. He is also working on a potentially much larger scheme to regenerate an area of the old Caledonian Forest in the northern Highlands. Northern and western Scotland is rightly regarded as one of the great beauty spots of Europe. Yet it was denuded of its original forest cover in the 18th century by sheep and deer farming and only 1% remains. In areas such as Glen Affric, where a small patch of forest is preserved, the real Scottish Highland landscape can be experienced; it cries out to express itself to the world once more. Alan envisages the regeneration of this exquisite environment in a 600-square-mile area north of Glen Affric. Some local landowners are already interested, and the first tree-planting parties have gone out, using plastic sheathing in the absence, as yet, of fencing. Without the protection provided by fencing, deer and sheep eliminate young tree growth. Alan's vision has been wholeheartedly supported by the Findhorn Foundation, but the project is far too large for our own resources. At present, the Forestry Commission, the Nature Conservancy Council and some private landowners are supporting pilot fencing projects. Natural regeneration can be supplemented by the cultivation of local seed in protected tree nurseries.

Scotland has, as yet, no National Park. The area where this forest regeneration work has started, which is of outstanding natural beauty and very marginal agricultural value, would be ideal for one. Through this project we are tentatively entering new fields of activity, expanding a spiritual view of human relationship with nature into the wider society. It is an innovative, inspiring kind of outreach.

Again and again in this book, I have emphasised that an inner-centred way of life is not about a perfected state of being, but about the release of energy that occurs when we begin to put the divine within into the motivator's seat. Our work with nature and ecology in the Findhorn Community is no exception. Working with love in this domain provides endless opportunities for action. Life is full, exciting. As we commence our journey towards Self, a bubbling spring of vitality wells up. The further we go, the more energy we have. How else can the blasé cynicism and aimlessness diseasing our civilisation be overcome? For us it is not, "How can we fill the time? What's on the telly?" but "How can we choose between so many exciting things to do?" Working to heal the planet is an inspiration *for* action. Instead of waging a negative struggle against powerful entrenched interests, which is wearisome, unrewarding work, let us awaken and mobilise an inner vision of healing for our Earth—one that will sweep over old boundaries, begin to unite unlikely allies, and stimulate hope and positivity. Such a purpose can move humanity beyond the sterility of perpetual opposition towards common human awareness on an honoured planet.

Newbold House
Forres

Chapter 11
It's All Happening—
From Foundation to Community

> *The inner significance of the Gita has to be understood in the context of human nature as it is expressed in the world, in the everyday activities of people. The most important objective of the Gita is to bring down the priceless, ancient wisdom to the level of the mundane world and to raise the worldly life to the level of the highest wisdom. Bhagavad Gita transforms Vedanta into daily life and elevates daily life to the level of Vedanta; it not only introduces philosophy and spirituality into daily life, but it also introduces daily life into philosophy and spirituality. Hence it reconciles spirituality and daily life.*
> —Sai Baba *Discourses on the Bhagavad Gita*

Letting Go and Holding On

The Findhorn Foundation began with a tiny core of people, meditating and gardening. Slowly others came and building began. Because it was felt that Eileen's guidance should be distributed, publishing started. More and more guests came and to feed them a dining room was built. To provide spiritual education for the guests, the educational programme developed. From small beginnings there has been continual diversification. The Findhorn Foundation has been like the eggshell within which the embryo community took form. Now the Foundation is becoming part of a larger whole, something even more accessible to ordinary people.

To provide a working demonstration of the Divine in ordinary life, structures have to develop in which individuals and families can express their inner spiritual discoveries and learn in a variety of independent activities. The Findhorn Foundation itself is a relatively restricted body which has a degree of control over its membership. In the last instance, people can be asked to leave. But the emerging Findhorn Community will have to open itself to a variety of new forms of communication and collective governance, in a situation where no clear control can be maintained. The

Foundation eggshell will have to break. Quite a lot has already happened, but in 1989 we are still at the beginning of this new stage in our growth. On the whole, it is still the Foundation which people wish to join when they are attracted here and it remains the dominant organisation.

But this is changing. In order for the community to grow, two anxieties have to be released: a fear of loss of control on the part of the members of the Foundation collectively, and a fear of independence on the part of individuals. For this reason the steps are gentle. The Foundation is transforming at God's pace. Although times are changing fast, we are not in a hectic hurry. Each new step requires a good understanding of how it naturally develops from the old. The less we are governed by fear, the more rapidly the change can occur. Sometimes I feel we encourage decentralisation with one hand and discourage it with the other. One of the small businessmen I interviewed for this chapter told me: "I don't have a very strong connection with the Foundation, but I do have one with the 'Angel of Findhorn'."

Perhaps the Foundation itself will one day be decentralised out of existence. Then it will indeed be the Angel that connects us in our various activities. But that is down the road. In 1969 Eileen received the following piece of guidance:

> *It will progress in stages and expand very rapidly. Expand with the expansion. The foundations go very deep and are built on rock; therefore it now does not matter how fast the growth takes place. It does not matter how great it grows. Let go of all fear of it getting out of hand. I can assure you it will not. But it will grow and flower and flourish and glorious will be the results for all to see. All will recognise My hand in everything that takes place.*

> (*Foundations of Findhorn*, p. 152-3)

Within the Foundation itself, some activities have a natural autonomy. Cluny Hill College seems slowly to be heading towards the independence that Newbold already enjoys. The process has begun with the initiation of the new Experience week in the Park, reflecting some of the differences between lifestyles there and in Cluny. *One Earth* started off as a Foundation newsletter, and gradually became a new age magazine in its own right. It has been within our umbrella because it was not financially self-supporting, but is now changing its form. The Audio Department may transfer to our trading division, New Findhorn Directions; the Pottery could naturally become an independent craft venture; the Game of Transformation is already semi-independent; and our Publications Department is another candidate for independence. There have even been proposals for an autonomous Accounts Department, although this has at present been rejected.

In the future we may see the food services of the Park (a restaurant, the Green Room Cafe and a food supply system for them and for individual members and associates) combine with the whole-food shop to become an independent cooperative, supplying everyone in the wider community. The gardeners may form a group—supported by everyone who benefits from their work in keeping the area beautiful—and sell their vegetables to the food co-op. Another company might provide maintenance and building skills. An accommodation service might rent space to a whole variety of individuals and groups, including independent workshop leaders living in the area. Perhaps the Hall will become a local centre for drama, and could be hired for events. A group running the Hall might reach out to schools in the local area to teach drama.

If this sort of thing happens, the Foundation would find itself merely an administrative and spiritual centre, sending its guests to have appropriate working experiences in the independent businesses associated with it, who would be paid for their spiritual training role. But at present, the Foundation is still dominant. Let's take a walk around the Park, as the tours for casual visitors do each day, to see what is going on in our emerging village community.

Growing Pains: The Community Business Culture—*The Wood Studio, Bay Area Graphics, The Apothecary, New Findhorn Directions, Weatherwise, Alternative Data*

In the Park live three groups of people: members and guests of the Findhorn Foundation; holidaymakers in the summer, most of whom have little or no interest in what is happening in the Foundation; and people who live year round on the site but are not Foundation members. A small number of this last group have been here since before we became the owners, and they also have no interest in the community. As and when they leave, we hope that people who do have an interest will buy their caravans. But the majority of those who live in the Caravan Park are part of what is going on, even though they are not members.

Another group of people interested in the Foundation live in Findhorn village, in Forres and in the surrounding countryside. In 1988 a rough survey showed that there were more than ninety of them, plus another hundred supported by the independent businesses—already more than the total number of Foundation members and their dependents. They include therapists, 'change-of-awareness' practitioners and healers, and craftspeople. Others are unemployed or study in local colleges. A single mother was drawn to live near the Foundation because she felt her baby wanted to be born here. At present such people can become Associates of the Foundation for a small subscription which entitles them to use many of our facilities. They have as close or as distant a relationship with the Foundation as they choose. Some work a shift or two with our departments. A few are ex-members.

* * *

Just across the main Findhorn road, by the bay, is the house and wood studio of *Richard Brockbank,* a master-craftsman and artist in wood. The sales of his very beautiful work support his wife Diana and their children. Richard and Diana did an Experience week in 1980 and immediately felt a pull to come and live here, but not as members. Richard, who had a background as a furniture-maker, took part in a workshop at the Foundation called 'Hidden Talents'. It gave him the confidence to explore living as an artist in wood. 'By chance' the house across the road where they live now was up for sale, and three months later they had moved in. Although they still felt it was right not to become members of the Foundation, both of them did the Orientation programme in order to strengthen their links with the community and understand better what was going on.

When he started, Richard hoped to make a lot of money from his work. Up to now, that has not happened, but there has always been enough to survive. At first some Foundation members were a little suspicious of someone who was independent, earning his own money. There was a caution, an anxiety that he was not 'under control'. The Foundation remains very important to the

Brockbanks, though, and Richard still does a cooking shift once a week to 'keep in touch'.

The main challenge lay in setting up and running the business itself, a theme echoed by others I interviewed. "It is easier to be a businessperson and incorporate spirituality into your business than to start spiritual and come to terms with the world of business," commented someone.

For Richard, spirituality is central to his work. He meditates daily in the Foundation sanctuary to find inner inspiration. In the same way that in the Foundation we talk of the 'Angel of Findhorn' as representing the energy flowing here, Richard feels there is a creative energy in his studio which is 'like a being', and he seeks to work in harmony with it. Perhaps a genuine work of art captures spiritual energy in form. Looking around Richard's workshop I certainly feel a kind of intensity. It was a great inspiration for him when a visitor wept with emotion as she handled one of his boxes.

Richard's personal vision is to become an ever clearer instrument for God's work. He would like to see a group of spiritually inspired artists and craftspeople here who could work together for mutual stimulation and inspiration, and combine to give workshops. They would possibly have enough resources to employ someone to take on the job of marketing their products—a very time-consuming task for the craftspeople themselves. Richard feels that his work, including the classes in woodwork that he gives, provides a bridge to the wider locality, a theme also taken up by other independent businesspeople here.

* * *

If you walk back across the community and along the Pineridge road, you come to our original design studio on the left. For a long time now it has been *Bay Area Graphics*. It is run by a couple from Germany, Ronald Morton and Claudia Klingemann. Both were formerly members of the Foundation, working in the Graphic Design Department. They felt invisible there; their work seemed too much behind the scenes. The department was self-regulating as it tended to work irregular hours to meet deadlines, so they decided to see if it could be run as a private business. At first the Foundation was reluctant and attunements brought up doubts about their business partner, who has since left. It took a whole year of negotiation before, in July 1986, they had their way and began paying rent for the studio on a five-year contract. Although they give the Foundation preferential rates and make their profit almost solely from 'outside' work, they still sometimes feel judged because they 'make money'.

Setting up Bay Area Graphics was a real adventure. Neither Ronald nor Claudia had business experience or management skills; for Claudia it was her first job outside the Foundation. The three following years were a process of becoming more professional. Claudia comments: "We had many hard times, especially with our business partner. Everything we had learned about group process and group work in the Foundation was put to the test."

They also had to learn about pricing, and to promote an appreciation of the value of quality design work in the local area. They used government business grants and training schemes, employing people with no connection with the Foundation. To get such a business going requires determination. Both estimate that they work more than double the hours they were expected to as members of the Foundation, but they enjoy the feeling of independence and responsibility.

For Ronald and Claudia, spirituality in business is a question of attitude, motivation and atmosphere. The principles of Foundation life still guide their behaviour, but learning the technical requirements of their profession is a challenge. The business gives them feedback as instant as that from a spiritual teacher. Claudia says: "If I work on myself, it reflects in the business. If I neglect my inner life, that shows up too. Feedback is instantaneous."

The employees enjoy the friendly atmosphere of the community, and are interested in what is going on. Ronald and Claudia want to work as a team, but haven't introduced attunements up till now. They aim to make a reasonable profit, but they don't have ideas of a much larger business; rather they would like to have the time to do other, more artistically oriented work instead of commercial graphic design.

In Morayshire low wages and unemployment are widespread. Few people who need printing work done have paid much attention to design; it's usually left to the printer. Spreading the idea of excellence in art and design work contributes positively to the

186

quality of life in the local area. Ronald and Claudia would like to specialise in designing presentation material for smaller organisations and companies, to bring more quality into their own work.

* * *

Back by the Park entrance is a group of businesses which are perhaps the nucleus of a future 'industrial area'. The old toilet block just north of the entrance, where Eileen once meditated, has been cleaned and renovated. It now houses the *Findhorn Bay Apothecary*, a workers' cooperative. From its tiny space a vegetarian cafe operates, together with a herbalist, a herbal bookshop and a mail order business. It also has its own guest programme. At first, the Apothecary was a private business; then it became a partnership. Only in Autumn 1988 did it become a cooperative, so it is in the process of finding its own identity. Its members are in the initial stages of learning to live and work with each other. Overdrafts are the order of the day, but things are not desperate. The mail order trade seems to be the main area for development at present, and if it is successful a planned extension to the building could be financed. The members attune at the beginning and end of each day, Foundation style, and also have a weekly meditation and sharing. They lack experience in business management but are hoping to get support from other community businesses through a series of meetings now being organised at Minton House. The vision statement for the Apothecary is very similar to that of any Foundation department, with experience in learning and education receiving as high a priority as selling. It is 'a place where people learn to love each other, to work as a team, to realise that everyone has a role to play, something to teach and something to learn'. The statement goes on to say that time should be given for spiritual development, and future emphasis should be on healing and guest programmes. Thus, in this enterprise material success is secondary to the aim of spiritual education, making the Apothecary more like a tiny version of Cluny or Newbold, with its own special focus, rather than a business per se.

* * *

Just across the road—an old war-time runway for the air base—is a caravan bravely sporting the sign 'New Findhorn Directions'. It is not an office space which most businesspeople would envy, but from it are administered the businesses which have become independent from the Foundation in order not to violate its charitable status. The directors of 'NFD', as everyone calls it, are all members or ex-members of the Foundation.

New Findhorn Directions was registered as a legal entity in 1979. The idea was that just as seedlings start life in a greenhouse, are moved on into a cold frame and then into the garden, so individual enterprises would spring up in the greenhouse of the Foundation, move into the supportive cold frame of NFD and then become independent. For four years the only 'plant' was Weatherwise Solar. But in 1983 we purchased the land where the Foundation is based and with it the commercial caravan park. In no way could this be considered one of our charitable activities, so it naturally became a part of NFD, employing professional managers who had formerly been members of the Foundation. In 1989 the Phoenix shop and the Trading Centre left the Foundation to become part of NFD, largely for the same reasons.

The 'greenhouse' vision of NFD was never realised. Instead of individuals nurturing businesses into independence under its umbrella, it became a holding company for ventures which help to finance the Foundation. Bay Area Graphics went independent without NFD, and Weatherwise Solar had its greatest crisis *after* it went independent.

A challenge for NFD is that on the one hand it is pressured to feed profits back into the Foundation, while on the other the businesses themselves have been undercapitalised and need a lot of investment if they are to flourish. Another discrepancy is that whereas the Phoenix and the Trading Centre use attunement and sharing and regard themselves in effect as independent sections of the Foundation, the commercial section of the Park has some employees who were never part of the Foundation, and the business operates more like an ordinary small company, although perhaps in a more friendly and supportive way.

To steer a path between these different aims and attitudes is NFD's challenge. There is a further dilemma too. The Trading Centre, which sells our nature calendars, cards and books by mail order, was not profitable last year. If losses continue, to what extent should it be supported by the other two divisions? Shortly the Wind Park project will become another division of NFD, managing the windmill and the sale of electricity to the whole of the Park. This also may well involve deficit financing. We are being asked to provide answers to business problems from a spiritual perspective. For Alex Walker, who is now managing NFD, the demonstration of spiritual principles in business is part of a vision which also embraces ecological awareness and the idea of reasonable livelihood.

We have had one warning that caution and clarity are necessary in the development of such business ventures. NFD tried to set up a time-share scheme in the Park as a means of financing other building work and providing better, more permanent guest accommodation. From the outset it was dogged by problems. The simple timber chalet design was criticised by the Park Environment Group and George Ripley, the architect of the Universal Hall, was hired to do another design, but this did not find favour either. Expensive advertising brochures sent out at the start of the venture had to be replaced a year later. Take-up was very poor and the community was divided on the project. At the end of 1987 it was abandoned with a loss of £10,000, a large sum for us. With hindsight it can be said that the project was too ambitious and too similar to commercial time-share schemes which depend on high-pressure selling techniques for their success. Perhaps if we had simply asked supporters all over the world to buy a small apartment which could be used by others when they are not using it, as is the practice in some Indian ashrams, the idea would have worked.

There is no automatic guarantee of success in enterprises connected with the Findhorn Foundation, as these accounts demonstrate. It is all a very delicate balancing act, an opportunity to work 'from the inside out' in small-scale, complex business situations.

* * *

Walking further along the same road we come to a large wooden hut. At the far side of this hut, whose self-esteem is bolstered by the name 'Medway Building', is the office of *Weatherwise Solar*, usually called 'Weatherwise' for short. The company is owned by Lyle and Liza Schnadt and employs six people—none of them connected with the Foundation—to provide insulation, plumbing, central heating installation and solar panels. 'Weatherwise Solar' is something of a misnomer, as solar panel construction comprises only about 30% of the business at present. Nevertheless, it is in this area of work that the company has been innovative with its own highly efficient brand of panels. Lyle has a vision of expanding production of this environmentally friendly energy source for export to sunnier climes than ours. If it succeeds, the 'solar' part of the company's name could once again become the main focus.

Lyle started out as a theological student in the United States, and became interested in community living. He came to the Findhorn Community in 1971, when he helped to build the original community centre, and then returned in 1974, taking a large share of responsibility over the next five years for the construction of the Universal Hall. In the late 1970s he developed the idea of spreading aspects of the Foundation's ecological message by starting an insulation company. The community supported Lyle in this venture and NFD was set up. Since another business, a crafts marketing enterprise, did not really get off the ground, Weatherwise and NFD became almost synonymous for several years. At first, when the company was doing mainly simple insulation, Lyle employed ex-community members, but as the more specialised solar panel fabrication and installation work developed, he began to take on local people who stayed longer and had the necessary skills. They did not appreciate things like attunements, however, and these fell into disuse.

Then Lyle and Liza took the business independent. Instead of having been hardened out in NFD, though, the 'plant' wilted and in 1985 they were virtually bankrupt. They had to cut back and re-focus. The Foundation helped: ex-focaliser François Duquesne became Weatherwise's business adviser and we guaranteed a bank loan to tide things over. In the last three and a half years all loans have been paid off and at last the business is large enough to pay corporation tax. It is a constant challenge to keep it viable. It supports Lyle and Liza, their family and their employees, but is not otherwise profitable.

As a result of his experience, Lyle strongly advocates bringing spirituality into existing business rather than starting from a solely spiritual standpoint. "You can't integrate spiritual principles until you know how to run a business," he avers.

Perhaps this is because of the predominantly non-spiritual character of existing business practice. Each environment creates its own set of demands and challenges. The Foundation is sheltered and taking its principles out into the wider society is hard. But it represents the way forward.

Although there are no overt spiritual practices involved in the running of Weatherwise, Lyle has created a harmonious atmosphere in the firm, with no back-biting or gossiping and a sense of cooperation rather than a hierarchical structure. He would like to develop a shared ownership scheme, but at present his employees are not interested. For Lyle, the company's location in the Park is supportive and stimulating, and the employees have gradually got used to it and come to respect community members they have worked with—Weatherwise has just finished a big contract installing new central heating at Cluny.

Lyle would like to have time to develop himself further but business and family fill his life now. Liza, who works part time in the company, helped Eileen Caddy to write her autobiography. For the last two years she has been developing the community's links with the Soviet Union. Groups of members and friends go there twice yearly and Soviet visitors are coming here in increasing numbers.

* * *

Adjoining Weatherwise, in the same building, is a business of a very different kind: *Alternative Data*. Here computers hum and click in an atmosphere more redolent of a corporate suite than a large wooden shed.

At the end of 1985 François Duquesne, the ex-focaliser of the Foundation, and Stephan Wik, a young, independent businessman from Sweden, both computer buffs, were working to develop an effective computerised accounts system for the Foundation. They installed their equipment—two up-to-date Apple computers—in a small hut known as the 'Apple Shed', next to our Reception office, and began work.

Around that time the technical director of Apple UK was visiting Edinburgh for a conference. He had heard about the Findhorn Foundation and happened to have a free day, so he got into his car and set off up the A9. Arriving at the Foundation he called in at

Reception, just like any other casual visitor. As he walked past the 'Apple Shed', he heard the familiar sound of computers at work and, peering in, was suprised to see two of the latest models of his company's product in operation. A member introduced him to the two enthusiasts. 'By chance' Stephan had received the day before, by satellite connection from the USA, the latest specifications for the machines, information which even the director himself did not yet have. He was favourably impressed.

The company wanted to develop a 'user-friendly' package of information for purchasers of their computers. The budding 'Alternative Data' operators had the idea of providing this information through a computer network. The project, like Topsy, just grew. Stephan describes Alternative Data as a tiny organisation with very big friends. A further development was that British Telecom decided to provide the Highlands of Scotland with an up-to-date communications system based on a huge mainframe computer in Inverness, so that small firms can relocate from the stifled south of England. The Highlands and Islands Development Board naturally wanted to support this process, and gave cash support. The information package that Alternative Data was working on for Apple was designed to demonstrate the use of an Apple computer for information retrieval. The mainframe computer involved in the British Telecom project, however, had a very complex command system, quite different from the simple system used by personal computers. Alternative Data worked out a translation method which would give an Apple computer owner anywhere in Britain instant access to the large information bank in the Inverness computer, simply by using their own computer, a modem and the telephone network.

On the day I visited Alternative Data, the first successful bug-free demonstration of their creation had just been given to the Apple directors. The system was designed as an optional software extra which could be purchased with the computer, and Alternative Data would receive a percentage of profits from sales. They might make a great deal of money . . . .

Alternative Data employs two people apart from its founders and is in the process of hiring three others. At the start the Foundation gave support by financing half of the building and supplying food and accommodation for François and Stephan. Foundation members continue to provide a personal support system, and the atmosphere in the Park is stimulating for the business. In return the new company has helped with equipment and software for the Foundation's expanding computer system. Up to now, Alternative Data's personnel have tried to have attunements on a regular basis. Stephan says that if under stress of work they neglect these, it immediately shows. He feels that the 'Angel of Findhorn' is an active partner in the business and won't allow bad practices to continue. They have had and are still having to work very hard on personal relationships. Indeed, for François this is the greatest challenge he has faced in his whole time in the community. He sees business as involving a great deal of manipulation of power, finance, authority and status. Particularly in situations where one is in interaction with large corporations, personal relationships and one's own self-awareness are crucial areas of spiritual work.

As this book goes to press, I have heard that Apple has awarded the coveted contract to one of Alternative Data's much larger competitors at the last moment, leaving the business in a crisis. Being dependent on big friends may bring its own risks!

Examining the Findhorn Community businesses so far in existence, one is struck by the variety of activities, conditions and forms of ownership. Putting our principles into practice outside the nest of the Foundation, among people who don't necessarily share those ideals, provides a challenge to the spiritual centredness of the participants Sometimes the new businesspeople lose their sense of direction or feel that what they discovered in the narrower community doesn't apply in the larger one. But if we hope our guests take with them something of our way of life on their return home, surely we have to demonstrate the same thing in our own wider community. Expansion into business enterprise provides this opportunity.

There are tentative moves to set up a business organisation for mutual support and understanding, but even this is too much for some of the new businesses who feel almost overwhelmed by their own problems. It must come, however. As individuals we cannot do without an appropriate support network, and people running businesses need it just as much as anyone. In facing the problems of conducting business in a spiritual way we shall have to overcome our pride and seek help and support from others in similar situations. Life in the Findhorn Community is a preparation for centredness in a world that has lost its way. If that preparation is to be effective, it must work in the least favourable conditions as well as in the easiest.

Caring Organisations—*Newbold, Meadowlark, the Moray Steiner School, Minton House*

Now we climb into the community bus and ride over to Cluny. We get off at the bottom of the drive and walk for another few minutes along the main road till we reach the entrance of *Newbold House*. Newbold sits firmly on the earth, solid and impressive. The story goes that the house was built for a retired military officer and his wife at the end of the last century. They lived there with their 15 servants. In the extensive greenhouses was a coal-fired heating system, which enabled tropical vegetables and fruits to be grown all year round. Even now an aged grapevine is slowly dying as its greenhouse disintegrates around it. The house eventually became a hotel. In the seventies Foundation members occasionally went there for a meal and one of the Cluny members helped out with gardening, so a connection was already established.

Because of the large number of members in the Findhorn Foundation at the end of the seventies, we were always in need of extra accommodation for guests. For a time we had the use of a house called Cluny Bank, which was owned by members, but when they left it became a private guest house. Then we were offered Newbold by its owners. At first the Foundation decided to rent it for the busy summer season. During our internal conference in October, when the decision whether to continue renting Newbold had to be made, Harley and Cally Miller felt the call to acquire the house. There was no Foundation money available to pay for it, however. Harley and Cally had £1000 and borrowed another £2000 in order to continue paying the rent. There was still one workshop booked for Newbold. It was very successful and using the proceeds from it Harley and Cally were able to pay off the £2000 within six weeks. They became the focalisers of Newbold, and in 1982 the newly formed Newbold Trust, a charity, purchased the house very cheaply by means of donations and three major loans, the last of which is still being paid back.

In 1981 one of Newbold's guests challenged Harley and Cally: "If you trust in God, why do you charge people?" They accepted the challenge and since that time Newbold House has operated exclusively on donations from its visitors. It has flourished, and was recently able to install a new central heating system without further borrowing. A superb conservatory at the side of the house is being restored meticulously. One dreams of seeing the greenhouses in the walled garden functioning again, but with solar instead of coal heating.

In 1983 Harley went to live in Berlin for a period. In 1984 Cally came back into the Foundation. Newbold's 'parents' had left.

Newbold is very like the Foundation, but with a special flavour. It has its own membership scheme and runs its own workshops. Foundation guests visit it during their Experience week to discuss a passage from David Spangler's writing and to tour the house. Many return to stay, either for a few days at the end of their time in the Foundation or for a special visit. Kajedo Wanderer, who has focalised the house since the Millers left, has introduced his own flavour, with workshops on T'ai Chi and Vipassana meditation. Life at Newbold also emphasises Native American culture, and there are often sweatlodges and chanting ceremonies.

More recently there has been a division within the membership. One group of members, supported by the majority of the Newbold Trustees, wanted to continue with the family-oriented atmosphere of the original Newbold. Kajedo's vision, however, is for a more retreat-centred house. It is his vision that is now being implemented, but at some cost—a group of members has left after a tense and difficult process. One proposal put forward by the Trustees was to use the assets of Newbold as a basis to purchase another similar house, so that both groups could find satisfaction, but the members opposed to Kajedo's vision have dispersed. I have to say that when I visit Newbold now, I do not experience it as having lost its previous atmosphere. I always take my workshops there to do Sacred Dance—preferably, if the weather is fine, on the beautiful lawns in front of the house. It is a pleasure to visit.

The Foundation tends to take Newbold for granted. More Newbold members visit us than we them. We have never given them financial support, except by sending a few guest groups in the earliest years. This was a blessing in disguise, though, for it forced Newbold to be totally independent and to develop its own style of financing, from which the Foundation may have much to learn. Newbold has always considered itself an integral part of the wider

Findhorn Community.

* * *

Returning to Cluny, we walk for exactly seven minutes through the woods of Cluny Hill to Drumduan House. I know it's seven minutes, because I lived at Drumduan for two years and did the walk summer and winter, till the trees along the path became old friends. Now things have changed, however. The sign at the entrance to the grounds I once tended says *Moray Steiner School*.

Already in the late seventies a 'children's group' (actually a group of adults) was discussing the idea of alternative education, and playgroups, a creche, a toddlers' group and a youth programme developed from their work. In 1983, when two Steiner-trained teachers who were members of the Foundation expressed their willingness to help start a school, a number of concerned parents, some of them Foundation members and others close associates, took up the offer. It was decided that the school should be a Steiner one because the central role of spiritual education in the Steiner system is close to the philosophy of the Foundation, and there was the added advantage that the school would be part of the wider Steiner school network. Other people from outside the community also took an interest and by September 1985 the first class, for six-to-seven-year-olds, began in a small building in Pineridge called the Family House.

By the end of that year it became clear that trying to fulfil the responsibility of membership of the Foundation as well as running the school placed too great a demand on the teachers. In order to concentrate on their teaching work they became independent. It soon became obvious, too, that the Family House in the Park was too small and rather isolated for parents who did not live locally. In May 1987 the school began to lease Drumduan House from the Foundation. It provides an almost idyllic atmosphere for the children and their teachers, with its spacious rooms and expansive grounds.

At present there are five classes at Drumduan, ranging from 6- to 11-year-olds, together with a playgroup and two kindergartens operating in the converted basement. About sixty children attend. Although only a fifth of these are the children of Foundation members, many of the other parents would consider themselves part of the wider Findhorn Community.

The Steiner approach to education considers the spiritual development of children as of primary importance. It emphasises the different stages in the unfolding of human faculties, and seeks to flow with a child's evolving consciousness rather than to impose upon it. Work in the early years concentrates on the child's will, encouraging curiosity and explorative behaviour. Emotional development is emphasised in the 7-14 age range, with extensive use of art work. It is only above this age that the system concentrates on the critical and rational faculties. The general emphasis is on building a social environment, learning to cooperate, and sharing and acknowledging the strengths and weaknesses of all. There is little sense of a hierarchy of skills; the development of all skills is equally valued.

The situation of the Moray Steiner School is special in several respects. Firstly, the Findhorn Community provides an international pool of teachers and pupils. This makes for variety and stimulus, but also sometimes for language difficulties. Secondly, the 'Angel of Findhorn' does not neglect to operate on the teachers, who find themselves thrown into a transformative process which can be unsettling for those without a Foundation background. Thirdly, although it is usual for parents in Steiner schools to give a great deal of attention to the school and its culture, here many have somewhat divided loyalties, as the pull of other community activities is very strong.

The school has had problems in attracting teachers, as the salaries it can afford are only meagre. The teachers have found themselves in extensive personal process, and a counsellor with a Steiner background has had weekly group meetings with them. Conflicts have arisen between some of the parents and teachers too. Over and above this, some parents have little idea of the meaning of Steiner education and they themselves require an educational programme. In these difficult early years parents have sometimes become teachers at times of staff shortage, while others assist with administration.

But the school is established and functioning. The immediate vision is to remain in Drumduan, perhaps eventually purchasing it from the Foundation, and to develop the school till there are three kindergartens and eight years (6-14) of education, after which the state and Steiner systems are not so dissimilar. A stable core of teachers needs to be formed. The Findhorn Community is a centre of example, not theory, and for the venture to be successful the spiritual concepts taught to the children will have to be embodied by both teachers and parents. This is a principle that applies as much to activities in the wider community as in the Foundation itself. A higher logic is operating in the development of this centre, and it will not be denied. This is the special challenge to and opportunity for the Moray Steiner School.

* * *

To reach *Meadowlark* involves a longer walk, to the south-west corner of Forres. It is a modern nursing home for 31 mainly elderly residents, built by David and Lizzie Mead. They visited the Foundation three times in the early 1980s and felt drawn here. He was a doctor, she a nurse, so the project of a nursing home embodying the primary principle of love in caring seemed a natural one. At the time they decided to move to the area, the Steiner school was forming, which they felt was important for their children's education. They came up, and within one week had found land, an architect and the spiritual support of the Foundation for their venture. They sunk all their savings into the project and went to the bank for a lot more. Weatherwise did the site layout, plumbing and heating, and a local building firm took on the construction work. The Meads went ahead in faith—the financing was not okayed by the bank until the roof was on!

At Meadowlark meticulous attention has been paid to the physical surroundings. Each resident has a beautifully decorated individual room with its own colour scheme. The public rooms use special Steiner-based colour effects painstakingly painted by a community member. David says, "I couldn't feel good about giving people less than I give myself. We seek to embody the spirit of the Findhorn Foundation in the way we work and treat our staff."

The first patient was an elderly Foundation member for whom living in one of our tiny, damp caravans had become just too much. Within two years of opening Meadowlark is full and has a waiting list, in spite of being expensive, which suggests that David and Lizzie have found the right way to do things.

Meadowlark has a large staff, mostly from the local area. The Meads make no secret of the inspiration they find in the Findhorn

Foundation. They seek to create a working environment of fun and enjoyment, empowering staff by consultation, listening, meetings and teamwork, and by raising their confidence through a 24-week training programme. They work to overcome employee deference, traditional in the locality, and seek to lead without control ('focalise'). Meadowlark's first birthday celebration, for 75 staff and their families, was held in our community centre in the Park. Many of the staff had never visited us before, although they live in the locality, an indication of the caution with which we are regarded. But all the staff are now either supportive or neutral about us. How far the link with the Foundation would continue without the Meads is not certain. The success of Meadowlark has only whetted their appetite for more ventures, and they are considering re-financing the project to start a housing association. Hopefully, through Meadowlark, as well as the other institutions I have described, more interaction between the community and the local area can be developed.

* * *

The last stop on our tour takes us back to the Park. Opposite Cullerne are the large grounds of *Minton House*. Long ago, Eileen Caddy had a vision of this pink house as a place of healing. Now that vision has been fulfilled. Judith Meynell, who owns Minton, sees it as supplementing the Foundation's work by providing a retreat space where people can calm and rebalance themselves, with advice and support if necessary. The house also runs a programme of workshops, mainly on weekends, emphasising alternative medicine, but also on themes such as social responsibility in business. At present the house can comfortably accommodate 12 guests in excellent conditions. Judith is keen to relate to more 'establishment' people, for whom the Foundation may at first be too unorthodox. The regional health board uses the house for meetings, for example, and there are 'quiet days' organised for the local clergy. The brochure of Minton House states that the intention is 'to interface in a responsible manner the alternative and the conventional modes of living'.

Judith hopes to form a limited company for Minton, with a group of people sharing financial responsibility and running it as a non-hierarchical group, with herself as focaliser. Those who

199

currently run the house meditate together in the mornings, and guests are welcome to join them. But there have been problems in creating a working group, and the aim has not yet been fully achieved. A 'work-scholar' programme has been started in which people can relate to the atmosphere of the house over an extended period, sharing in its work and spiritual life.

Apart from doing an Experience week, Judith has not taken part in the ongoing life of the Foundation, and has sometimes felt a sense of reservation from us because of this. Mutual trust and respect have slowly developed, however, as we realise that expansion beyond the confines of what we can control is something to be welcomed, not feared. In the busy summer period, the Foundation rents space in Minton for the workshops and Experience weeks that overflow from our own facilities.

* * *

Clearly the Findhorn Foundation is but one of a number of institutions in a diversifying community. As yet it is the most dominant, but the trend is obvious. Over the years decentralisation will increase, as will new structures for interaction and mutual support, to create a spiritually centred, self-governing community. There are indications in Eileen's guidance that, as this happens, expansion will continue:

> In the days ahead as this centre of light grows and expands, more and more souls will be drawn here. Each one will have something specific to give to the building of the whole. They will have to find out themselves what they have to contribute and then give what they have. You will find that many new and wonderful gifts and talents will come to light and each one must be used and developed. This is another way in which a completely new phase of the work will develop.
>
> (*Foundations of Findhorn*, p. 100)

A lifestyle based on a selected group in a specially limited community such as the Findhorn Foundation stimulates personal transformation. To develop that lifestyle into a set of interacting working institutions and living situations provides a more realistic model of a way of life that can be adapted to the wider world. *The foundation has been laid. Now the community constructs itself.*

200

Cullerne House

Part Three
Lives and Situations

Introduction

This part of the book tells the stories of twenty of the people for whom the Findhorn Community is presently the centre of their lives. Each of our personal histories could be a book in itself and in such a few pages there is the opportunity only for an outline. Yet even in such brief accounts a fascinating variety emerges. The common theme is that of a quest—not a quest for the Findhorn Community as such, but a yearning for something which has led the individuals involved to the community, where they could find a measure at least of what they were seeking.

Gathering the material for this part has given me great pleasure. Each life demonstrates in microcosm an aspect of the struggle for understanding that is required of humanity at this time. Many of us in our search have broken codes of conventional morality and occasionally even the law. We have learned to forgive ourselves and change, however painfully, reaching towards the discovery that we are the image, in form, of God. That discovery, that new direction in life, becomes the guiding light, the star that draws us towards our truth, giving us purpose and determination as well as an increasing joy. Only our resistances along the way are painful. Some of us have developed such clever defence systems . . . .

These stories demonstrate the trust with which people in this community reveal their personal histories, a trust which is developed in the sharing and support system here, where people are not condemned or judged for who they are but lovingly assisted to become something more. The accounts are grouped thematically in relation to the present situation of the people involved, so that each one can be read either as an individual life history, or to illustrate an aspect of community life.

Pride of place in these accounts must go to Eileen Caddy. For me she is an anchor of our community. She feels that a greater power has prevented her from leaving here, although at times, as the interview shows, she would have liked to. Because she has already published an autobiography, and her background is outlined in the chapter on the history of the community, I asked her if she would concentrate on the current state of her life.

Lives & Situations

Eileen Caddy—An Anchoring Figure

We met one morning in the living room of *Eileen Caddy*'s small caravan. It was an emotional interview, as Eileen talked of the challenge of reconciling two aspects of herself.

"I have an affirmation: 'Joy comes with service, and service comes with dedication.' Nowadays I'm constantly prompted to reread what has already come through me. My job is to pass it on. By teaching these truths, I am told, I can help millions of people to embody them. I have to recognise that I am a world teacher. I need to stop being afraid to face this, because it is the truth—I'm a world teacher of God's word. I wasn't given these wonderful messages for nothing. The task now is to live them, be them, demonstrate and embody them, until they are me and I am them. I work on this constantly.

"People want to learn what I have to share; yet I still belittle myself. I have a very precious message to pass on to humanity and I need to do it fearlessly, with joy. I am indeed mightily blessed—I give thanks for everything. I ask to be shown how to share what I have been given with the millions, to be open to any change, to the God within.

"You know, I find it dreadfully difficult. I have this awful thought that I'm a hypocrite; yet it wouldn't have been allowed to come through if I was. I do want to live the Truth, to be the Truth —I am the Truth. But doubts come over me now and again. Why should I have been chosen? I accept that God needs channels. I accept that Peter needed me so he could be used to create the Findhorn Community. But sometimes it feels as if it's not *me* at all. I have to prick myself to make sure that it's me, as if there is a war going on inside me. It's been like this all along, right from the word go. One side wants to retire, to live a quiet, peaceful life. The other says, 'You're here to serve; get on with it!'

"I had a dream. In it I was dead and in my coffin. They were putting the coffin into its grave. I was trying to attract someone's attention and a girl picked up my message and said, 'She doesn't

206

want to be buried, she wants to go to hospital!' So they took my body there, and I saw surgeons dissecting me, taking my organs for experimentation. Watching them I started to laugh my head off. I said, 'Service until the very last— now I'm free!' Thinking of this dream helps me a lot when the idea of retiring comes up.

"Even in the sixties when I meditated so much the conflict was there. Meditation was wonderful, hours of just being, just waiting in God. I was in an incredible state of bliss. But when I went back to Peter in a raised state of consciousness, it was hard to have a normal married life. Peter complained; I found it very difficult to go to bed with him.

"One of my children wrote to me, 'Dear Mum, your work in future will be more and more concerned with communicating the word of God to millions like a gentle shepherdess. You are going to guide the flock through a new gate and attain a oneness and attunement seldom experienced by incarnated souls.'

"What I want is to put God first. I know God is in me; there is no separation. But I can only be who I am and when the messages come about reaching the millions, I get scared. Wouldn't you?"

I reminded Eileen of Christ's words in Gethsemane: "My father, if it be possible, let this cup pass from me; nevertheless, not as I will, but as Thou wilt."

"It's not a burden," continued Eileen, "it's a responsibility. That's what hurt me when Peter and I split up. We were responsible for so many lives. We were chosen to do this work, there were cosmic ties. Now, for me to do work on my own awakens a sense of responsibility I have had ever since my childhood. When we travelled I looked after the others, tickets, money. Responsibility became engrained in me. Dad expected it of me.

"I deal with my dilemma by working with the Christ energies. That's how it will be resolved. I use affirmations: 'I am a beautiful, Christ-filled being.' 'I claim my Christ-light now.' 'I claim Love now, unconditional, universal Love now'—always now, because there's no time like the present. I am enfolded by, infilled with this wondrous Love. Let this love flow all around me, out to the whole community, out and out to the whole world. It's part of me now, and I can say that in front of people. I'm not afraid to share any more, because the affirmations come from within.

"Let me turn to the community. It's like my biggest and most unwieldy child. I had the same trouble with my son Jonathan, having to stand back and let him find his own way. I was told to stand back and not interfere in the community's adolescent stage. That's what I did. They didn't want to hear about guidance and I was told, 'Leave them, they have to learn from their own mistakes.' Until about two years ago it was an incredibly difficult time. I felt responsible for everything. I knew what needed to be done, and I'd be told, 'NO!' When a child goes towards a dangerous thing, it feels awful to hold back, but I had to. It's easy to break a relationship, but it takes years to build it up again and I didn't want that to happen with the community.

"Recently, I chose to join the new Core Group. I had resistance to it. I didn't want to work with a group—in all the years I've never done that before—and I didn't want to work with young people. I felt resistance from some members of the group towards me and what I stand for. But I came through by prayer, meditation and just being.

"It was a good choice. I'm enjoying working with them now. As I am open and vulnerable, they become so, too. They're far more spiritual than I thought they were, thank God. They have tremendous wisdom.

"My advice to everyone, the community and the world, is: turn within. Find the Divinity within, and more and more have your being from that Divine centre. That's what's happening with the Core Group. They're taking more time to go within and meditate. You need to go into stillness, to take more time to be still. Prayer and meditation are the two keys to the doors within. Everything is within us, but these doors need to be opened. The little book (*Opening Doors Within*) has it all there. Particularly for new communities my advice is to concentrate on creating the spiritual foundations. Without them, it will break up. For three years at the start of the Findhorn Foundation Peter and I lived a little like hermits. But we were creating the spiritual foundations—good foundations.

"As for my future, I just feel I'm here to serve. I have to keep myself open to serve in any way. I see a lot of travel, contact with people, giving. I feel terribly humble in being used in this way and I still ask myself, 'Why me?'"

Crying, Eileen continued, "I constantly say, 'Thank You, if You can use me in any way.' I say it first thing in the morning. It is 'any way', because I don't want it to be conditional. It has to be unconditional. It's strange, isn't it, really? Some people would give their lives for something like this, and yet I haven't chosen it. I don't feel it's a natural thing for me. But if that's what God wants, then use me, use me! One day my two sides will come together and there won't be any separation. It will resolve itself."

* * *

Craig Gibsone—From Addict to Foundation Focaliser

On breezy days when the tide is in you are likely to see the sails of wind-surfers racing across Findhorn Bay. One of them may very well belong to *Craig Gibsone*, the current focaliser of the Findhorn Foundation. He comes from Australia and is 48 years old, though he looks younger.

"I was born in South West Australia on an isolated small property without running water or electricity. My father worked in the government agriculture department and was away a lot. My mother looked after us—my two sisters and me. She was a very sensitive, intuitive person.

"I had a rather isolated childhood, in close contact with nature. I used to leave my toys out for the fairies to play with! I remember strange experiences which I now realise were spiritual—a powerful nightmare in which I was falling into a whirling mass of humanity, becoming denser and denser, more and more constricted, losing spirit to life. It was as if I were drowning. Doris Lessing describes something similar in *Briefing for a Descent into Hell*. Then one night my sisters and I all woke up at the same time to see three luminous eyes hovering at the end of our beds, looking at us. I put my head under the covers, hoping they'd go away, but for a long time they didn't. We were terrified. I know my sisters and I chose to incarnate together. One is a powerful clairvoyant —her spiritual awakening happened at the Foundation. The other is a gentle woman, sensitive and much loved.

"School began in a very traumatic way. I was dyslexic, but nobody knew that—I only learned it when I was 35. I spent my time in slow-learner grades, and was treated as if I were mentally handicapped. When I was eight, we moved to Perth. It was a tremendous shock, and set me back even further in school.

"My family were high Church of England, and for a time I felt support from the church. I discovered the power of prayer, and thought I might like to be a priest. But that got swept under the rug of 'sex, drugs and rock 'n' roll'! I think I must be a natural addict; my father and grandfather were alcoholics. Much of my life has been spent overcoming addiction—especially to alcohol.

"As an adolescent I spent a lot of time on the beach, surfing. Then at 17 two things happened that changed me. I went to art school, and for the first time started to enjoy intellectual and creative life (*Craig is a fine potter—CR*). I also read *Lord of the Rings*, which moved me deeply. I travelled with it for a year all round Australia. But I didn't give up sex and alcohol. When I came back to Perth, everything seemed the same as it had always been, so I bought a ticket and headed for Europe, still with Tolkien's book. The experience of Europe traumatised me some more. Having been taught that Australians were God's own people, I hit five thousand years of European culture and felt very small and inadequate. I reacted by drinking more heavily.

"After four years of wandering I ended up in London in the mid-sixties on a path of self destruction, as an advanced alcoholic with lymphatic cancer. Two weeks before I was to go for a cancer operation, someone gave me a tab of acid (LSD). It opened me up in a remarkable way and led me into a three-year experience with psychedelic drugs. I came out of hospital, gave up the cobalt radiation treatment they had recommended and dropped alcohol. It felt as if I was being given a last chance. I changed my diet and my attitudes to life. Without knowing what I was doing I started to sit meditating in the lotus position.

"At that time some psychiatrists were experimenting with psychedelic drugs. A group of us took acid in control situations with schizophrenics. It was a way of going into my own insanity. After three years I was ready to create situations in my life without relying on stimulants. I read a book by Idries Shah, *Tales of the Dervishes*, and began to look around. I helped to set up something called the Arts Laboratory and had an exhibition of painting there but I got stoned and gave all the work away. Then I went to the Samye Ling Tibetan Centre in the south of Scotland for a week and only left it three years later, although I spent the middle year guru hunting in India, without success.

"At Samye Ling I learned of past incarnation, yoga and meditation. I thought I could escape the cycle of life and death through intense meditation. But I learned also of the Bodhisattva cycle, commitment to rebirth for the redemption of suffering humanity.

"In late 1968 I visited the Findhorn Community. Somehow I suddenly knew that everything I had discovered would be implemented here. I found out about the Western mystery tradition while having cups of tea with elderly people who reminded me of my family but talked about things like flying saucers, St Germain and the devas. That was an eye-opener! When I went to a talk by Peter Caddy I started hallucinating without drugs, seeing him change to a Moses figure, then to a being of light. However, Samye Ling was in difficulty and called me back for a year, so it was only in 1970 that I arrived at the Findhorn Community again, with £10 in my pocket.

"In the early days, the Foundation was like an ashram, with Peter in charge and Eileen as the guru. At first I accepted it but later David Spangler emphasised turning within to find our own wisdom, and Myrtle Glines helped us to get in touch with our emotions, which hadn't really been done till then. I became Peter's right-hand man, helping to stabilise things. I was the first of the new focalising group.

"There were lots of traumas. A woman I was in a relationship with left to have an abortion and someone told me it was so I could be free to give my energy to the community. That disgusted me, so I left and spent a year at the Lorian Association in the States. But in 1974 I came back for another cycle.

"Peter travelled a lot, and I focalised when he was away, learning to listen in groups and trying to develop group responsibility. When Peter came back he took control again without really honouring what had been achieved while he was away. They were lessons in humility, a key to my true spiritual growth. Once I went with Peter, Eileen and Roc around Britain to meet many of the major people behind the esoteric movement and to activate power points. It was an amazing journey. I observed and learned as Peter and Roc did their thing, while Eileen held the energy. It was inspiring to watch dynamic intuition at work. Many times I felt like a mouse in a lion's den. They seemed to embody much greater power than I had experienced in my own life; a most remarkable group.

"Once, when Peter was away and I was focalising, we had the chance to buy a house called Cluny Bank. I was trying to build a sense of collective awareness, not just do Peter's will. The old Core

211

Group looked at the house. We loved it, but the meditation was negative, so we didn't buy it. A similar situation happened with Drumduan. When Peter returned, he criticised us and said we were afraid. But Cluny Bank was bought privately by members and was available to us while we needed it, and someone bought Drumduan a year later and donated it to us. The attunement process worked, but I didn't like being criticised. There was pressure in the late seventies to get 'yes' to buying any property that came up for sale.

"1978 was a crisis year for me. First my mother was killed in a car accident. Then the woman I was living with drowned—once more somebody's channelling said it was so I would be free for the community. The crystal incident took place (*see Chapter 5 —CR*). I felt the community had been so lured by glamour and illusion that it seemed to be going backwards into magic. There was also a problem with dope. We had a clear rule that marijuana was not to be used. But some people were smoking it and it was actually growing behind the pottery where I worked. Eileen and Peter didn't know about it. It was all part of the illusions of the seventies. I felt I had to leave, and stayed away for four and a half years.

"I needed to reconcile myself with my friend's drowning. I went to sea, sailed across the Atlantic and lived in the Caribbean to be in touch with the water. Then I worked as a building instructor in communities in the States. Finally, my inner self told me to come back to the Findhorn Community.

"When I returned there wasn't a room for me. I lived in a garage for a while, then reconstructed an old caravan in the vegetable garden and lived in that. I knew that I would focalise the community again, but my first job was to revitalise the Park, re-creating communication between people and developing new forms of group integration. It was a time of rebuilding for myself as well. Old patterns of leadership weren't appropriate for the eighties. I let go of my reaction to the glamorous guidance of the previous period, and learned to accept guidance as a natural, ordinary function of life, as normal as going to the toilet, a tool to assist us and to work with.

"When the chance to focalise came, I was unsure. I asked the community to trust that I wouldn't re-create old systems. I wanted to stimulate inner meditative work as the substance of the community, but in a group context. The age of the guru is waning. The teacher today is one who turns you back within yourself. We're only on the edge of what we're becoming, at the beginning of a new cycle. The realm of attunement and guidance has always been present in spirituality. Now it's entering wider society as materialist forces recede. For me, the key is the ecological crisis; people are starting to realise that if they continue to consume, they'll consume themselves. We have to learn to value ourselves whatever our living standard, whether we have a Mercedes or a push-bike. Will we in the community be able to maintain our level of consumption below that of our society and demonstrate a rich and vibrant social and spiritual life at the same time? If we retain real fulfilment in spirit, the weight of materialism won't surreptitiously draw people back towards the material level.

"I want us to feel once more the importance of the Findhorn Community on a planetary scale. As we dedicate our lives by service to it, we are working with archetypal patterns within humanity. Changes in our community structures parallel what is happening in the Soviet Union. Personally, I have the challenge of finding my own individual creative centre where I am empowered and vital, and of giving myself willingly to something greater in collective situations. In fact, by surrendering to spirit and the larger collective purpose, you don't lose anything; you're empowered by it, enhanced. I want to continue the inspiration of François and Jay, the previous focalisers, for the growth of the Findhorn Community. This means maintaining the spiritual education of the Foundation as part of the vitality and life of a diverse community situation, privatising aspects of the Foundation and helping people to let go. The experiences of the seventies have affected my attitude to property nowadays. The Foundation doesn't have to own and develop everything. We should be open to sympathetic people working alongside us, trusting them to do the right things. I think properties can be embraced by the 'Angel of Findhorn' without being owned by the Foundation. That has its educational role, and will become a smaller political, social and spiritual body. There are too many people dependent on the Foundation. We need to create lifestyles outside it. Vitality in nature is strongest where there is as much diversity as possible. That applies to us too. Also we must acknowledge the devas, the elementals, the angels—the unseen beings that have given the Foundation the resilience to move

213

through major changes that could have destroyed it. That link is sometimes remembered, sometimes forgotten.

"One of our real challenges is to define what is the Foundation and what is the open community. On the inner level, it feels as if the 'Angel of Findhorn' has got much bigger than the Foundation. It imparts its vitality to more and more people around us, helping both those in the Foundation and in the Community to find a sense of self-worth and value. We have to continue to keep the level of co-creativity with spirit in the substance of both Foundation and Community."

Finally, I asked Craig to say more about how he had overcome his pattern of addiction.

"It was through Buddhism. I understood something of the world of 'Maya', the illusoriness of sense gratification. Even when I lost the power to overcome my sensory desires I came back again and again to realise that the true reward is in the spiritual context—there is no substance in illusions. Somewhere along the line I came through the veil and saw them for what they were. One has to be disciplined, a soft discipline. My meditational practice is the key. Even when I lost myself in drugs or emotions, there was still a part of me which watched. I keep coming back to that centre—the observer. Then there is a multitude of help, if I invite my personal guides and guardians, the angelic kingdoms, the elementals. Counselling can help, too. We have to do both deep spiritual and deep therapy work because of the level of intellectual and educational manipulation and indoctrination we receive from early childhood. For me a blend of Western therapy and Eastern mystery traditions is a wonderful symbiosis."

* * *

Elfreda Coy—Senior Citizen

Often when I am eating lunch in the Community Centre, and there are lots of guests and conversation, I like to sit down next to *Elfreda Coy*. It is not that we don't talk, but amongst the bustle she is always herself and that is calming. She is white-haired now, and a little frail, but she is still very much part of the community. Elfreda is from my parent's generation. She reminds me of afternoon tea with my mother, at half past four, with triangular sandwiches. She was even brought up in the same area as I was. Elfreda has spent her last 17 years at the Findhorn Foundation.

"My mother always encouraged us to go to church, and to the Sunday School at the vicarage. I belonged to the Junior Imperial League Bible Group. As I grew older, I was in the Bach choir at St Albans Abbey. I used to go to the Abbey for silent retreat weekends with the nuns. I've always gone to church, but here at the Foundation I began to go daily to sanctuary instead. I feel if I need any help I can go within and it will be there.

"I was married for twenty years and brought up two sons. It was a terribly difficult marriage. Finally it ended in divorce. After three years we met again by chance and he asked me to remarry him. I agreed, but it was a complete failure, and only lasted three weeks. Then I worked in all kinds of jobs: the Civil Service, in a gown shop, for Boots the chemist. I trained to become a beautician and manicurist. After a while I moved to Letchworth to be nearer my brother, and met my best friend there; she and I shared a house. We both had the same interests and were treading the same spiritual path, which was wonderful. We had a small group which met three times a week, meditating, giving healings, reading and discussing.

"One day, I went to visit my brother. Some friends of his who were there were going off for a holiday, and when I asked where, they said, 'To the Findhorn Community—why don't you come with us?' So I did. That was how I arrived, for ten days, in 1972. I thought it was wonderful. One wet evening I went to the sanctuary alone, and stayed on to hear a tape that Peter was playing. In the middle I suddenly realised that *this community* was to be my home. I had actually come to stay. There must be work for me somewhere! Next day, I told Peter about my experience and he said, 'Well, that's right, then—the only thing is, you'll have to buy your own accommodation.'

"An aunt of mine had just passed away and left me enough cash in her will to cover my expenses. In the sanctuary, I had a clear image of the caravan I was going to live in, and I did find it waiting for me among the old caravans for sale at the bottom of the Park—a beautiful, *new*, pale blue and white one. Peter showed me a site for my caravan and the boys started digging the foundations, but Eileen got a message from upstairs saying they were digging in the wrong place, so they had to stop. They showed me another site, but my car wouldn't fit in. When Peter came back from his tour, he gave me the site I'm in now, opposite the community centre. I asked David Spangler to come and bless it. He went round everywhere and then invoked healing energy in the middle of the living room floor. For weeks afterwards people knocked on the door to ask if they could sit on my 'power point'!

"My first work was in Peter's office, looking after the switchboard and doing odd jobs with Dorothy Maclean. After three months I went to the weaving department and made clothes for the shop. I worked in the kitchen and the garden, too.

"In 1975, Peter took some of the older people up to Cluny Hill just after we bought it. It was in a state; there were cobwebs everywhere. Peter asked me to upholster the Cluny sanctuary chairs, and after I had finished I did the same work for the Hall for the next three years, upholstering three to four hundred chairs. After that I started to focalise the finishing department in Publications, where I stayed till 1984."

I reminded Elfreda that she'd been doing that when I came for my Experience week in 1983, and she'd seemed to me to be quite a martinet.

"That was my Civil Service training. A few years ago it got too much for me; I had to organise the preparation of 32,000 brochures and no one was hurrying to get them ready. The strain was too much. Barbara (*another older member who has since died—CR*) took me into her home for a rest cure, which I needed. Since then I've been community centre hostess.

"I'm semi-retired now but I find plenty to do even so. I love it here. Everything that has come up has been God's will; there have been testing times for all of us, including me. One of the exciting surprises was on my eightieth birthday. I didn't realise anything was going on, because the other members kept it all out of sight. They took me into the community centre lounge—there was no one there at all, but then suddenly the whole community appeared and sang 'Happy Birthday'. I was taken into the dining room and there was a whole table covered in presents, a bouquet of flowers so large I couldn't carry it and a huge cake. They gave me a card with goodness knows what on—I've kept it so I can look at it when I'm too old to do anything else.

"After the 1988 conference agreed to set up spiritual groups for members, I started to go to one every Wednesday evening. We're mostly older people. We concentrate on oneness, unity and love, so we are able to work as one towards helping the community. We've got to know each other very well. I couldn't live without a spiritual life now—every other kind of life seems so boring. I meet so many people who can't understand how we can be so united and so loving. They feel it as soon as they come in the entrance. It's because we live as one family—I've told lots of people that. I wake up every morning and think, 'Another lovely day with my family. Good show! Thank You, Beloved!'"

* * *

Managers—Alec Whittam and Alex Walker

Alec and Liz Whittam live in 'the Burrow'—Cluny's sub-basement —in two sunny rooms on the lower south-east corner. It is quiet and secluded, but insecure. If the sewers block, the Burrow is the first place to get flooded. Since Alec focalises Cluny he is, as it were, the one who gets the divine feedback. He is 54.

"I was born and raised in a working-class area of Manchester by working-class parents. I was the first person from our neighbourhood to pass the 11+ and go to grammar school. After my national service, I specialised in physical education at Loughborough teachers' training college. I got married right after that—it lasted four years, as did my first teaching job in Kent. Then I moved to London to teach, and remarried. In the early sixties we emigrated to Canada and after a while I joined the physical education staff of the University of Manitoba. Later I worked on recreation management for the provincial government.

"Then, in 1974, came a traumatic time for me. My marriage broke up after 16 years and my wife and four children moved to British Columbia. I wanted to move to be with them, and resigned from my job on the expectation of another in the new area, but the politician who had promised it to me was voted out of office. I was unemployed for the first time at the age of 40. It was a real turning point, and I made a number of decisions. Up till then most of my fulfilment had come from my career, which contributed to the failure of my marriages. When Liz and I met, I was determined not to make the same mistake again. We spent 11 years nurturing our relationship. My career had much less priority.

"Soon after I met Liz we made friends with a Dutch couple and invited them to our apartment. Albert, the husband, said, 'What are you working on?' I looked blank, so he got up and went out to the local '7-11' store, picked up a self-help paperback and said, 'I think you're at this level—read it!' After that I began to attend workshops. We joined a Gurdjieff group; it started us searching and questioning, but we found it too severe. Over the next years I searched round a lot, going to workshops and taking courses. I had various jobs, but after a while I began to get itchy feet. I wanted to live on a boat and travel, but it seemed too complicated to learn everything about that, so I settled for a van instead. Liz didn't like the idea but she did want to travel in Europe to explore our cultural roots. My sister suggested we compromise and travel around Europe in a van.

"At that point the Findhorn Community came up. All at once someone gave me *The Magic of Findhorn, My Dinner with André (a film in which the community is mentioned—CR)* was showing locally, and Peter Caddy was interviewed on local TV. We contacted the Findhorn Foundation Resource Person in Vancouver and she came by to talk to us. Then we sold up everything and left for Europe, with the idea of visiting the Foundation, but also to head for the sunny south. We bought a camper van in London, thought, 'We'll go to the Foundation first', and arrived for our Experience week in May 1984. By about Tuesday, we were both saying, 'We need to spend more time here.' It seemed as if people here were trying to put into practice all I'd learned about in my workshops. Liz loved it—here was practical spirituality. For both of us it felt as if we were coming home.

"But we hadn't given up our quest for the sun. We visited our old Dutch friends in Holland, all the time feeling that we really needed to be back at the Foundation. Trying to follow our plan, we moved south. We got as far as Brittany when the van's clutch burned out. Nobody seemed to be able to repair it. We spent eight days camping on a dealer's lot in Rennes and finally decided to turn back north to the Foundation. The clutch was instantly repaired and gave no more trouble. We did an LCG month and had interviews. I wanted to see my children before becoming a member and we had no money for fees, so we went back to Canada. It took us two years to get the money together; it was only in 1986 that we did the Orientation programme.

"There was a theme for me in coming. I had recognised that the only way I could get anywhere spiritually was through surrender.

At that time I thought I had to surrender to a system, a person or a belief. I asked, 'Is this a place I have to surrender to?' After I had been here for some time, I realised that I had to learn to surrender to the inner God; to surrender myself to my Self.

"Another important aspect was our relationship, our energy as a couple. I felt strongly it was a gift we'd brought with us. The gift has been given back in the strengthening of our relationship, although it hasn't been easy. My reaction to my earlier trauma had turned me towards a close world in which we centred on each other. Coming here marked the end of that decade. We were asked to turn and face forward side by side. We started focalising Home-care together and enjoyed it. But when the chance to focalise Cluny came last year, it was right for me and not for Elizabeth. That was all right intellectually, but I struggled with it on a 'scared child level'. I was being asked to take up a position that made the same kind of demands as my career jobs had, demands that had helped to break up my earlier marriages. The spiral had turned once more and said, 'Are you ready now?' I was scared that things might not work.

"The major challenge in focalising Cluny has been the emergence of my 'scared child'—I've had to recognise it. The position of focaliser invites isolation; it's a department of one. I have to struggle daily with other people's projections—those who want someone to tell them what to do, and those whose authority buttons are always being pushed. Treading such a delicate balance has often brought up a feeling of impotency. Often I didn't say what had to be said; I suppressed it, and then it emerged in an exaggerated form. For the first two years in the community I'd looked around with some arrogance, watching others work through problems. 'I'm glad I'm mature enough not to have to go through that,' I thought. Now I'm forced to do the inner work I didn't do then. I'm taken and shaken till I do examine how I have to change. My new breakthrough is to seek support—I'm having sessions with Michael Dawson and Lee Oldershaw.

"Whenever I get into insecure states, the bottom line is that I'm not finished here. I'll spend time twisting and turning and thinking I should go away. But it's just not on—internal feedback is instant. I announced that I was leaving, but my whole body and insides screamed 'No!'—the pain was instantaneous. I thought my ego was screaming because of my attachment, but it wasn't the case. So I'm going to continue to focalise. Try as I will, I can't deny the inspiration of this place. I feel excited a lot of my time. Maybe it's a management meeting or something else that inspires me. My heart is really here in Cluny.

"I have a vision of Cluny as independent, but I've learned to be careful how I use the word and in what context, because it evokes very emotional reactions. At present, the Findhorn Community is a speck in the heart of the Foundation. In a while the Foundation will be a speck in the heart of our spiritual community. I want to take Cluny to independence within that context, not in a context of separation. I speculate that we'll move to a stage where membership at Cluny will require particular skills. The tenor of our work here is educational, but we are also the training ground for the membership of the rest of the community at the moment. Gradually our autonomy will increase. We need to persuade the Foundation we can have a separate accounting system. A lot depends on the trust that Cluny is in safe hands. We work with a two-handed gift: new members with a lot of exuberance and the fire of youth, but not balanced by the spiritual strength of people who have been longer in the community. It perturbs me that young members are focalising major demonstration areas for our guests. For some, being thrown in at the deep end may be good, but it's a haphazard way of running an educational facility. By attracting longer-term staff members from the Park we could upgrade the skill level of staff at Cluny.

"There's another challenge. Newness and change is swirling everywhere. We're going to make some mistakes. I don't want us to get punched into the past—circle the wagons again. It was necessary at first, but no longer. We need to be open. For instance, we formed a support group recently—it was supposed to be an instrument of empowerment for me, but what's actually happening is an experiment in group focalisation. The bottom line is that I may go down in the annals as the focaliser who got rid of the individual focaliser. We need to try new things. The energy wants to come through—so what is the best vehicle for it? I find it very exciting.

* * *

Alex Walker got married to Pauline Akhurst in October 1989. It was the community 'wedding of the year'. After six years in a relationship, they felt ready to make a more formal commitment. I asked for Alex's story largely because of his long experience of community management. Alex is 33 and Scottish.

"My parents moved from Glasgow to England when I was three. They were what you could call first-generation middle class. We moved from Lancashire to Birmingham and then to Yorkshire, where I stayed till I was 21. Eventually I went to Leeds University, to study geography. I liked that subject because it's wide-ranging, connected to geology, meteorology, maths; to the way the planet is. In my final year, I began to want to go back to Scotland again, to discover my roots, and I was accepted on a postgraduate town-planning course in Glasgow. It was a lively time politically, because of the Scotland Act, and I quickly became involved in the Scottish National Party. It was fascinating. I enjoyed discovering the streets of Glasgow and its way of life. I felt I understood it much better than Yorkshire.

"On the other hand, at that time there was still a lot of depression in Glasgow, a lot of poverty and ugliness, and after a while I became disillusioned with politics. It didn't seem to do much either for the struggling, unhappy people I met, or for myself. I picked up *The Magic of Findhorn* on Edinburgh Waverley station one day, and shortly after visited the community. The lifestyle rang clear bells inside me; it seemed to be an ideal community. People from different backgrounds were getting on, trying to work in harmony, and in harmony with the earth. It contrasted strongly with my political activism, which was mostly about arguing *against* things. This was more constructive!

"However, I couldn't understand the community's attachment to what I took to be a mushy and inconsequential spirituality, so I went back to Glasgow, continuing to visit the Foundation from time to time. As I spent more time here, I began to have profound inner experiences which opened my door to spirituality. I found myself having sudden, deep, unexpected heart connections with Glasgow, sometimes with Scotland, sometimes with everyone. It convinced me that I had to experience spirituality further, and needed to try to provide an example of a better life rather than to persuade and exhort others. Most of my friends thought I was going crackers. My childhood in England must have disturbed me!

221

"I took the plunge and joined the community in 1981. Since then there have been two major strands to my involvement in community life. The first is my relationship with the world of business and finance. I soon discovered that all was not well in the Foundation. There was a traumatic financial crisis. Of course, I was asked to join the Accounts Department and we had a torrid first year or two, with an embattled atmosphere. There was too much debt and a static income. On the one hand our creditors were 'baying at the door'; on the other disgruntled community members couldn't have more money for their departments. Our job was to clear up the problems left by overspending in the seventies and to learn financial realism. I found taking responsibility exciting and challenging. I was on the Management Group after a year, and looked after finances for five years.

"The second major happening was that I met Pauline. She'd been brought up in the community, but had gone away and then returned in 1982 with her three-year-old son, Barnaby. We've been together since early 1983.

"I have also participated in and led various workshops about astrology and the tarot. For me the community was like a spiritual supermarket, with all kinds of different 'products' on the shelves to sample. Meditation, for example. Years before I had been instructed in TM (Transcendental Meditation). I have meditated regularly ever since, but it took me a long time to feel I understood it. At first I used the mantra I was given in TM for calming and centring. But at the Findhorn Foundation I started realising the variety of different applications of meditation, including using group meditation as a decision-making tool or working on specific problems by receiving information from higher planes. Only in the last two years can I say I'm beginning to understand the different applications and possibilities of meditation.

"Past life regression work has also fascinated me. In one regression I became a boy in 11th-century England. My father had died at an early age fighting the Normans, but as I grew up I became a quartermaster in the Norman army. Late in that life I realised that this dual loyalty explained why I had always felt inwardly troubled. The regression helped me to understand my ambivalent attitude to England, and also to my adopted son, who has seen very little of his natal father. The experience in regression of how difficult such disruption can be gave me a lot of insight into our relationship.

"From 1987 on I got more involved with the private sector of the community. I set up a small film production company, Silver Cauldron, and later became managing director of New Findhorn Directions, where I have worked ever since. I wanted to help the wider development of the community and, with others, set up an Open Forum group for those not in the Foundation. Now I'm working with a fledgling business network here. I'm also still on the Foundation's Management Group, as well as being a Trustee.

"At present the community is in a very healthy state, economically, socially and spiritually. It's a diverse, growing, attractive option for an increasing number of people. A major task is to marry business and spirituality, both within enterprises and in relation to outside organisations. Should there be a collective spiritual practice? Will the Foundation's central organising role change? One option is for it to become more specialised in adult spiritual education with a more professional attitude to life and work, and to improve the material lifestyle of its employees.

"Another option is to develop the 'mystery school' environment, like a Western ashram, cultivating an observably simpler life than the average in the Western world, or even than in the rest of the community. I think there's a tension between these two ideas. Perhaps it will be resolved by doing both. There are advantages in being more professional, also in having a more dedicated lifestyle, yet an ashram suggests spiritual elitism. Perhaps it's a reflection of who we are—part material and part spiritual. The answers will emerge, not be decided. For myself, I'd like to see both happening. It is a challenge, though, as the building programme starts. What lifestyle should it reflect?"

* * *

Student Members—Helen Martin and Jean Prince
Helen Martin was part of the Orientation group that I co-focalised in autumn 1987. She is 35 years old, a quiet, introspective woman with a gentle intensity. When Helen speaks of her angelic connection and of her experiences of communication with the Divine, I have no scepticism or hesitation in believing her. She has complete integrity. Since our interview she has become a staff member, working in the Park garden.

223

"I was born in a small town on the west coast of Scotland. My mother was a housewife, my father an engineer. I had two brothers; my older brother died when I was an infant, but I had a closer bond with his spirit than with my younger brother here. All my life I've had a closer connection with the spirit world than with what maybe you'd call the real world. From a very early age, I've always felt God's hand in my life. When I was five, I had a big argument with Him in school, inwardly crying and saying, 'Why do I have to go to school, when I've all the knowledge and wisdom I need?' He said, 'Well, it's just not like that this time; you have to learn as you grow.' I closed down. I couldn't understand why people didn't understand me. I still struggle with words and with how to express myself verbally.

"For a long time, I felt I didn't have much control over my destiny, for when God intervened He was there in all his pomp and circumstance, directing me. It's more subtle now. I'm moving more towards God, moving more towards being a co-creator. It's a gift I've received at the Findhorn Community. As I move into the light, my thoughts and actions are more aligned with my purpose.

"When I was young, church was a very comforting place for me; I loved to go with my parents. I also used to go with the deaconess to arrange flowers. I would sit watching her and listen to the angels singing. The first book I was given in church was called *The Littlest Angel*. From that moment on I felt my essence was angelic. On my eighth birthday (Good Friday) I saw a film of the crucifixion and realised how awful humans could be to one another. I had my first real understanding of who the Master Jesus was. I promised Him at that moment that I'd dedicate my life to humanity. When I was ten, I remember hearing Jesus preach through my minister. I knew what was happening. Some years later I was told that my minister had had a vision of Jesus as he entered the pulpit that day, and had opened himself to be spoken through.

"My relationship with the church changed when I was 18. One day, when I was taking communion, I looked into the gallery and a shaft of light appeared. I felt the Christ energy and heard the words, 'It's time to come.' I left the church and started looking for alternatives. I spent 11 years as a teacher, and during the holidays I travelled a lot, often visiting Greece—I felt very much at home there. I went to the Soviet Union and Scandinavia as well. Holidays abroad were my big bid for freedom.

"I was given *The Magic of Findhorn* by a friend. I was totally shocked by the story and couldn't understand what God was doing with Eileen. The Findhorn Community wasn't something I related to. Later I went to a fortune teller in the south of England. She told me of a place I'd live, described people I'd meet, their names, the colour of their hair and eyes, and their jobs. The names were those of people in my Experience week. She even told me the sacred dances we would do, the department I would work in and the name of my work department focaliser, but she didn't get the name of the place. It wasn't until five years later that I did my Experience week. Three days into it, I remembered everything she had told me.

"I felt compelled to be here and came back as an LCG. But rationally I didn't feel it was the right place for me to be. I had a more comfortable alternative in my teaching—it was meaningful work that I enjoyed, and my life was balanced and creative. Then, one day back at work, I was suddenly out of my body, observing myself teaching. The words came through to me, 'Now do you see the creative power?' It was time to leave teaching. That part of my life was complete.

"But I wasn't ready to come to the Foundation! I booked an air ticket for Australia, thinking, 'As long as I spend all my money, I won't have enough to go to the Findhorn Community.' God was gracious. For six months I had a job, was given a house and a car to look after and reconnected with friends. Life was wonderful. I decided I'd go to New Zealand for six months. There everything went wrong. I loved New Zealand, but I couldn't get work and wasn't happy with where I was living. I was walking one day, contemplating what I should do about my situation, when my body was filled with light and a voice told me to 'go home'. Going home at that moment meant the Findhorn Community. I looked in a shop window and there was the book *The Littlest Angel* again. So I got the first flight out of New Zealand and wrote to Personnel. I spent two months near the community with friends, helping them in their garden, feeling very close to nature; then my parents gave me the money I needed to join. Two years on, I'm still here.

"I didn't have any perception of what I wanted to contribute. I was happy to be part of the attunement process and attuned to cooking in the Cluny kitchen. That was a hard shock. I enjoy cooking, but all of a sudden I was asked to focalise meals on a large scale. I felt there were enormous expectations, considering I had just landed. It was the beginning of an intense experience of human behaviour and attitudes, my own included. As I settled down, I enjoyed being part of the transformative energy that is the kitchen's work.

"At the end of the first year I agreed to focalise the kitchen. It was quite a different level of experience. I resisted for a long time, then I chose it from a place of love, wanting to support Cluny from within the kitchen and to create some sort of synergy in the department. For most of the time I felt that trying to get support for the kitchen was like clutching at straws. Although I could feel part of the vision coming together, Cluny as a whole seemed too big and too dynamic for me to deal with. I brought the kitchen to the point where its members had come together as a group; I'd done what I was there to do. The next step was for someone else. My life had been the kitchen for one and a half years. My whole process was a group process—the kitchen's. It was only when I stepped out of it that I began to reconnect with myself. I'm still stepping back and looking at what has been going on for me in the kitchen. I slowly begin to see where I was feeling blocked, where I was struggling, and why.

"I had clear inner guidance when to leave the kitchen. Within a week I began the children's programme for the summer holidays. The difference between working with children and adults, for me, is that with children you can walk through the veil. There's a total acceptance of just being together.

"My work with the children has given me one of my greatest insights, about working with intent. I visualised myself creating a space that would embrace the children, and that intent alone created a wonderful work experience. Everything was easy; I was supported on all levels, from all areas of the community, and the work I was doing really made my heart sing. I want to continue to work with the children in some capacity.

"At present I'm filling in on Cluny Reception while Lucia is on holiday. The decision as to whether to become a staff member is coming up. I'm ready for the level of commitment, but I'm not sure what I have to give and what there is in the community for me to step into. It isn't my project to save the planet, or the trees or the dolphins, though of course I care about these things. My way is to connect on the level of human consciousness. My relation-

226

ships with the people here inspire me. I have close supportive friendships with several members from my Orientation group. They are wonderful teachers and friends. Primarily it is the people connections that will influence my decision to stay.

"When I look back on my life as a whole, I realise there's been a kind of blessedness there. There's always been a group of angels around me since I was a child. When I've gone through difficult or emotional times, they've been present. Being sensitive to this energy, I acknowledge and work consciously with the angelic presence."

* * *

As Helen is quiet and introspective, so *Jean Prince* is outgoing and dynamic. They were in the same Orientation group but whereas Helen's life has been mostly at Cluny, Jean lives in the Park. She will be 46 this year. As this book goes to press, she has just taken on Public Relations for the Foundation.

"I was born in the East End of London—Bethnal Green. My family was always short of money, and I never had a teddy or a bike. When I won a place in the local grammar school in Stepney, my mother had to scrub floors to earn extra money to keep me there. By the time I was 17, I'd made a decision that I never wanted to be poor again and I worked hard. At 25 I was running the promotional department of the *Brighton Evening Argus*. Five years later I started freelance feature-writing and public relations. I moved towards a materialistic world in which it was the outer trappings that mattered. I remember having some doubts, even when I was twenty: something was missing, but money was then the greater pull.

"I did well. With my second husband I had a home in Kensington, another in Spain and a holiday home in the South of France, and I drove a Porsche. Then he left me and took everything. I came back from Spain with no money, no work and nowhere to live. After a four-year legal battle I gained possession of our flat in Kensington. I started a consultancy business in London, doing PR for clients like the Ritz casino. But my heart wasn't in it in the same way. I began my search for that 'something' that was missing. I did a workshop with Robert Hargrove on 'Relationship' and another on 'Leadership'. That changed me. I took more personal

227

growth workshops and almost became a workshop junkie. I did yoga and a nine-month shiatsu training, and I went to White Lodge for spiritual development—I was out doing workshops almost every weekend.

"During that time I heard about the Findhorn Community. People said, 'You'll love it there,' so I got a brochure, but didn't come. Two and a half years ago I spent five months travelling round the world, a working trip with 32 writing assignments. When I came back, I went straight into a fast pace of PR work and three months later I was so exhausted I felt I needed a retreat. Cleaning out my bureau I found the old Findhorn Foundation brochure again. This time I came. I did the Experience week and the 'Creating the New' workshop. Instead of a retreat I had the two most intense weeks of my life, but I knew that what I wanted was here. I went back to London for a month to check out how it felt in the old environment. After ten days I wound up my projects and my business with my clients. I came up in April 1987. It caused a lot of family upset. My mother thought she'd never see me again; that I was going to some sect that would take me away for ever, but after a while she visited, saw what it was really like and loved it."

Jean showed me the gardening clothes she was wearing. "I've been through huge changes. I don't earn money any more, I am happy in old clothes and with a second-hand car. I don't even buy books. None of that is important any more. My London friends say there's a new lightness and gentleness in me. Years ago I came across as hard and tough, but now I'm getting to the essence of who I am. I just love being here.

"The first two years at the Foundation have been a mixture of intense challenge and opening up to an inner peace which I've never known. I've been working through my ego and my habit of work-oholism. Peter Caddy called this place the 'ego burial ground'! In my first year I focalised Homecare at the Park and I wanted people to know how good I was, to like me. My challenge was to find a true motivation for action. I could feel love and joy when I was doing the 'beautifying' parts of homecare, like flower arranging. But it was different when I was cleaning the toilets. I read Eileen's guidance constantly, and was determined to achieve an equal love doing both toilets and flower arrangements. It took me nine months. After that time I actually wanted to do the toilets and cleaned them with true love.

"When I moved to Cullerne garden, the same problem came up in a different form. After I began to grow dried flowers I slid back into commercialism. I saw them as a way of making money for the department and tried to find new ways to maximise profit. It all changed when I prepared flowers to take to a big local country fair. When we seed the flowers, we give them love, bless them, ask the nature spirits to energise the seeds. The same happens when we transplant them and later when we plant them out. The colours become vibrant, and they are cut and dried with love and joy. I suddenly saw that the flowers absorbed those vibrations and provided a way to send love and joy out into the world. That was the whole reason for growing them, not to make money. Spreading love was the only important thing.

"As I work more with love, my old patterns are challenged and PR is flowing back into my life in a new way. At first I thought I could do PR for the community with the old view of 'It's a product—with creative ideas you can promote anything.' After a year I realised that I still had a lot to learn before I could promote this community. This year we did a display of organic vegetables and flowers at Brodie Castle fair. People were amazed at their vibrancy and we got talking about the community and our way of life. It's a new way of doing PR that promotes the Findhorn Foundation not as a product or workshop programme but by example and inspiration.

"I think the spiritual impulse running through the community is strengthening. In our department a more powerful spiritual energy is coming in. We're opening ourselves through deeper sharings. It's not what we do, it's how we do it—that's what the guests come for. Sharing this 'how' is what I want to commit myself to in the next years. I see us moving into a new way of being, and some members are being forced to look at and heal old pain as we move through the transformation process. We're being asked to deal with our unfinished personality problems in order to be clear, open channels to pull in Light. I'm now in a spiritual group whose purpose is to pull in and ground the Light. We try to develop this consciousness in our daily life and work.

"Soon after I came to the Foundation I did a workshop called 'Tools for Self-Discovery'. It introduced me to art. It's been amazing for me to work with art as therapy. For two years I've been working regularly one-to-one with Hannah Albrecht, using art

229

to heal past relationships, work through blocks and process problems. It's the main form of therapy I've been attracted to. At first I couldn't put my anger into colour. Now I can express any emotion in a few minutes. Working with art has developed tremendous creative energy in me. I'm learning to weave. I make earrings and dried-flower arrangements. I have sewed party dresses for children and Pauline's wedding dress and I'm making baskets. Even.in practical things I'm keen to try something new. When we had a blocked drain in the garden, instead of asking the Maintenance Department to deal with it we dug down, followed the pipe till we found the block and cleared it ourselves. The fun is in the trying; that gives a lot of satisfaction.

"I see the Findhorn Foundation as my home. I'd like to stay for a considerable time, and plan to build here next year. Many experienced and successful businesspeople in their late thirties are joining. I think our careers aren't accidents—we are being asked to find different ways of doing business. A new way of doing Public Relations is forming in my head. There was a reason for my 15 years in PR; but first I had to let the old ways go."

* * *

Living in the Park—Mari Hollander
Mari Hollander is 38, a tall, active American woman. A central focus of her life in the community is family, children and work on the infrastructure of the Park, where at present she deals mainly with the energy system. She has been very active in the Moray Steiner School; she gave me much information about it for Chapter 11. Her story illustrates some of the challenges, and blessings, of bringing up children in the Findhorn Community.

"I was born in the Netherlands, and my parents were Dutch. I was the eldest child. We moved to the United States when I was five. Although we moved around a lot, I settled well—home life was secure. Even before I left Holland, I was drawn to the church. We were in the social, liberal wing of the Presbyterian church, so I learned about God as loving and kind; I loved Sunday school.

"By the time I was 12, when I had a friend whose mum worked in a bookshop, I started to read esoteric books about things like Atlantis and reincarnation. My father started reading too, which connected us. We chatted about cosmic theories. My mother wasn't so interested in such things—she was just a nice person.

"As a student, I was involved with radical politics for about four years at the end of the sixties, more through taking drugs like marijuana and LSD than by being active. I became disenchanted with the politics, though, and a year or two later gave up the drugs too. At university I dropped the church, although I still had a sense of service: I felt it was better to serve than just to think, and I had a flash to do a nursing course when I graduated. After my training I worked for three and a half years, taking long holidays. I had a skill I could use anywhere in the world and I travelled through the US, Canada and Central America. Then I made a trip to Europe, and I haven't left since.

"I had heard a report on a feminist radio programme about two women, 'Divina' and 'Elixir' (*pen names for Eileen Caddy and Dorothy Maclean—CR*), who had a 'magic' garden in Scotland. When I contacted the station about it, they were very vague but gave me the title of a journal, and the Library of Congress found the reference for me. I wrote to 'Divina and Elixir' in Morayshire, saying I wanted to visit. Soon after that I moved house and forgot about it. Then one day I was reading *The Secret Life of Plants* and just as I was on the last chapter, which is about the community, a reply letter from the Foundation was forwarded to me. Just after that my sister gave me *The Findhorn Garden*. I felt a new sense of hope.

"I decided to come to Europe to do a midwifery course and visit the Findhorn Community, planning to be away for two years. When I got to the community, I thought my Experience week was revolting. There were 45 people in it and I didn't even like groups! But I met a nice couple from the Auroville community who convinced me that group life was important. In spite of the Experience week, I returned for the October conference in 1976 and stayed to do the Essence programme. I thought it would teach me centredness and group consciousness. I just stayed on after Essence, focalised Cluny Homecare for six weeks and then became a member. I wanted to go into the children's programme, but didn't. Like a temple slave, I felt healthy just working hard. I had enjoyed working with patients in hospitals, but I'd had problems with the administration. Here we were working 100% towards something good.

"A year after I joined I came to the Park to work in the creche,

231

the result of our mini baby boom in the late seventies. I met Loren and we found ourselves working on the same shifts and rotas for the next three months. We began a relationship and talked of having a baby. It was strange, as if our as-yet-unborn children said, 'You have to co-parent us!' We both chose and felt chosen to be parents and I became pregnant immediately. I discovered it on Erraid during a first visit with the community children.

"Next year we went to Erraid again with our daughter Ona, and felt it would be right for us to live there. I grew up in the suburbs and went to regular schools that taught nothing about nature. I'd always wanted to live on a farm. On Erraid I could live out that fantasy, learning about homebuilding, boats and caring for food animals; how to take care of myself on Planet Earth. We visited the States, I released my work in the Foundation and we went to Erraid. We moved into a house with no heating or running water. It was a heroic gesture! We took on one of the worst houses to do up, and struggled through a long winter.

"On Erraid I learned about living in a group where we were totally dependent on each other. For the children it was an ideal environment to grow up in, but my relationship with Loren was rocky. We split up for six months on Erraid, but living on the island provided a stability that the Foundation didn't and we came together again. I knew at Ona's birth that there was another child to come—even his name, Teva. But I wanted to wait at least three years to enjoy the first one. Teva was actually born on Ona's third birthday. I had some resistance to the pregnancy at first, because we were trying to improve and rebuild our relationship, yet it was as if I was fulfilling a contract. After Teva's birth, the relationship was just acceptable, but our work together was brilliant. It's still a good working relationship with a lot of rivalry, like one between siblings.

"After five years on Erraid, we moved back to the Foundation. We had helped to set up a healthy group life and created a good bridge between us and the owners of the island, assisted by my Dutch background. The Erraid group was strong and harmonious when we left.

"When we got back, I worked on the food-shed system for six months; then my plan was to begin a 'real' job in Personnel, with Loren supporting me by helping to look after the children. I had a strong sense that I was doing it to find out who I was. Three days after I began he fell in love with someone else. I was shattered. In the previous two years I'd surrendered to the relationship, and wanted to see it through. On the negative side, I'd lost my identity as Mari and become 'what the family needed'.

"I reacted furiously. I blamed C (the other woman), met her and told her to back off. She wanted to be friends but I just wanted to hiss, spit and claw. Somehow, to be able to carry on working, I had to blame her. Later I forgave her and was furious with Loren. But I eventually became balanced. I remember thinking, 'How is Lebanon going to be solved if I can't deal with my own stuff.' I did lots of counselling to own my anger and find myself again. The children were upset by the separation. Teva got uncontrollably angry, Ona needed lots of reassuring. The children and I moved into a new, smaller place. It became a metaphor for putting myself back together again. For the first time I lived without any other adult. Painting and fixing up the cottage was fixing myself up, too. But I wanted to leave the community, so Loren and I could get away from each other. There was a turning point when I found forgiveness. I gradually regained my self-respect and no longer felt a victim. It took me about two years to recover.

"I realised I loved being in the Foundation and moved more into the planning side, as well as looking after energy. Then I met Richard; it felt good and we started living together. The family is in a dynamic cycle. We live across the road from Loren and his latest partner. Everyone gets on well.

"Ona is ten and a half now, and by her choice she's moved in with her father. There was a four-month preparation, but it was hard to face and I'm still upset sometimes. I have to struggle with an old model that says I'm failing if my daughter doesn't want to live with me. I don't subscribe to that model intellectually, but I feel it. Just now it's a real balance, not to feel rejected and not to reject her. She comes over often. Teva showed his upset by fighting with her. We fought, too—it seemed to be a means for us to express our regrets. It's an open-ended situation, so Ona could come back any time. I find it hard work—I need to be constantly vigilant with myself. Nevertheless it also feels right. She should be with her father for a time. Loren's partner loves the kids and is very good with them. Through Loren's relationships there is another child involved and we include her in our family. I want Teva to learn that it is possible to work through things.

"Apart from my family, my work here is concerned with build-ing the Community. I'm in the next step of that process now. I'd like to give up the energy work and have more to do with the development of the vision. My experience here has given me a many-sided training through Erraid, Personnel, the school, energy involvement and as a parent. I'm also working with the Game, which helps me to curb my outer impatience and to make neces-sary changes inside.

"I plan to do some hands-on work by building an extension to 'Rose Cottage', where we used to live—finish the plans, do the costing and take part in the building. That will be a training to be part of the Development Wing. For me, this developmental work on our land is a mirror of my own self-transformation, as well as of planetary transformation. I feel closely involved with issues of social ecology and architecture, nurturing what supports life on our planet, as well as in our community. Could some of the whole-ness and self-sufficiency of Erraid be transplanted here? It makes me excited."

* * *

Letting Go of the Past—Barbara Hellenschmidt

Barbara Hellenschmidt lives in Cluny, where she has been a member for a little over a year and works in the garden and dining room. She is 49. From her story I have emphasised the aspect of release of the past, something we all have to do if we are to embrace the God within.

"I was born in Brandenburg an der Havel in the eastern part of Germany. My father was a solicitor, but in the war years I saw very little of him. Of all my family, I was closest to my grand-mother—when I was very small, she used to take me for walks in the woods near our house and tell me about nature beings. We'd often walk silently, too. I was convinced that sunrise and sunset were arranged by the nature beings. It was their special time in the day.

"When I was five, the Russians came. We were taken and locked in the cellar of a neighbour's house. All the women were repeated-ly violated. After that my mother had times when she was almost out of her mind, and we were looked after by a young village girl. My brother was only seven weeks old then—he would have died if the girl hadn't cared for him. After we were let out, we often had to stay overnight in our own cellar while bombs and shells were falling all around. I remember wounded horses dying in our garden, screaming and waving their legs, everything lit by flames. All the old men and young boys, however sick, were taken off to work by the Russians. They were driven with whips with the soldiers shouting, 'Davai! Davai!' Then the refugees started coming in endless streams from East Prussia, dirty, injured, hungry, carrying what they had on their backs.

"Once Grandfather was taken away. We didn't know if he was alive or not. He didn't come back for weeks. Then one night, the house door opened. Everyone was afraid it was the soldiers again, but it was him, broken, white and old. He went to his chair without a word, took out a big handkerchief and put it over his face—it was so we shouldn't see him crying.

"There was very little food. People tried to steal things from the troop supply trains, but if the Russians saw them, they were shot. When I was six, my mother took us to Thüringen to her sister's, where there was more food. It meant leaving my grandmother. The journey took two days. We had to walk a lot of the way. We lived three years there, without ever being welcome. One day my father came back, but he didn't remember me and I didn't remember him. I was so disappointed. My mother was still terribly affected by her experiences and could not be close to him. It was also a very hard time for me. After five months my father moved to Hamburg and we finally went to West Germany to be with him in 1949.

"My joy in life was to visit my grandmother for holidays. Every time I came back to my family from these holidays I would get ill. I began to develop a hatred of the Russians and of communism, projecting the pain of my unhappy childhood onto them.

"One day my parents brought us children together and told us they were going to divorce. It was a shock, because there hadn't been any rows. My father used to say, 'Only the mob shouts.' I, too, learned to hold on to my feelings, lock them inside. My father remarried a much younger woman. Although I didn't get on with my mother, I felt for her, and began to hate and distrust men.

"After I left school, I trained as an industrial manager. It was then that I met my husband. I was so suspicious that it took four years before I'd say I'd marry him. That time and the first years of marriage were the happiest of my life. My need for love, and his need to escape from being over-protected seemed to fit nicely together, but gradually I began to lose my own sense of identity and live through him. A few years after our daughter was born we began to separate emotionally, and eventually were no longer able to talk to each other. I went to a therapist, who was a minister, and that brought me back to Christianity. Being in a church congregation gave me a lot of support. My husband simply wouldn't talk, and after three years I got a divorce and trained as a teacher. It was a hard time. I kept going and tried to live my feelings through my daughter. But she reacted to my withheld emotions and I was afraid of hers, so our relationship was often fraught.

"In 1983 I went to a workshop in Hamburg given by an American Indian. He challenged my victim consciousness, and my belief that the events of my life were due to chance. I tried to understand my childhood and forgive my parents. It also broadened my Christian beliefs. It was in these workshops that I first met people who'd been to the Findhorn Community. I was given *The Magic of Findhorn* and reading it reawakened my childhood belief in nature beings. I had the chance of going either to the Findhorn Community or to Finland for a holiday. I had a dream in which I was buying a ticket for the north of Scotland. That decided the issue!

"During my Experience week, I was overwhelmed by the love people showed here. Then I did Eileen's 'Learning to Love' workshop. I determined to put love in centre place in my life. Back in Hamburg, my relations with my pupils improved, and I opened up to love human beings. But I knew I had a long way to go. I took a year off, to come to the Foundation—at least, I thought it'd only be a year. When I came I had a bad knee for three months. I had one leg in the old, one in the new! I pushed myself further—I went to Sai Baba and to the Himalayas. Baba brought up all my shadow side for me—at the ashram I had to face my envy and my dependence on people. But after I left and managed to free myself of resistance to the different culture, I had a wonderful time trekking in Nepal, just me and a guide.

"My life in Hamburg didn't seem so important any more. I did more workshops and began to release my old life. It took me a year to let go. Then I came and joined the Foundation in July 1988. I knew I had to open up to my feelings, and I did a three-month Bioenergetic and Gestalt workshop. It was hard work, but it pre-

236

pared me for the major reconciliation I still needed.

"I brought very few things from Hamburg. I wanted to release my old life. But for some reason I took a little Russian doll. For the first time some Russians came to our conference here at the Foundation and I met them. All my old pain, hate, fear and guilt came up again. Slowly I began to work with it. I read *Perestroika* by Gorbachov, and then came the chance to go to the Soviet Union with a Findhorn Community group.

"When we arrived on the plane in Leningrad, for some reason we weren't allowed off straight away. Soldiers with machine guns patrolled outside. It brought all my childhood terrors to the surface. When we went inside the airport, all the police looked like soldiers. If I could, I'd have flown straight back. I kept talking to myself, saying, 'Stay in the present . . . .'

"In Moscow I met two Soviet Sai Baba devotees who had released all their war experiences. It was time for me to do the same. But I also met Russians who didn't want to talk to Germans because of the war. One of our guides spoke incessantly about the German destruction of the Soviet Union. I began to feel totally guilty, even in our group. I shared what I was feeling, and others shared too, giving me a new way of seeing things. Because I'd bottled everything up and never shared about it, I'd been blocked from really hearing anyone else's opinions either. It was such a relief to let go. Then I thought of a journey I'd made to Israel. I had felt compassion and sadness, but not personal guilt. I realised that my guilt feelings were connected to my hate and fear of the Russians. I was responding to my own suppressed emotions.

"I opened to the warmth of the Russians I met. At the end of two weeks, I could look into the faces of the young soldiers and actually see the friendliness there. I returned filled with a sense of inner peace. And something else happened. My right shoulder had been stiff with a kind of arthritis for years. Nothing would cure it. After the Russian trip it became flexible and free.

"I still have a tendency to lock myself up when I get hurt. Staying open and sharing is a daily exercise for me. I've begun to give massages, which bring up feelings in those I work with; I can support them by using the experience I've gained in learning to open myself. In the future, I'd like to join the guest department and work with groups. I'm sure I won't go back to school. I want to stay in the Findhorn Community.

Youth in the Community—Shirley Barr

I talked to *Shirley Barr* in between her return from a highly successful cross-cultural youth project in Botswana and her departure
to begin a three-year drama school course in London. She was just
coming up to her nineteenth birthday. Her personal story includes
something of the story of our Youth Project, which is run by young
people themselves. Shirley will be missed in the community.

"I was born in Dundee but we lived in Carnoustie for the first
eight years of my life, near the beach. My mum ran a post office,
and my dad worked for the health service in Dundee. They were
happy times.

"My dad became the administrator of a convent for the disabled
in England, so we moved and lived in a large house in the
grounds. I was happy there, too. For the first time I had a room of
my own. The convent grounds were beautiful. They had an animal corner for children, and my brother and I looked after the animals—a donkey, chickens, rabbits and guinea pigs. There was a
tiny village school with all-age classes which took some getting
used to, though.

"When we were living in England I first visited the Findhorn
Foundation. I did the Children's week while my parents did the
Experience week. I fell in love with the community. The children
seemed so free and happy—I was jealous. We only stayed in England for a year, then when we were on holiday my dad said,
'Would you like to move to the Findhorn Community?' I was very
excited, but the others weren't so sure. We decided to come up
and see if there was somewhere to live. After the interviews
—even we children had them—a caravan for the family was available, so we went home and started packing up our belongings.

"I was very excited about living in a caravan. We moved up in
the summer holidays, and I spent three weeks making friends. I
fell straight into the children's life in the community. It's an
incredible place to grow up. I pulled away from my family
because I spent so much time outside with the others. It's impossible to have a tight-knit family here—there's so much to do. There
are no main roads, and lots of people to care for you. We could
help in the kitchen, or cleaning—even working was made fun. I
also liked going to the primary school in Kinloss.

"Around the time I started at Forres Academy things changed.
Several of our young people were there and there was a lot of

judgement against the Foundation, which we hadn't found at primary school. It was horrible for Foundation kids—we got teased every day. I began to question why I was living in the community. I tried to make friends at school and for the first two or three years attempted to conceal where I lived. I tried to do what the others did. At school everyone was like a closed box. Then I'd come back to the Foundation where everyone was open and happy. For people of my age it was very hard, so we rebelled and some petty thieving started in the Foundation.

"I'm very adaptable, but for some of the others it was more difficult. We were all involved in what happened. For us, it released aggression and confusion, but it made things in the community difficult and people didn't trust the teenagers. There came a stage where all the other young people left and I was on my own, so I started making friends with older people—lots of them put me 'under their wing'. There were also older young people around, and some of them invited me to spend time with them. When some of the others returned to the community, I was more balanced and didn't feel like a young person any more. I stopped trying to fit in at Forres Academy, wore the clothes I wanted to wear and said what I wanted to say. I concentrated on working so I could leave school with qualifications as early as possible.

"Because of the difficulties with the teenagers Craig started meeting with us. Their experiences had made most of them more mature as well, but we still weren't trusted. We were watched everywhere, especially at Cluny. That created more aggro—a 'Catch 22' situation. Craig wanted to make friends with us, but he also wanted to find out what was going on. Then Allan Howard started coming to the meetings. He could see it was getting nowhere; he saw we had to organise things ourselves.

"We had our first Youth Project meeting over at Cluny. It made an incredible change in our lives. From then on trust between us and the community started growing. We began with a youth exchange with young people from the Easterhouse housing estate in Glasgow. We stayed there for five days and then they came up to stay with us. Together we organised 'Terra Nova'.

"Terra Nova was a conference for activists. We invited people from housing groups, social-work-type groups, youth groups, people in working class areas. We had black poets and a Rasta group. The idea was that everyone would get together and we'd create a network. Each group shared what they'd done and how, so by hearing each other they could find solutions for their own problems. It all took place in a huge marquee in the lower Caravan Park, and most of the delegates stayed in caravans. It rained all the time and the marquee nearly blew down, but it was very successful. About 200 people came, but they represented nearly five million others; it was mentioned in Parliament. At the end of the conference we set up a computer network. A lot of community members helped during the conference, and we used the Hall for lectures, but it wasn't officially organised by the Foundation.

"It was an incredible confidence boost to pull it off. We went on to do smaller things—work projects in the community like cleaning leaves from gutters, picking up litter, painting; just helpful things.

"For our next big project, we started working on an exchange with Native Indians from Canada. We spent a year arranging for them to come over here and in 1986 they came. We spent the first week on Erraid, then they did a sort of Experience week at the Foundation; a very flexible one. We all spent the last week in a hired coach touring Britain. They were singing and drumming everywhere—they appeared on the 'Blue Peter' programme on TV—and they allowed us to sing and dance with them.

"When they left, we spent another year fund-raising to go over there. We spent three incredible weeks in Winnipeg and followed the Pow-Wow trail across the Rockies, camping. We did sweat-lodges, met a medicine man—the whole point was to share cultures. It was hard to come home again.

"I'd just left school. It was too late to go to college and I didn't really want to. I was living at Cluny. I decided to stay on another year, working half time in the Education Branch and half for the Youth Project. Then I met Andy and we got together, which created total explosions in my family. I got really close with my mum in this year—she became one of my best friends. I did an audition for drama school but got turned down, so I still stayed on in the Foundation, co-focalising summer youth programmes which were developing more and more. When Kim, the other focaliser left, I trained Jessica to focalise them.

"Then came the Botswana project. The idea of it was to take young people from three different cultures and put them in a situation alien to all of them. We came from the Soviet Union, Western

240

Europe—actually Britain and Sweden—and Botswana. The point was to learn to cooperate whilst discovering our cultural differences. Thirty-eight of us, including facilitators, were in the travelling party—14 Europeans, 8 Botswanans, and 12 from the Soviet Union. We travelled through Botswana, observing the ecological situation and then, as part of the de-briefing, we gave presentations to the Kalahari Desert Conservation Society and to the Botswana Wild Life Department.

"We really discovered the cultural differences! Apart from the scenic beauty, which we all loved, group interchange was incredible. We had group meetings and smaller 'family' meetings every two days. Each family had a couple from each culture, and families took turns to cook for the whole group and clean up. We squabbled over who was working and who wasn't, just the pettiest things, but as we got into arguments we found that there was much more behind them. In 1990 the second part of the trip will take place, starting in the Ural mountains in Russia and doing work projects, then going by train to Sweden for a week of travelling around, and finally coming to Britain to visit the Centre for Alternative Technology in Wales and to spend the last week at the Findhorn Foundation—five weeks in all.

"As for me, I'm going to drama school in London. For the next three years that's where I'll be. It's a big move, but it really is time to go. Everything's worked perfectly, so I know it must be right. I've got a grant and a room in a flat with two other girls. It's the perfect thing to do, even if I don't end up being an actress. I've learned here that I can take the space to follow up my interests."

I asked Shirley about her approach to spirituality.

"When I first came here I didn't know what it meant. Being brought up with it all around me, though, all the good things came into me without my realising it. I learned to attune and meditate in meetings. It wasn't drummed into me, but it was just there. I don't sit and meditate, but some of the things I do are meditation in action. Sometimes I wonder where all the things I know come from, because I've never been taught them. I guess I'm probably very aware for my age. It's inbred.

"The only problem with being brought up in the Findhorn Community is that you grow up too quickly. Maybe it's because you're taken as an equal from the start. I feel I missed some of my youth. Being a young person is important—I think I'm too old for my own good. For me, personally, I wouldn't want to see the situation different now, though. It's pretty perfect. My worry is for the kids who go to the Steiner school, because they're missing out on the reality of the world. The Foundation is a pretty protective place. Even though I struggled through my education, I'd rather have been at those state schools than at a Steiner school. Maybe when these kids finally go out into the world, they're going to get a big shock. Still, I think the Foundation's a perfect place for kids to grow up. I wouldn't have wanted to be anywhere else!'

* * *

Healers and Educators—Michael Dawson and Angela Morton

In 1988 we started an experiment, for the first time supporting staff members as full-time educators. *Michael Dawson* took up one of the positions. He is a healer and regularly gives workshops entitled 'Healing the Cause' for the Foundation. He is also a member of the new Core Group. Michael is 45.

"I was born in Enfield, near London. My parents managed various shops—newsagents, tobacconists, that sort of thing.

"I've always been fascinated to discover how things work. When I was only four, I tried to find out how light bulbs work; it began my interest in electronics. I had fears of going to school and was a bit of a loner, loving nature and animals. At the age of eight I joined the RSPCA. My father and my brother, on the other hand, loved soldiers and my father shot pigeons. My other love was science fiction. I joined the British Interplanetary Society at the age of 12. I was the youngest member attending their lectures at Caxton Hall.

"School became less threatening as I got older. I was bullied at first, but at some point I learned the power of silence, to use my eyes so that I didn't need physical force to protect myself. I did well at science, but was put off religion.

"My parents divorced when I was 13. I felt a separation between us; they were more human beings than parents. After the divorce I became cynical about life for a period of about a year, challenging everything in myself and others. I didn't want girlfriends. I was depressed by the hypocrisy I saw and enjoyed the freedom of being left alone.

"I left school at 16 to study electronics with the Post Office, but I

242

found it boring and soon switched to the Merchant Navy where I eventually qualified as a Radio Officer. I felt alienated from the interests of my fellow officers—mainly pubs and brothels—so I started to study radar and then taught it for nine years in Decca Radar.

"In spite of questioning the value of marriage, I married and, three years into it, found myself with a good house, a car and two kids. My wife wanted a bigger house and more money, but I felt there had to be something else. I found a book in the library by Yogi Ramacharaka—*Fourteen Lessons in Oriental Philosophy and Occultism*. It was a turning point. I read it in the kitchen while my wife watched the TV. It was the first of a collection of more than a thousand books on occult and spiritual subjects. I devoured them.

"After two years as an armchair occultist, I decided to apply it and chose the Theravada Buddhist path. Christianity had no appeal—it seemed too simple and I was governed by my intellect. My friends called me 'Spock', which I took as a compliment. My wife, realising that she wasn't with the person she'd married, fell in love with the man next door, decamped with the kids and moved in with him. For two years she lived next door, testing my philosophy of life. But a year after she left, I met Barbara Gillians. We found we could grow spiritually together in a free atmosphere. We were still together when we came to the Findhorn Foundation.

"I fell in love with the idea of being a teacher, picturing the children hanging on my every word, and began a teachers' training course. After two months the retina in my right eye became detached and I had to have an emergency operation. Three months back in my course it happened again. When I returned for yet another attempt at the course, the retina detached for the third time. As I lay in bed after the third operation I realised I wasn't seeing something. Of course—I'd never be happy with the system of discipline and restriction on freedom in schools. It was sledgehammer guidance! I phoned the teachers' training college from the hospital and resigned. Two days later I was offered a job at the college where I had studied before, teaching electronics.

"So I had a further seven years' teaching in good conditions with a short week and long holidays. I began to visit new age communities and studied and taught astrology. One day I was driving with a friend when she spontaneously began to channel a message that it was time for me to simplify and purify my life,

243

give up teaching and find trust to let life unfold for me. I began crying for the first time in many years, and couldn't drive any more. For three weeks I stayed in an altered state of consciousness, writing poetry, loving nature, my students . . . . Then I resigned from my job. But, still wanting to secure my future, I began planning to start a jewelry business. Just before I was ready to launch it, in the middle of a 'Star Wars' film, I heard, clearly, three words only: 'Don't Sell Jewelry!' I gave up and existed for four hard years as a supply teacher in difficult schools in South London. I learned to pray in the toilets before class, and once more used the power of silent looking to keep order. The kids nicknamed me 'the Vicar', which was appropriate because Jesus was becoming my model as a healer and teacher.

"Eventually I came to the Findhorn Foundation. While I was scrubbing potatoes in the kitchen during my Experience week, it came to me to stay on a further week. In the second week I decided to do Essence. My mother had died and left me just the right amount to pay for the programme. Essence was an opening and joyous experience, but I resisted membership. Finally Barbara wanted to visit and I returned because of her, hoping to be a healer at Minton House. After two weeks we both had an urge to become members. Our house had been on the market for a year, but after the decision it sold within two days. We had the money!

"We joined in 1984. I worked in Cluny Maintenance for more than a year, and focalised it for half that time. Although I didn't have the skills to maintain Cluny, with prayer and manifestation it was a graced and happy period.

"I had done a little healing for many years, but at the Foundation I developed it, helping people to reach a relaxed state where they could contact their higher selves for information on the psychological roots of their problems. Through forgiveness they could then move towards healing. I co-focalised a six-week healing workshop with Karin Werner, which challenged me to let go of my science-teacher background and become open and trusting. I started to work in the Health and Wholeness department giving healings to members and guests, and took the opportunity to co-focalise our Healing Conference.

"I have stayed in Cluny all the time, but Barbara and I split up and she went to live in the Park. It was sad, but we both knew it was for the best. The relationship had lasted 16 years.

"After the conference I joined Personnel. It was a real growth period. I hated upsetting people. Now I had to put my truth across in a loving way and sometimes face their disappointment. It gave me confidence in my own inner attunement. Now I'm working as an educational staff member, giving not only my 'Healing the Cause' workshops—I've done eight now—but also working with *A Course In Miracles*, which has had an electrical effect on me. I sense that the development of my work will take me out into the world as well as here in the Foundation.

"Last year I joined the new spiritual Core Group. I didn't intend to. I only had eight votes and felt no strong draw to it, so I sat relaxed, watching the selection process in the Universal Hall. Someone said I should be on the group, so I went down to the centre of the Hall to say why I wasn't going to be. To my surprise, when I got there an energy arrived to bring me onto the group and I followed it. I stayed with an arduous selection procedure, and finally was accepted. In the group of eight, I'm the only one from Cluny. Most of the others have been in the community longer and know each other. It took me time to feel empowered in the group. Now I find our one-hour meditations powerful and nourishing; what I give to them I get back—giving and receiving are the same. The Core Group is like the spiritual root of the Findhorn Community's tree. Our job is to maintain the spiritual purpose in the direction of the community, to be a secure reference point. As a member of Core Group I've taken the focus for community meetings, helping us to revive inspiration, move in new directions and anchor spirit.

"My external success in healing, workshops and friendships is not enough to satisfy me. The fruits are in the inward journey. That's what is important: learning to trust in God, to simplify life. My major task is to keep my heart open, to say 'yes' to life. Joy comes through service. I can fall into the illusion of sacrifice by thinking there's too much to do, too much is asked of me. But nothing is asked of me—I choose. I feel I'm going back home, to a spiritual home I once left, where I can find peace of mind. I have a strong sense that things are speeding up on the planet; the earth needs a great deal of education and healing. I believe I incarnated to help with that."

* * *

Angela Morton lives, like Michael, at Cluny. She is 33.

"I was born on March 4th, 1956. March forth! How I live my life is connected to that birth date.

"I grew up in Hamburg. I can't remember very much, except that I loved flowers. I could lose myself in them and stroke them for hours. My parents had a vegetable shop, but my father died when I was five and that started the era of growing up. There were three of us: my elder sister, my mother and I. It formed my view of independent women. Without being negative about it, men aren't needed. It just seems natural that a woman is fully equal. My sister and I are very close. She's the one person in my life with whom I experienced a totally unconditional love that allowed me to develop my spiritual being, because I could be anything with her and she still loved me.

"I liked school at first—I was among the best in my class—but gradually I lost interest and accepted mediocrity. I loved reading, especially adult books. Looking back, I don't think I understood half of them. I used to like going on holiday in adolescent camps. The groups gave me a sense of independence from my family.

"My mother thought my sister and I were more capable than she was. She expected us to take responsibility at an early age. By the time I was 16 I found the family rules irritating. I just wanted to leave. Talking with my mother didn't solve it. I made a suicide attempt, a cry for help and attention. I stayed two weeks in a psychiatric hospital, not wanting to go back home. But I had to, and I lived for another tense year in the family, ill with psoriasis. The illness was so bad, I had to go to hospital, and a doctor there saw the psychological link and encouraged me to leave home. She made me phone my mother from the hospital to tell her I was leaving, and waited with a glass of brandy to fortify me after the phone call.

"Although I was still at school, I supported myself by working in the afternoons in the kindergarten and with slow learners. It taught me that giving love helps in education. But the life I saw around me seemed full of ignorance, unconsciousness and selfishness. I didn't see any ideal to live by. I disliked commercialism, so I became involved in left-wing politics, but I found the same untruths there too, so I left.

"I shared a house with two young men. We loved each other a lot and wanted to understand what life and the universe mean.

We talked about it a great deal. Once I had an experience in which I recognised the omnipresence of God—he was so small that he was in everything, so he was the biggest thing of all. It reminds me of our recent community meeting on God—I received the message, 'God is everywhere, God is even in nothing.' At that time I called God 'It'. Growing up in the sixties, I couldn't easily recognise God.

"I thought I should train for a profession. University didn't interest me, so I learned bookselling. It was enjoyable to help people choose literature. It brought up the question 'Who am I?' It was as if I was a different person for each customer, so I reasoned, 'If I live in a community with all sorts of different people, I'll have to be myself.' I started little communities, but they all fell apart over silly things like dish-washing.

"I began a relationship with one of the two young men I was living with. He'd heard about the Findhorn Community and gave me a book about it. I was very judgemental of spirituality centred on gurus and although I wasn't attracted by the idea of talking with nature devas, the idea of long-term community life did seem attractive.

"Our own attempt at building a community collapsed, but we had saved a little money and decided to use it to travel, starting at the Findhorn Foundation. We did our Experience week in 1981 and, basically, I've never left since.

"At the beginning, I was scared. All the members seemed like goddesses and gods. They folded the sheets so slowly and carefully in Homecare, and I thought, 'That's love.' Then I cut carrots at the same speed in the kitchen and people didn't like me. In my second week I did my first KP with Karin Werner, another German, working with the dish-washing machine, and she worked at my normal speed. It sounds silly but it felt wonderful.

"After a month my partner and I both wanted membership. The Findhorn Community's gift was to bring love for God—rather than just having the 'It'. God came down from my head into my heart, the greatest gift one can have. I knew I could put myself to good use as a member, but I didn't think I was ready. In the Personnel interviews I was pushed to overcome my fear.

"After Orientation I worked in the Cluny dining room, which I liked. I soon focalised it and discovered that it had an angel, the 'Dining Room Angel', a higher source I could learn to listen to.

247

There was always time in the dining room to share with guests who needed personal attention and support. It was the way I made the basic connection with our guests.

"My friend and I split up. We had a vision of becoming holistic people, but in practice we supported each other's insecure behaviour patterns. Now I understand that we had fulfilled our contract with each other. Being alone was a drama. I didn't know what to do and I quickly got into a terrible, painful relationship. I prayed: 'God, if I'm supposed to be by myself let me know; if I'm supposed to be in a relationship, let me know with whom!' I dreamt of Eric and after two weeks he sent me a bouquet of flowers and asked to connect with me. We're still together.

"I did the accounts at Cluny for a while, which opened me up to what was going on in the wider community, and then moved into the Guest Department, learning how to work with guests—how to create an atmosphere of support and safety so people can open up to what is within them, just as I had with my sister when I was young. When you're working with a group, it requires skill and an ability to establish a strong connection with the higher being of the Findhorn Community and the higher selves of the members of the group. I felt myself become an instrument and co-creator—I often had to raise myself above my average level of being and become 'more than me'. Working with all the different group forces, you have to live in the here and now. In the beginning I tried to do with a new group what had worked with the last one, and fell flat on my face. You just have to keep the connection to higher beings and trust. I began to learn self-confidence, one of my greatest lessons in life. After two summers focalising the Guest Department I joined Education Branch.

"In 1984 Eric read a book about Sai Baba and tried to persuade me to read it. I didn't believe in gurus, but suddenly I was bombarded with Baba from every quarter. Five guests in an Experience week were devotees. I had dreams about Him. Then an Experience week co-focaliser was a devotee, so I decided to check it out with 'my own' God—who told me to surrender. Finally, I made a decision to go with Eric and a group from the community to visit Him. Now I'm convinced He is God on earth. He's helped me to become a better person, more loving, more caring, more confident. I'm happier, and have great hope for the future of humanity and the planet. He talks about three stages of spiritual development. 'I

248

am in the Light'—that has been most of my life. 'The Light is in me'—that is the last three years. Now I'm working with the concept 'I am the Light'. I haven't fully grasped that. There's a difference between the mind 'knowing' something and every cell knowing it.

"The last period I've spent working as an administrator in Ed Branch. At first I designed the Guest Brochure, then I became Ed Branch co-focaliser. That's the most responsible job I've had. Before we had the new Core Group, I feel, a lot of the spirit and vision of the Foundation was held in Ed Branch. The focaliser had responsibility for the spiritual integrity of our educational work, creating the channel for the energy to move in. Now the Core Group does that. I also developed a beautiful friendship with my co-focaliser.

"When it seemed to us right to step out of the focalising role, no one came forward. It was a powerful lesson in trust. I had to be prepared to let whatever I'd done collapse if need be. It didn't collapse, but it changed. In retrospect I can see that changes are happening which couldn't have taken place if I'd stayed. The group has re-formed with a co-ordinator instead of focalisers. I've taken on responsibility for our Outreach programme. There's a great potential for our programmes to be carried out to other places. Most of them are relevant everywhere.

"I believe that I create my own reality—a lot of it unconsciously. It is an understanding that has come with my spiritual development. Because I am a part of God and God loves me, everything that seems to happen to me is my creation and is for my good. That helps me over periods in my life which are difficult. I try to see God in everything: what I touch, who I meet. It's more important than the *events* in my life. When I achieve that change in perception, it alters my response and it gives me the strongest feeling of safety. You can't get lost. There was a definite time when this way of understanding started. I was working in the dining room —someone walked in before me at a meal time and said, 'Oh God! All those many people!' Something in me made me answer back, 'Oh dear! All those many Gods!' It shifted everything; I had an experience of bliss."

* * *

Gardeners—Ian Sargent and Judith Bone

Ian Sargent has begun focalising the Park garden this season (1989). Earlier we worked together in Drumduan and I developed a great respect for his gardening skills and for him as a person. He is 47. He is a quiet Englishman and, as this book goes to press, he is going back to the south of England he loves as the gardener of Chalice Well garden in Glastonbury, another famous 'new age' centre.

"In my childhood we lived on the Surrey/Sussex border in a house in an acre of garden, with a back gate leading to a field and a wood. My father was an aircraft fitter, my mother a housewife. I had no brothers and sisters of my age, and I spent a lot of time in nature; I was a bit of a loner.

"When I started school at the age of five, I just wanted to be out in nature; it felt as if my freedom was being taken away. Perhaps it would have been better if I'd gone to school at seven, like they do in the Steiner schools. But as it was I left school at 15 without any qualifications. By then we'd moved house twice, but I went to live with my grandmother near where I'd grown up and got a job as a cinema projectionist. After that there were various jobs, till finally I passed my Public Service Vehicle driving test and became a bus driver.

"In the meantime I'd taken up gardening as a hobby—my grandma said I had green fingers and I'd spend hours helping in her garden, learning from her.

"I got married in 1969 and had two children, a boy and a girl. We settled down and I worked an allotment, as well as an ornamental garden around the house. In the early seventies my young sister emigrated to Australia. She said it was wonderful and persuaded us to give it a go. As soon as I stepped off the plane I knew it was a mistake. It was a tough time and put a strain on our marriage. We were homesick, so we returned to Britain, but the lure of the money drew us back to Australia again. My wife missed the house we'd bought.

"But our lives began to drift apart; in the end we separated and divorced. During that time I read *The Secret Life of Plants* and was very excited by the last chapter about the Findhorn Community. Later on I found Eileen's *Foundations of Findhorn* in the local library and couldn't put it down. I loved its simplicity and power —it was as if I'd been searching for it all my life. I knew I had to come to the community. The time in Australia taught me not to put material things first, but to appreciate the simple things of life, things which are free—our inheritance from God. I give deep thanks for this lesson.

"I did my Experience week in 1984. I worked in three gardens in that week. No one mentioned the devas or nature spirits, which disappointed me, but I felt very good and experienced new things that I'd never done before. Working in the gardens was a joy! I needed to go away to absorb it all, but by June I already wanted to come back. In September I started working in Cullerne gardens. Everybody seemed to be sorting out their differences in the attunements; it was mostly about personal growth and empowerment. There was an aspect missing for me—the connection with the nature energies. I thought, 'I'd like to bring that back.'

"I did Orientation and went to work in Drumduan garden. At that time it was a beautiful old garden, gone wild. The first time I saw it I knew it was my place. Three of us started working there. Every Monday morning we'd do a meditation to welcome the new guests. We connected with each other and with the nature spirits, and then showed the guests round the garden so they'd know everything that was going on.

"When we planted things, we attuned to the beings of the plants to bless them. We were really cooperating with nature energies. If we forgot, the plants didn't do so well. Even in the first year we had very good results; there was a great vitality about everything that I'd never experienced before. We dedicated an area as a wild place for the nature spirits. No one ever went in there. It was on one side of a path we'd built through the woodland. At the end of the season, a line of bright red *Amanita muscaria* mushrooms grew along that side of the path. We knew the nature spirits were symbolically acknowledging us—traditionally gnomes sit on toadstools and red also says, 'Stop! Do not enter!'

"In 1986, when the other members left the garden, I took over the focalisation. In the beginning I missed their support but soon drew another member to work with me and the connection with the nature spirits continued. A year later I attuned to looking after Traigh Bhan, our retreat house on Iona, for the summer, when the guests visit. It was challenging to start with, living with a new group of guests every week. As I got used to it and released the feelings of responsibility, I woke up to the magic of the island. I walked all over it and discovered the energy centres, which have been described as chakra points. While I was sitting on the one called the 'sacral chakra', tears came welling up in me, seemingly from nowhere. I felt I had experienced one of the mysteries of the earth's energy.

"On Iona I had time to think over all that had happened to me, and decided to leave the community. I went to an aunt's in Dorset and got regular jobs, first as a meat packer, then as a maintenance man at a private school for boys. It was a secure job, with good pension prospects, but that kind of life wasn't satisfying for me. I heard that Eileen Caddy was visiting Glastonbury. I went to hear her talk, in a cold, dirty old hall with hardly anyone there. Eileen was wonderful, shining like a beacon. I suddenly saw the Findhorn Community with a light radiating from it. I knew I had to return and a month later I was back.

"After a little hesitation I attuned to the Park garden. I felt there was a lack of connection with the nature spirits there, and that my role was to bring that energy back. We've slowly formed a new group and worked through a lot of personality problems, but we are making the connection with the nature spirits again. You can see it as you walk around the garden and look at the vibrancy of the plants—the original quality of the sixties is returning."

I asked Ian how the Foundation had changed him.

"Before I came here, I was sceptical and questioned everything. Now it's as if a door in me has opened. Also I had a tendency to try and please people. Here I've been given a chance to break through that and do what's right for me. Workshops I've done have given me the support I needed. I was shy of talking in groups—that's gone. Now I lead meditations and do nature sharings with guests. My sensitivity to nature has grown tremendously here, especially on the etheric level. Although I've never seen them, I know when the nature spirits are present. But, you know, something changed in my life from the moment I read Eileen's guidance in Australia. Even then I tried to put her teachings into practice in my daily life as a bus driver. I used to have a lot of pretty hard customers. It worked—the impossible happened and my life became a joy.

"Sometimes I feel that it would be nice to be married and live an ordinary life. It can be lonely here, and there are certain authority figures—people who talk all the time, so that the shyer, smaller person isn't heard so much. I find that difficult. I've also had feelings of insecurity about lack of money. I'm trying to work with the quality of trust, to believe that all my needs will be met.

"I find it's best if I take one step and not look too far ahead. I try to live a day at a time and enjoy that day as if it were the last. I'd like to plan next year's garden, learning from this year's mistakes. I feel grateful for the Findhorn Foundation, and privileged to be a member. It has taught me a lot. And if ever I leave, my life will have been really enriched by being here."

* * *

Judith Bone is the focaliser of Cullerne gardens, our largest garden area. I am happy to see how they are flourishing, for in 1984, when I worked there, it felt as if they were at the beginning of a long period of healing—of the soil, of human relations and of relations with the Foundation. Judith is 41 and English, a thoughtful and self-questioning person.

"I grew up in the north-east of England. My parents were fairly regular churchgoers, but church was not a big part of their life. I went to Sunday School, was confirmed and was also a member of the Young Anglican People's Association. As I got older, I was influenced by humanism and by the age of 15 I stopped going to church. I drifted away from religious ideas, and when I went to a women's teacher training college in Cambridge, I even became an atheist for a time, under the influence of the educational philosophy classes. But I was interested in what made the world tick.

"I taught for one year at a village school. I felt very immature to be a teacher—it was a challenge to be 'Miss'—so I decided to travel. I thought of doing Voluntary Service Overseas, but my family weren't keen. I went to Germany instead and fell in love with a German. I stayed there for the next six years, working as an au pair for a while and then teaching English as a foreign language. I had a good job and was comfortable, but it wasn't enough. I wanted to do something important and right, something valuable. Part of me was constantly searching.

"I read a lot and began to realise that many of the things I took for granted came from my Christian upbringing. I was living a conditioned way of being. I went travelling in India and Japan and stayed nine months in the latter country, teaching English. It was a big opening to see different ways of living. People in Japan have a Zen way of looking at life; they take it as a discipline and really work on it. Back in Germany I started T'ai Chi in Munich with a Japanese teacher. He also taught me Zen meditation.

"I first visited the Findhorn Foundation in 1981. It felt like coming home. I was searching for a community of like-minded souls and saw it here. I was very inspired by the people I met. For me it was also a very beautiful place—I was tired of city life. I intended to come as a member, but I began a relationship with Joshua, an Italian, and spent a year in Rome with him. Although I came back to do the Essence programme, it wasn't till 1986 that I was ready to join.

"I've worked as a gardener all the time I've been here. It's important to me to be outdoors in the fresh air, in touch with the earth. It has been a quietening, centring experience. Working with the many guests at Cullerne has brought me really into the present. In my background, diplomacy, charm and tact were values. In the honesty of the community, I've had to work a lot on being clear. The biggest challenge for me has been that I came here with Joshua and now I'm a single woman again. I have had to look seriously at my way of being in relationships, to learn to express what I feel. The separation was a long process. I moved out because I was no longer aware of what was Joshua and what was me. We couldn't support each other. But all through it was the underlying feeling that it was right to split. For the first time I'm learning who I am and what I want without relating to someone else. Long-established patterns in me have been challenged, but when at times I have felt like closing down, I've always been pushed back into staying open and loving. In a difficult patch I did rebirthing, which helped me release things I'd held inside for many years. Now there's a new way for Joshua and me to relate to each other.

"In the middle of it all, my mother died. I was with her for the last three weeks. The vision of the world I have learned at the Foundation gave me a lot of strength to be with her. I received so much from seeing my mother releasing. It was so obvious that only her physical vehicle died. In a way my mother was more available to me after her death; geography and location no longer separated us. It has also helped me to become my own mother to myself.

"After only one year in the garden I was the most senior member of the group! If I hadn't focalised, someone from outside would have had to come in. Fools step in! I felt very unqualified, but I was supported by the rest of the group. Now I feel competent on a personal level and with the guests. On the gardening side there's a lot to learn and always will be. My ideal is for the whole group of gardeners to be empowered. I see spirit in everything we do. The plant and animal realms are all part of one world with us on an equal basis; the way of connecting it together is love and appreciation. A lot of lessons in the garden are in understanding interconnectedness. Invisible energies are present and there is a mystery in growth. I find it, for instance, in compost-making. Although I don't see nature spirits, I become more and more aware of them: in the plastic tunnel with the tomatoes and peppers I've felt a real presence beyond something I could see. By learning to work with and trust my intuition I've become able to receive messages from the 'Angel of Cullerne'.

"With the guests I don't do a lot of talking but work more by example. Letting them have their own experiences opens their awareness of what is present and possible in the garden.

"I love the diversity of life here. I have involved myself with Sacred Dance and the Game of Transformation. I already studied dance when I travelled as a teacher, so Sacred Dance appealed to me from the outset. Spirituality is a lot about joy, and in Sacred Dance I can feel the magic of moving together. I like leading it for Experience week groups. I focalised a Sacred Dance workshop with Anna Barton recently and want to do more. I like the way that people have realisations about themselves and move through them in a non-verbal way.

"As to the Game, I'm a facilitator for the 'Game-in-the-Box' and a chronicler for the workshop Game. I want to become a qualified Game guide. The Game gives me a powerful experience of working with unseen beings; there's an element of magic in it, how things are interrelated—a clear purpose creates an equivalent experience. It's been one of my biggest transformational tools, and I use the language of the Game to express the process I've gone through here.

"During one game, when I was chronicler, another player shared that she procrastinated about getting in touch with God. I realised I did it myself. I would intend to meditate, then start something else instead. I caught myself doing it and made myself sit down. Suddenly I *knew* that God was Love, that the greatest force was Love. It was a total inner knowing. The experience lasted several minutes. It was sublime."

* * *

The Environment Matters—John Talbott
John Talbott is a difficult person to catch, particularly at this time, when the complex process of wiring the windmill into our electrical system is occupying him. He is 37, but seems ageless, a practical visionary who has never capitulated to cynicism.

"I was born in Wiltshire, so I have British roots. But my parents were Americans and moved back to Portland, Oregon when I was less than a year old. There I remember the trees in parks near my home, giant old Douglas firs, the remnants of huge forests. I used to go and walk among them and felt a wonderful sense of peace, but also a sense of their trauma at the loss of the great forests which had been cut down. Even as a tiny child I felt a deep friendship with them and made an unconscious commitment to them. When I was about three and a half years old, as I was walking to the local kindergarten, I declared to the trees, 'I've got a lot of work to do!'

"I was brought up a Catholic, and the church moved me a lot when I was young, yet it didn't hold me, and by 12 or 13 I was already a sort of atheist. In my mid-teens I reconnected with nature, in the mountains and forests of Oregon. I was hiking once when I was 19 and sensed a presence come out of the forest and walk around me. I couldn't see it, but I could hear and feel it. I was awed and not a little frightened, and I never told anyone about it.

"At university I started off studying English, but later chose engineering. A few years later, as I got a job with a big multinational company, I also began on my conscious spiritual path. After work in the business world I would go in the evening to meditation groups or others exploring spirituality. I also did dream work. Dreams have always been very important for me. After two or three years someone gave me *The Magic of Findhorn* and I then realised that my experience when I was 19 had been a meeting with an elemental being. Two months later I was at the Findhorn Foundation. I stayed for some weeks, but only in the last week, in a workshop called 'Revelation', did I receive one—and knew that I would be coming back. Returning to the States, I began meditating every day, establishing an inner discipline.

"At work I was a budding young star, climbing the ladder. I was appointed to be project engineer for a major project at my plant and was sent to the corporate headquarters in Chicago. Flying in, while we were stacked waiting to land at O'Hare airport, I felt something say, 'Now is the time we need you.' It was a call from spirit and I knew it meant *now*. I gave notice the next morning, spent a couple of months clearing up my affairs, finished my professional exams and came to the Findhorn Foundation. I thought I'd give up engineering and work in the garden, but after one week I was in Maintenance, and I've been in that and building ever since.

"For the first two years I felt fantastic. I had left a city of half a million people and come to a tiny community. But I had a dream that I had left a tiny place and come to a vast one. By working with my dreams and with the Game of Transformation I connected with one of the archetypes of the Findhorn Community, the aliveness and intelligence of nature, and all the early memories of the trees of my childhood reawakened.

"1982 was a key year. I heard of the idea of the 'planetary village', creating a human ecology in harmony with nature as a model for the planet. It felt like my life calling. I also met Frances and dreamt that I had found my life partner. We were both inspired with the idea of a cooperative venture with nature expressed as a local planetary village. We lived together for three years and then felt God wanted us to make a deeper commitment, so we married. But it was a commitment to a larger vision and purpose, too.

"Until four years ago my main focus was on developing myself. At the beginning I had a dream which said, 'You'll be able to work on construction after you've worked on reception!' I realised it meant 'receptivity'. I received a lot of healing. In 1985-6 I felt the initiation was over, my apprenticeship was finished, and I moved more into a leadership role, working on the Management Committee. Now I felt like a journeyman, and began to use more of my professional skills. I developed a workshop called 'Dreams and the Spiritual Path' and led it for several years. I learned to be a guide for the Game of Transformation and I still lead Game workshops—it's a good balance to the physical work.

"But the main thing has been the development of a nature-related ecology. I have a sense of tremendous excitement in the nature kingdoms at the possibility of working with a conscious humanity. It is my main motivation. I experienced the magic of this co-creation when we reconstructed Traigh Bhan, for which I've been responsible for seven years. We had a very difficult re-roofing job that lasted more than a month. The weather there is extremely wet. At the beginning we prayed not to have rain. We felt a sense of willingness. It rained the day before we started, then for 38 days there was no rain at all. Each morning we meditated and asked the weather devas that if it was possible for it not to rain, we would be very appreciative. The day after we finished, it rained. We felt that when we climbed up on the roof, a greater energy was with us as well. That energy is in the Findhorn Community too, waiting to be called on.

"The expression of that co-creation here is in the development of a planetary village in the Park. This isn't the only planetary village. It's one of thousands that are growing, to demonstrate a sustainable lifestyle. What is needed is a combination of four elements: spirituality, ecological awareness, economic sustainability and a nurturing cultural and social atmosphere. Here we are working on all four elements; other places tend to emphasise one or another. The spiritual impulse began everything in the Findhorn Community; our cosmology gives us a purpose and a location on Earth; and there is already a rich community life. Where we're breaking new ground is in economic diversity. The final expression will be an ecologically sustainable lifestyle, which will involve the development of the businesses. As yet, we've still a long way to go. We have only just begun to make real the idea of ecological housing.

"We're translating all the ideas into form by understanding what's here and blending our needs with those of nature. We're studying soils, geology, what kind of materials to use and how buildings are to be placed in the landscape. At the moment we're at the point of changing from the development of an overall plan to actual building. It's taken longer than we thought, but in retrospect the timing is just right. The community has to be ready to release old ideas and be open to the new.

"We are bringing together a building and landscaping team. It's been hard to draw people that have the skills we need—builders and landscape architects—grounded in spiritual awareness. That is the special synthesis required. At present we have 12 people in the building department, and eight others working with planning and design. We've formed a Development Wing to make it real. It's distinct from the educational wing of the Foundation, but still part of the charitable trust. We're all volunteers with a spiritual motivation. What has to grow is a building and landscape school where we're teaching a new way of building and landscape design that focuses on the practical expression of 'work as love in action'. A self-build group is coming here to help us with the building school in 1990 and we'll hopefully expand that into landscaping and gardening. The first windmill of our wind park is up; our vision is for a sustainable, non-polluting energy supply, roughly 70% wind, 20% solar and 10% wood based. We are investigating a new system for sewage treatment so that all organic waste can be recycled on site. It may also provide energy—we hope to start a pilot scheme next year. We'd also like to develop our own water supply and purification system and increase our food production.

"From 1990, we should be building five to ten houses a year, using non-toxic local materials. They will embody passive and active solar heating systems and be energy-conserving as well as beautiful and nurturing homes, sensitively designed and placed.

"The images of the founding group of the Findhorn Community are still very real for me. The concept of God is alive and accessible; nature is intelligent and is ready and willing to work with us. We all have our own Eileen and Dorothy within us, giving us a way to connect with God and the nature kingdoms in our daily work. I feel that if we're to be successful with bringing this planetary village into reality, it will really involve that level of cooperation."

* * *

Independence, Music and Dance—Barbara Swetina and Anna Barton
There are many musical activities in the community, most of them connected with singing. There is a barbershop group; a local choir, the Culbin Singers, to which several community members belong; and our own choir. But there are also other, more informal, musi-

cal events, which are often organised by *Barbara Swetina*. She may be playing the piano in a recital, an accordion at a summer festival, a flute at a dance, or singing at a celebration of devotional music. She is 34.

"I was born in Vienna to parents who were both graphic designers by trade, and I had a very happy and unperturbed childhood. Music was always important in our family. I learned the recorder when I was six. When I was eight, I saw my first piano, at a friend's party, and discovered I could straight away make melodies on it. Next Christmas a friend of my mother was selling a grand piano and my parents bought it for me as a Christmas present. Of course, many children learn to play instruments in Austria.

"I had my own theory of reincarnation in those days. I thought we all came here three times. My friend, who saved her chocolate, was obviously in her third incarnation but I, who gobbled mine up, must be in my first. I used to imagine myself on a cloud with the angels, watching my life like a film. Sometimes it was scary to see, but I knew it was only a movie and that I'd eventually be back with the angels. School was boring to me, but at the piano I could dream. I wrote my own compositions and loved to distinguish the different classical composers.

"At 17 I went to a special school for music students. It was a difficult time. I was confused and turned to my boyfriend for closeness and affection. I could not communicate well with my parents and tried to hide the truth about this relationship from them. Adult life seemed very dull and neither sex nor my daily piano studies could fill the void which I felt inside. I turned to marijuana which seemed to give me magic and sparkle in this inner darkness. Although I wasn't sure if God existed, I prayed for help.

"Soon I met a man who did yoga. He introduced me to Huxley's *Doors of Perception*. I realised that the reality we saw wasn't the only one, and that to open oneself through meditation was better than through drugs, because the results didn't go away and there were no side effects. I started yoga and began to read Jung and Steiner. The knowledge of the invisible worlds brought the sparkle back into my life, without the drugs.

"I moved to Salzburg to train to be a primary school teacher, but I never taught. One day I visited some master classes in music and saw a student from Japan playing Bach solo sonatas on the violin.

I had a deep experience—for me it was an invocation of the Divine. I had to get back into music. I trained in the piano and recorder, earning some money by busking. I was involved in the Steiner community and it was there that I heard about the Findhorn Foundation. I read *The Findhorn Garden*. I liked not only the pictures but the love and care with which the book was produced. In 1978 I booked a ticket and came here. I was 23. I felt I was coming home, as if there was five times more of me than I'd experienced before. But I wanted to finish my music training. I wasn't ready to join.

"Seven years later I had moved to Munich and had a relationship, a nice house with a garden and a marriage proposal. I decided to visit the Foundation just once more—and then the chapter of my 'normal' life closed. I didn't run away from it; it was just finished.

"I was preparing to do Orientation when the 'Angel of Findhorn' gave me another option. I was invited to be part of an Argentinian music group, Los Incas, and become a 'star'! I played out my dream and toured with them for a while, but it didn't satisfy me. Although I had missed out on Orientation, I was in time to do the Essence programme and in those days you could become a member after taking part in that, too. It was a difficult period for me personally, but I found a lot of love and support in the group.

"Three of us from that Essence programme joined the Foundation, but when the rest of the group left it felt lonely. It was a hard start. I worked in the kitchen. Gradually I started introducing songs and musical games into the shifts; although I was shy, if I pushed myself I found it created togetherness between us and uplifted us. From the guests I started collecting songs, rounds and chants from different cultures.

"After a time I was invited to lead an evening with a departmental guest group, to share music. Some Germans who were there invited me to do something similar in Germany. I tried it, as a step in faith. Three people came. But one of them was a yoga teacher, and she organised another workshop inviting all her friends. That time there were thirty. They asked *their* friends and I found I had become a workshop leader.

"After two years in the Foundation I felt I needed more time for music. My soul was crying out for it; I wouldn't be satisfied without it. Personnel supported me to go independent, though I had no idea how I could stay. Now, two years later, I own a caravan in the Caravan Park and two or three times a year I go on tour in Europe. I do little things here like giving lessons, and I get some meals by working for the Publications Department. I work with our Ceilidh band too, and we've produced a tape. I'm always putting on informal concerts, or providing music for meditations, celebrations and conferences. I've become the community musician!

"People get inspiration and healing through the work I do. Music and singing is a sort of spiritual hygiene that is lacking in the lives of many individuals. I once did a workshop with Danaan Parry on life vocations—I felt that my piece of the puzzle is to bring more song and dance to the planet.

"My dream and hope is that we are developing a sacred society, a society that is in touch with love and truth. My work is to create sacred spaces where we can encounter one another in a new way of being and see how we like it. Music heightens a sense of joy and ecstasy that heals us from within. The more I deepen my connection with music, the more I sense it as a form of prayer, making the Divine tangible between us. My vision is that my music helps to bridge gaps between nations, remove barriers between religions. We're all children of one Divine Being."

* * *

In *Rainbow Bridge*, the community's internal newsletter, one finds from time to time articles from places like Paris or Bologna or Stuttgart. They are extracts from *Anna Barton*'s travel journals, lovingly sent in to keep us in touch with the events of her Sacred Dance workshops abroad. Anna is 53.

"My father was a policeman. In the war we were evacuated to Surrey, otherwise I was a Londoner. I was the eldest of four children, so I was expected to be responsible, something that's bugged me ever since. We were Church of England and that's stayed with me too, although I don't believe in the confessing and 'miserable sinner that I am' bit. I still tend to see God as a father figure, who rewards me when I'm good and punishes me when I'm naughty. I'd like to grow out of that, because it's not true. There's also a part of me that believes in God within, working from my own centre, knowing that that is God. I can find that place more easily than I used to.

"After school I trained as a secretary and worked as a telephone operator/receptionist for six months. But my heart wasn't in it, so my parents allowed me to train as a teacher at Lincoln Training College. I had a horrible probation year with a difficult headmistress in Romford, and then I got married. That was the end of my teaching career!

"Dick was in the Air Force in Cornwall. Because of his job we travelled a lot, having children every two years till finally we settled in Cornwall and bought an old water mill, which was big enough for his parents to share with us. We lived there for more than eight years. I became part of the local scene, started a preschool playgroup and trained to supervise it. I learned to paint pottery and loved it for the creativity. I wasn't so interested in money; voluntary work was more important to me.

"Towards the end of the time, Dick was posted to Kinloss air base. He wrote home about the Findhorn Community and Eileen, whom he repeatedly visited. He told about amazing encounters with nature spirits and spirit beings—though he didn't believe in them! The rest of us decided to come and see the place. It was 1972. I loved the way people were. I'd had a fairly conventional and uptight life. Here were all these flower-power people, singing and dancing. I worked in the pottery. At first we just visited; our life at the mill was too good, and we'd done so much work on the house and garden. But we began to feel a pull. We had a family conference about it. I decided that if anyone was against moving, we wouldn't go, but all of us agreed. We waited till Dick's retirement in 1974. In the meantime we started a new age group and set up the mill as a craft centre with candles, macrame and pottery.

"It was quite a wrench to leave it for the Findhorn Foundation. Eight of us came up—four children and four adults. Dick moved into administration straight away. I did several jobs, among them focalising Reception and reorganising it. We all played a big part in the community. We developed Pineridge garden with the help of a JCB; we sang and played in sharings; I went on to Core Group. Dick and Fred (my father-in-law) became involved in Cullerne, but I didn't want to. I wanted to be more at home. Also, Sacred Dance was becoming more and more important to me.

"In 1976 Bernhard Wosien came to give a dance workshop. He originated Sacred Dance, collecting folk dances from everywhere and simplifying them into circle dances with a spiritual significance. Because I wrote down the dances at his workshop, I was made the focaliser of the ongoing group that formed. It was the Sacred Dance that kept me going in 1979, which was a very bad year for me. I had been ill just previously and had had several operations, our mothers died and my husband began a relationship with someone else. For a time we tried to 'do the new age thing' and accept a triangle, but it was hell actually. Eventually they left. I was 42, without a husband and my children were growing up. I thought my life was over, but dancing kept my head above water.

"In 1980 I did my first workshop outside the community, in Essex. Then I was invited to Paris and Florence, and my second career had begun—my first had been raising the children. The more I danced, the more I realised it was my vocation. With Dick gone, I was dependent on the community allowance; no car, no phone, no holidays. I felt like a little, dependent old lady. As the children left, I was asked to share my house but instead I wanted more independence. In 1985 I became a self-employed dance teacher. It was easy at first, but now I'm having to learn more about business. I didn't know anything about accounts and invoices. The more complicated it gets, the more alien it is. I think that life should be simple. I'm actively trying to get back to a simple life, doing eight or nine workshops a year. Fourteen was too many, last year. When I'm away so much I can't be with my garden, which I love.

"I like to share with the community when I'm away, so I write extracts from my diary for *Rainbow Bridge*. Here, I lead all the Sacred Dance workshops, also workshops in 'Meditation in Movement' and 'The Joy of Dance'. I'm responsible for all the Sacred Dance in the community. It's a lot of work to organise: an ongoing group Tuesday night, a casual group Wednesday night, performances for festivals and celebrations, making tapes, working out steps for new dances, answering all the letters I get.

"Since I became independent, I've pulled back from the Foundation somewhat. I don't eat in the community centre; I have a smaller group of friends than I used to have. I like to slow my pace down now; I need more quiet and relaxation between workshops.

"Looking back, I have suffered a lot of pain and loss here, but

I've gained more than I could ever have done outside. My perspective on values and beliefs has changed. I used to have a set of absolute values. Now I can look at a situation and search for the truth in it. For instance, when my eldest daughter wanted to live with her boyfriend at the age of 16, I said, 'No.' But when I thought about it, I realised that I was more concerned with what people thought about *me* than about her—so I changed my mind. Prior to coming here I would never have had a relationship with a younger man—I met Alain, my present partner, in the south of France in 1983—but now that doesn't matter to me. It's who the person is that counts, not their age. It has been valuable for my children, too. When they were ready to go to college, they were glad to get away. They had begun to see the community as their peers outside did. But once they were out, they realised how much they'd gained from their upbringing here. They had much more maturity than their friends.

"The last six years have been the happiest of my life, in my relationship and in my dance teaching. My main motivation in life is to spread Sacred Dance. It changed my own life, and I know it can help other people to change theirs."

* * *

The Newbold Focaliser—Kajedo Wanderer
Kajedo Wanderer has lived in Newbold House for eight years and focalised it for five. He is 32 years of age. At present he is the only member there who is also a member of the Foundation. His insights are very valuable for the community, for there are small differences in the lifestyle of Newbold and Foundation, and we can cross-fertilise each other by comparing ways of doing things. There has also been a subtle change in Newbold under his focalisation, with more emphasis on spiritual practice, its application and group focalisation.

"I was born in Kassel, Germany. I never got to know my father, because my parents split up when I was two years old. I only saw him once, when I was six. My mother played a central role in my life, as did my grandfather, a truly grand old man with long, white hair and a big heart. I still feel a strong tie to them. My mother remarried a politician, and I was expected to become one as well. I could soon keep up adult conversation, which made them laugh. I

265

have fond memories of grandfather's big garden with its ancient trees, and of old-fashioned aunts and uncles in cigar-smoke-filled, oak-furnished living rooms. My great-grandfather was a master tailor, and his mirror-lined workrooms had a great working table on which apprentices sat cross-legged, working with multi-coloured cloth. It transported me into a world of fairy tales.

"As a teenager, my childhood world collapsed and I went into a crisis. I felt a sense of uselessness in me and all around me that I couldn't bear, so I started drinking heavily. I was short and I made up for it by being tough—and drinking. My parents wanted to put me into a rehabilitation centre for alcoholics. Somehow I knew I had to help myself battle my depression and find meaning in life. I started hanging around groups of equally desperate people, but also the Hare Krishna movement and other religious cults and sects. I became fascinated by a group of Jesus people, who were concerned with living and applying love. They had a drop-in cafe for people like me. I went along and argued with them, at the same time feeling suicidal, drinking and getting into fights outside.

"Finally one of them said, 'We've talked for six months and nothing's changed. Now I'm going to pray for you. Come with me, if you're not afraid.' I couldn't back down on that challenge. Several of us went into their prayer room. Among them was a huge black American GI who started crying during the prayers. I realised he was crying about me. I ran out through the night and the rain, a 16-year-old totally frightened that a stranger could cry because of me. The next day I went back, desperate. I tried to speak to God, and said, 'If you exist, take charge of my life.' Then for the first time I consciously experienced unconditional love; every object and living being around me was directly communicating love to me. At that time I called it Jesus saving me.

"I stopped drinking and smoking and joined the movement. I trained to be a forester during the day, and in the rehabilitation centre in the evening I worked with junkies and child prostitutes. I learned the basic spiritual truths of the Bible. It's still my sounding board; when I read other teachings, they resonate on the basis of what Christ said and did.

"A group of us split off from the others because we felt they were getting too establishment-oriented. Four of us opened our flat as a half-way house for ex-prisoners and ex-junkies. I had endless energy. I worked as a forester all day and then till two in the morning with the street people. Money we earned we gave away. Once we spent all we had on flowers and went through the streets giving them to people and saying, 'God loves you.' Another time we made a huge Christmas dinner in a church basement and picked up taxi-loads of junkies and prostitutes to eat it. Four of my friends whom we were trying to help died from an overdose of heroin. At that time 'born again' Christians in Europe weren't a bad thing.

"But the established churches and the police were ambivalent, although we were totally clean of drugs. The police searched the flat. The churches refused us premises, but sent us their 'impossible' cases. Gradually we ran ourselves dry.

"While I was doing alternative military service in a kindergarten with Turkish kids, I met a 'wise being'—a very kind spiritual friend and teacher who took me deeper into spirituality and introduced me to Eastern religions and practices. Then I began learning from a Hindu monk. An old German lady taught me Vipassana meditation and for three years we met in her shrine room for Buddhist studies and group meditations.

"After five years in forestry and one and a half years in the kindergarten I gave up everything, put on a backpack and started on a three-year journey visiting monasteries and spiritual communities in Europe and Asia. I studied Zazen and T'ai Chi, and lived with Franciscans, Benedictines and Tibetan Buddhists.

"A very important experience for me was becoming a Buddhist in Nepal—taking refuge, it's called. The ceremony involved having my hair cut off and chanting with my teacher/Lama in front of a beautiful statue of the compassionate Buddha. During the ceremony I had a clear vision of Christ next to the Buddha, winking and smiling at me and giving the thumbs up sign. I had a sense of living in harmony between the Buddha and the Christ. Later, during a tantric meditation, I became very ill. I had a near-death experience and would have died if it hadn't been for the monks, who looked after me. But during the experience I had a sense of pure consciousness, of God as Oneness, with no dualism.

"In my travels I had already visited the Findhorn Community. I had a resistance to the different type of spirituality here, but after three or four visits, during which I fell in love with Newbold garden, the sense came to me that I should stay. I couldn't resist for long. In a few weeks I was focalising the garden; after three years, Newbold itself. When Cally proposed I should focalise, I refused. It didn't square with my hippie self-image. But I knew that the underlying reason was fear. I stayed open and asked God. In the end I had to say, 'Yes. The answer is, "Not my will, but Thine".'

"I'm glad I did. It has been beautiful to watch Newbold grow. To live in harmony, you have to acknowledge the gifts you are given and not try to be someone else. It's taken me eight years to understand these gifts which make Newbold unique within the Findhorn Community and that they have a lot to do with 'root space', the dark, the feminine, the Earth as a living being. To grow our own fruit of spirit in this community we have to nurture our roots as well as stretching up towards the light, to care equally for yin and yang qualities.

"You must understand that we are an aspect of and inseparable from the larger Findhorn Community. I see the whole symbolised in the yin/yang symbol, with Newbold, Erraid and Iona being a focus for the earth and inward energies, while the Park, the Hall and Outreach are the outward, yang energies. For some things the intrinsic energies are in the Foundation, for others they are here. Our land and trees give a womb-like energy, whereas the Park is light, open. The Park is the residential and commercial area, Cluny is the university and Newbold might be a new model for an educational monastic setting. A Foundation Trustee once called it the ashram of the community. I spend 12 to 15 weeks a year in silence, focusing on our spiritual practices through the various workshops and retreats I facilitate. For many people silence is very scary. We make it safe here to deal with the undefined, feminine, not-yet-born, silent space.

"For the British authorities, we were comfortable to register ourselves as a religious institution rather than as a business, and that's what we are. This spring, we made a commitment to put spirit first in everything we do—to put being before doing, so that any activity can become prayer and worship. There are no great changes on the form level, although we have already had two four-week retreats this year, but the general energy and atmosphere in the house are becoming much more spiritually based, and there is a greater dedication of the members to spiritual practice. For us, the future is to grow in spirit; what form that takes is secondary.

"Our lifestyle here is one of sharing. More people are coming to live here for a longer time and 'common unity' is a strong theme in our programmes, as a form of spiritual teaching and message. At present more people want to share this than we can accommodate. We have started to invite spiritual leaders here. A Catholic priest shared a Eucharist with us in our sanctuary, and Native American teachers lead earth-sky ceremonies. Through these events a particular atmosphere is generated and we become a meeting point for many spiritual traditions.

"My vision for Newbold is that it may become more and more a place of refuge and learning, a place built on our love of God, shared with each other."

* * *

Becoming a Spiritual Businessman—François Duquesne

François Duquesne was the first person to elaborate the idea of the 'planetary village', an earlier way of referring to the wider Findhorn Community. Since one tends to have to live out one's ideas here, François became a community businessman, partner in the Alternative Data software company. It is interesting that he regards that situation as more challenging than anything he had faced before, even as focaliser of the Foundation, although that was demanding enough. At the time of going to press, François has taken on the challenge of working in the management of a big computer company and, for the time being at least, has moved away from the Findhorn Community. Many people see his leadership as having saved the Foundation during a difficult period.

In the interview I have not emphasised François's artistic side. He is a wonderful mime artist and actor. He says of mime:

"One is given permission to be totally open and vulnerable, to reveal oneself without making a commitment, without saying, 'This is me, here.' It may be me, but the white-painted face raises a question mark. It is liberating to express oneself without cumbersome words; a kind of therapy for me.

"I was born in Paris. After studying law my father, who had been a graphic designer for the press, built, together with my mother, their own real estate business. I don't have many childhood memories. I was a keen, hard-working scholar. I specialised in maths, physics and languages at school.

269

"My parents were spiritual, and at around 16 I began to read their library of the Eastern and Western mystery traditions. I loved particularly to study the spiritual practices of the East. But I resisted my father's views, and for a while argued everything in opposition to him. Finally I read a spiritual book that really spoke to me: Lobsang Rampa's *The Third Eye*.

"After baccalaureat I went to business school, and part of the course involved a study visit. I chose India, with the ostensible purpose of examining the effects of the green revolution. But my real purpose was to visit ashrams. I was exploring all the levels of Indian society and culture when I received a telegram from my girlfriend. She was pregnant! I returned to marry her, and then my son Philippe was born. My marriage closed the avenue to the East!

"Soon afterwards I read a pamphlet about the Findhorn Community. We came for a visit at Christmas 1971. It all seemed to be happening here—the Hierarchy had come down to earth! I completed business school and returned to the community in 1972. Roc, Spangler, Dorothy, everyone was here; it was buzzing and aglow with light—a tiny community, but very impressive. I immediately decided to stay and moved into the Accounts Department. But my wife wasn't so happy. We had tried to make the best out of the marriage, but love wasn't there. After three years she moved back to France with Philippe.

"I became concerned with accounts, administration and management groups. After Spangler left, I continued to develop the embryonic 'college' for members that he had started. Michael Lindfield, who later wrote the book *The Dance of Change*, and I gave all sorts of courses on 'The Grand Order of the Universe'. It was great fun. I also went touring for the Foundation.

"By 1978 relations between Peter and Eileen were very uneasy. Peter was being drawn to other women and their marriage gradually fell apart. He decided to leave Eileen and go to Hawaii. When Peter said he was off, I'd just come back from a lecture tour in the United States and I was planning to leave the community myself. Peter said, in effect, 'I'm going. Here's the baby!' I was 28. It was a challenge for me. I thought, 'I'll do it!'

"I inherited a situation in which the community was in crisis on three levels. Firstly, there was a spiritual crisis—of faith and of vision. The question was being put: Is the Findhorn Foundation past its heyday? Is it now going downhill? Secondly, there was a crisis of leadership. Peter's at times very autocratic style of leadership had created a general distrust of authority. Also people had idealised images of Peter and Eileen, and their separation turned those images to dust. The third crisis was financial. We were on the verge of bankruptcy. We couldn't even pay basic things like telephone bills; the phones were cut off at one point. People would start a project, spend money and leave. There was no budgeting, no strict accounting.

"We had to work on all three levels in parallel. To nurture a sense of faith required placing a new emphasis on meditation, meeting together as a community and developing the next phase of the vision, that of the 'planetary village'. It was essential to move away from the distortion of a glamorous new age hippie movement and recapture the sense of a high destiny in what we were doing. We started meditation groups and organised community meetings about our vision and purpose, and in 1982 Roger Doudna and I focalised a conference on the theme of the planetary village.

"In regard to leadership, we started to put democracy in place, but the community membership halved in a period of two years and the 'village council' that we set up became superfluous. We placed much more emphasis on the focalisers and started the staff programme, for which we negotiated new visa arrangements with the Home Office. We tried to create structures of some permanence with a foot in the real world.

"Financially, it was essential to put controls in place. We started with an annual telephone bill of £12,000. After 16 months of locking phones and closing lines we were making a profit! We completed a new accounting system and made all the focalisers do their own budgets. On the one hand we had to stop the leaks, so our resources wouldn't flow out. On the other, it was necessary to put the Foundation on a solid long-term capital base. It could not rely purely on donations and guest fees. That could never provide the capital to finance expansion.

"All these themes came together with the chance to buy our land and remove a major symbol of impermanence. My expectation was that the Caravan Park would provide one third of our income. To raise the purchase money, we had a team of staff focalisers in place to pull the community together. We raised two thirds of the cost by donations and paid off the other third in two years, giving us a £400,000 asset.

"For me, this felt like a completion of my time as community focaliser. Now the Findhorn Foundation had a vision, was evolving its own method of self-governance and had the means to pay its debts. I felt complete. I was tired of interminable meetings—I was longing to do something. I wanted to leave, but I met Hannah, who was just coming into the community. It was clearly right for her to be here, so I stayed. My soul, however, was calling me to move out of the Foundation. I had eight bouts of bronchitis that year. Later I felt that I'd have lost my life if I'd remained a member any longer.

"I had talked so much about the planetary village, however, that I did want to be part of building it from the ground up.

"I spent a year in NFD putting a time-share scheme together in response to a request to finance a million-pound community centre complex, but the scheme was several times undermined (*cf. the account in Chapter 11—CR*). Then I met Stephan. I thought, 'I'm not going to waste my time in the Foundation—this time I'll build a business where I can be more in control of my own destiny!' So I became an entrepreneur.

"We started by working together on a new accounting package for the Foundation. Out of that grew Alternative Data. The challenge was to reconcile spirituality and business. I hadn't felt able or inclined to do that before.

"Business is the dominant institution of our culture. It needs people with consciousness, or nothing will work. I wanted to build a successful cooperation with spirit in business from the ground up, making a contribution by demonstration. There were so many workshops on new age economics. There are plenty of consultants. But could we transform the institution of business *from the inside*? I wanted to try it.

"The actual experience has been difficult, although the project itself has been exhilarating. Our business colleagues and partners are great people. The company is in God's hands—we've many times been on the brink of collapse and have been picked up. It's the human relations aspect that's been a shock. I have come to realise to what extent violence can be legitimised through business. Not physical violence, but psychic violence through the exercise of power. Generally, only one part of a person's identity can function in business. The whole system is based on status hierarchies. I'm suddenly in the middle of it and I think, 'No wonder the world doesn't work.' Power is the most difficult human transaction, and it's constantly battled over in our office.

"I thought meditations on Monday mornings and being nice to customers would do it; instead, I had to deal with intense personality conflicts in a system where power is also equated with money. Yet there is great excitement. All the problems have had to do with perceptions of power. Power to stifle and manipulate, or to create, enliven and challenge. There's no other way of dealing with power issues except by bringing them out and working them through till there's some result.

"I'm going ahead in faith, trusting that this path also has a heart."

* * *

A Last Perspective—Mary Inglis

Preparing a list of people to talk to for the third section of this book, it seemed natural for the final interview to be with *Mary Inglis*, as natural as it was for the membership to support her on our Core Group. Mary has been here for many years, she is one of our Trustees and her presence is one of quiet integrity and balance. Her current work, focalising the Game of Transformation in the Findhorn Community, makes her both a part of the Foundation and independent of it. Leading workshops abroad gives her a broader view of things. Our interview lasted a fascinating four and a half hours, and it is sad to have had to drastically shorten my notes. Perhaps Mary will take the hint and write her own story as a book. She is 44 years old.

"I was born in Edinburgh, but my father was in the Colonial Service, so we left Scotland when I was one and I grew up in Africa, a couple of years in Nigeria and then in Lesotho. We used to live in what were called 'camps', administrative centres for the colonial government, with about ten white families and a varying number of black families. It was a very safe environment. I was out of doors a lot. I loved it. Later I was sent to boarding school in South Africa, and it was always a relief to come home for the holidays, take off my shoes and roam barefoot again. My brothers and sister and I all developed very tough soles!

"I was sent to an all-girls' school in Pietermaritzburg. I didn't enjoy it much until my last two years, but I liked learning and I did very well there. My father was well liked in Lesotho. He considered himself to be preparing people to take over the running of the country, and respected them, irrespective of colour. Segregation there had more connotations of class than race. It was in South Africa that segregation and apartheid really struck me. Partly it was the contrast between Lesotho, where segregation was breaking down, and South Africa, where it was tightening up and becoming increasingly enforced by law. I began writing about what I saw, thought and experienced, discovered the writings of Alan Paton and decided to be a journalist.

"At university I began working for the weekly student newspaper and became involved in student union politics through the National Union of South African Students. I wrote articles about student affairs for a liberal newspaper (which I joined a few years later) and when I left university I spent a year running the South African National Student Press Association, a news service for the student press, as well as working for the South African Institute of Race Relations. In the meantime Lesotho became independent, my father died, and my family moved to South Africa. The kinds of activities I was involved in obviously didn't endear me to the South African authorities, because my request for residency was turned down and I was asked to leave the country. I appealed, and after a lengthy process which included being asked to leave three more times, I received a permanent residence permit. By that time I had been working as a newspaper journalist for three years.

"In Lesotho my family had known a healer and she had an ongoing influence on me. When my arm was broken in a car accident and then had to be reset in a bone graft operation, she sent me healing and I recovered remarkably quickly. A group of us in Cape Town began to have ouija-board-type seances, in which we received spiritual teachings for about a year. One thing that was emphasised was that the motivation for political action was very important. If it was spurred by hatred, violence and judgement, it wouldn't help. At the end of the year we had a final message, telling us in effect that the seeds had been sown and that it was time for this phase of the teaching to end. The experience led me back into contact with the churches and, through them, to the movement for Christian Education and Leadership Training, which used group dynamics, human relations training and en-

274

counter techniques within a spiritual framework. I was excited by this work and by the transformative effect it had on the people in the multi-racial and ecumenical groups which CELT organised, and finally I gave up my job and came to Britain to explore it further.

"Over the next two years I explored a variety of approaches to individual and group work—Gestalt, Re-Evaluation Co-Counselling, massage, meditation, and T-group and group dynamics training. I spent a summer in Northern Ireland on a project bringing young Catholic and Protestant teenagers together both in work and recreational activities. A key time for me was spending six months with the St Mungo community in London, a group which worked with destitute men. All the tried-and-tested beliefs and ways of being I had developed over the previous few years were challenged there, and I found myself plunged into a devastating sense of hopelessness and despair, in which it seemed to me that we were all, at core, destitute. The only way I could deal with it was to stop thinking, to give up judgements and evaluations and to live in the present . . . and through this, amazingly and wonderfully, came a new sense of God's immanent presence, and an incredible joy. I began to feel I was receiving teaching, even through what by chance I picked up to read, or what I saw on the few occasions I watched TV. It was a pivotal time in my life.

"My mother had heard about the Findhorn Foundation and when she spent time in Britain in 1972 we visited the community together. The person showing us around was talking about angels and I felt someone lay their hands on my shoulders, but when I looked there was no one there. Elfreda said, "You'll be back. You belong here."

"I went back to South Africa, but had no wish to stay. Then I spent a few weeks at the Foundation; I was very drawn to the place but wasn't sure about joining. I wanted to be socially active; also I was uneasy that people in the community weren't working much with their emotions. I went back to London and a couple of months later was offered a good job in youth education with the Church of England. It was time to make a choice. After some indecision, I knew I was to come to the Findhorn Community. I arrived back to stay in August 1973. I remember there were chickens where the Hall is now!

"On the night I arrived, I had a dream. I was in my own, loved

275

house, and I was going to die at four o'clock. I put everything in order in the house, then sat in a window seat in the sun, ready to die. Next morning when I woke up, I had a new sense of myself.

"I came as one of a number of slightly older people, after the 'youth wave' of the early seventies. We had a lot to say about how we thought things should be. It was disconcerting to the longer-established people. We started a choir and wrote a Mass in D, for angels and humans—our understanding was that D was the note of the new age. There was no Orientation programme for new members in those days, but the experience in the choir provided the space and opportunity for us to work through many of the issues that are part of the integration process here. It was an intense group process which helped to insulate us from the rest of the community and also them from us! When we eventually proudly performed the mass, half the community went home feeling ill. Roc took us aside and told us that D was actually the note of purification!

"I began working in Publications and got interested in David Spangler's writings as I typeset some of his books. I have spent much of my time here involved with that department, editing, writing, publishing. I have also worked a lot with education. When I came there was little place in the Foundation for people's distress and there was a mistrust of support techniques. There was a sense in which the spiritual level was seen as 'good' and the personality level as 'not good'. A group of us—mostly women—with experience in emotional and group work became quite vocal and active, but we were seen as a threat and some of us were called up before the all-male Management Group to explain ourselves. It was clear we would have to find new ways of doing things or leave, so we started to develop experiential components for the programmes here, seeking to add them to the esoterics then being taught. We also began the 'group discovery' programme which is now part of the Experience week. Gradually these aspects became incorporated into the education and 'techniques' became respectable.

"After 18 months I became part of the Management Group myself. It met every morning. There would be a meditation, and then a theoretical discussion between Peter, François and Dick Barton. Other people didn't speak much and when they did, were not really listened to. My idea of circle sharing so we could really hear each other was resisted for months. When we finally did it, it was such a breakthrough that it quickly became standard practice. I was learning the spiritual context, but for years I was the spokesperson for the human context—giving space to all of ourselves. Nowadays, though, I sometimes feel we have to be careful not to get so caught up in the pull of personal process that we forget the spiritual context.

"For years I was involved in community administration; I was on and off the Management Group, and spent three years in the Personnel Department. But gradually my ongoing association with the Game of Transformation, which dates back to 1978, became dominant, and I began to focalise the Game in 1987.

"In 1988 the community supported me to join the spiritual Core Group. I was ambivalent about it at first, because I am no longer much involved with the specifics of the Foundation's work; most of my time and attention goes into the Game. But the community is very close to my heart, and I feel I have perspectives to offer. I also feel a very strong connection with the energy running through this centre, which I relate to as a friend and teacher. The Core Group is a holding and amplifying group for this energy, and we have had some very powerful meditations.

"In fact, the work of both the Game and the Foundation is very close. Both are about the transformation of human consciousness. I believe that transformation is about incarnating more fully, bringing more of ourselves into this world. We haven't fully incarnated yet, as individuals or as a human race. We're walking around in bodies, but we're not all here yet. As we open to spirit, to the fullness of who we are or could be, this puts pressure on points of ourselves that are resistant to spirit—and that's where personal work is important. It helps us clear away false identifications and blockages. Remember Moses and the burning bush—the fire that burned but did not consume. That, to me, is a symbol of incarnation. The more we incarnate, the more we bring ourselves fully present to each moment of existence, so the more do we experience the immediacy of the presence of God. Every bush becomes a burning bush; we become fully who we are, alive with the fire of spirit."

Conclusion

Big doors swing on small hinges. Tremendous happenings start from very small beginnings. I tell you, what has started at Findhorn in such a small way will grow and expand into a worldwide, universal movement; a revelation will become a revolution. My ways are very strange and very wonderful; they are not your ways. Walk in My ways in absolute faith and confidence, and see My wonders and glories unfold. The spring of the new age is here, bursting forth in perfect harmony, beauty and abundance; and nothing can stop it from coming about. There is a right time and season for everything, and now is the right time and season for the birth of the new age. So dwell not on the past, leave it all behind; and see what I have for you this new and glorious day. See My wonderful promises all come about and give eternal thanks for everything. Hold ever before you the vision of the new heaven and new earth.

—Eileen Caddy's guidance

As I write it is October 1989, a beautiful, mild autumn day after a wonderful summer. Even the good weather gives rise to some anxiety. Is it an epiphenomenon of the greenhouse effect, rather than just one of our occasional good years? We do not know, but the tides in the bay have never been higher; perhaps in 30 years time large parts of the area will be under water. We act and live, however, for the present and the community is a hive of activity. The windmill is to be erected this week, and members and guests have been trenching and laying 11,000-volt cable to bring the power from the site, about half a mile along past the Pineridge woods. The roofs are on two new barrel houses, and the gardens around the new community centre extension are slowly taking shape. Steadily, new people are moving into the area to live as part of the wider Findhorn Community. The 'summer season' has finished, but the guests are still coming. Thirteen of our male members have just returned, inspired, from a men's retreat in a house in the Cairngorms. At Minton House a small ecumenical group of Christians has been meeting to discuss the relevance of existing church structures in the coming period, and daring to question

279

whether those structures do, indeed, have much relevance. The British Green Party has adopted 'attunements' in its conference. Two more television crews are visiting this week. Our life of demonstration goes on.

One perspective on the Findhorn Community is to show its relevance to the social and political impasse of our times, in which the materialist world order is, basically, shooting itself in the foot. The first part of the book is written from this perspective. Another perspective describes our life, work and organisation to demonstrate that a spiritual way of living can be practical and effective. That view comprises the second part of the book. A third perspective approaches the Findhorn Community through the life stories of its members. They are the stories of ordinary people from different backgrounds, nationalities and religions, who have finally said 'yes' to the spiritual opportunities life has offered them. They have found a path through the labyrinth of greed and despair to become unpretentious demonstrators of the solution that will really work for humanity—life as the pathway to the God within. Their personal perspectives form the third part of the book. A fourth, visual slant is given by Harley Miller's beautiful line drawings and the photographs of Chris Giles and others.

A final perspective is provided by the *energy* this book shares with you. For I am concerned neither with an academic description of the Findhorn Community which leaves the reader distanced and unmoved, nor with cultivating the same passive reaction that people have to television's endlessly absorbing sequences of pictures. We are all part of the same global Noah's Ark now, a leaky ark that needs a lot of repair to survive the floods of cynicism and disillusion that threaten to swallow us. The way forward explored in our community does not leave individual human beings as minute and powerless ciphers in other people's political and economic enterprises.

By asking the simple questions, 'Why am I here?' 'What is it all for?', and spending a little time to find the answer, quietly, inside, seeking God's love as our own essence, the turn-around can begin; meaningfulness and excitement can re-enter ordinary life. If we turn away from that inner spark, dullness resumes control, the eyes glaze over once more, purpose is lost and we drive ourselves to act merely to blot out our loss. Then any amount of possessions will not help us; more vacuous television programmes will not assist; hooliganism, vandalism and drugs will give no satisfaction; the search for wealth, power and status will ring hollow; even excursions into the glamorous realms of sorcery, superstition and the occult will be of no avail—for where there is emptiness within, no outer or peripheral forms will satisfy.

The Findhorn Community represents the practical exploration of a truth—the Truth—whose time has come for humanity. *The purpose of human life is inner-directed, the disentangling of the Self, Essence, God-nature from the ego-self which growing up in a secular world superimposes on it. The external life of our sense experiences is our teacher in this quest for the real Holy Grail; our actions in the perceived world express our inner discovery.*

This is the theology which is appropriate now, not just for a monastic few, or for a tiny band of spiritual elitists; it is a practical theology, offered to all of us. Everyone can easily make this turn in their lives, in the direction of their Centre, freely, independently, without feeling coerced by established forms, and even in the most seemingly desperate political, economic and personal conditions.

This personal spirituality has become the only practice in contemporary life that can provide relevant answers to the current human condition. Slowly we will all learn this and realise that it is not a last-resort solution, but the way to joyful, challenging, vibrant human living. The real purpose of this book is to contribute to raising these issues for you, its reader, so you may perhaps question the direction of your own life and begin to realign it. There are many visionaries counselling change. In the Findhorn Community we are showing how it works in practice, and there are others like us in every locality, the world over. Where love is being expressed without dogma or condition, there they are —individuals, groups and communities.

It is quite wrong to believe that this turning within represents a selfish withdrawal from the great challenges of poverty, malnutrition and disillusion that plague the world. The stimulation of contact with the Real, the Love within, unleashes ever-increasing energy for action in the experienced world without; it purifies motives and eliminates cant and moralism. Mother Theresa's unstinting love and energy for the deprived of Calcutta and the world comes from putting God first, so she can see Him in all, whether they are Catholic or Hindu, deformed or diseased. And everyone, from whatever religious background, responds to her. When the God inside us becomes the focus of our being, our potential in the human form is enormous. Each extra iota of love that you can discover in yourself builds the foundations of your new identity; it may be expressed in any situation—your home, relationship, friendships, community, suburb, housing estate, office, factory, political activity—to begin the transformation of that situation and of the people around you.

As you follow this path there will be times when you feel like reverting to fear, anger, neediness and guilt. Do not judge yourself useless for shortcomings; notice that the path is not a short one, and use the opportunity to learn from your reactions. By using the insights you gain, you can prepare for your next step forward. The challenges you face are an opportunity to find more love.

Do not pretend to be loving when you are not. That is hypocrisy. It contributes to a phoney society, an inner Stalinism in which what is said is not what is felt, and what is done debases what is proclaimed. But never accept your non-lovingness; seek its sources and find the means and the support from others to remove it. This is legitimate self-examination which has the paradoxical advantage of soothing your ego as it dismantles it. And as you win, turn outwards again and experience the results. You are actively creating a new human identity which, collectively, will construct the appropriate civilisation of the twenty-first century.

God is on our side; the energies of nature are on our side. The physically experienced world is not objective or neutral to the spiritual seeker. We have demonstrated in the Findhorn Community, and continue to demonstrate, that as spiritual seekers we become participants in a magical game and, as *A Course in Miracles* asserts, daily miracles are the norm to those who seek the love that is their essence. Numerous small examples have been recounted in this book. They don't belong only to the origins of the Findhorn Community. The outer world appears static and impersonal only to those who take it as the sole reality.

Do not consider the progress or non-progress of others on this path as your own criterion. You are working for the provision of happiness and meaningfulness in your own life. By moving in this direction, you are automatically contributing to the transformation of the whole, as well as satisfying yourself. Do not dwell on the problems of the world, while not denying them. Place emphasis instead on the remarkable changes that are taking place, and realise that in changing yourself you are part of the energy that is causing them.

Here in the Findhorn Community, and in all the other centres of light over the planet, we are doing the same. Learn from us; share with us; teach us. But, please, share your life practice and only those of your theories which are fully exemplified in it; share how you are working to solve a problem, not your 'abstractions as to the theoretical manner by which problems of which you have no personal experience might be solved'! Remember that anything that leads you away from love as the centre and essence of your own identity is a backward-leading cul-de-sac. There are enough of those already.

At the Findhorn Community we have, I think, basically learned our lessons about glamour. We are living an exciting, stimulating day-to-day life, not one that denies ordinariness in the pursuit of exoticism. Day-to-day life here is full of wonder and small miracles. But they are the spice in our exciting diet, not the whole meal. Billions of human beings on this planet are concerned with an ordinary life. It does not need to be a seemingly endless, meaningless grind, punctuated by occasional circuses in which one may experience momentary oblivion, or by stories which tide one over the boredom of a few more months. At the Findhorn Community we are showing that an ordinary life can build vibrancy, creativity and ongoing magic from very meagre resources, if love is the motivator. Actually, every little child unconsciously demonstrates this to us in its play, if we care to look.

To quote one of Eileen's favourite phrases, 'All is very, very well.' Join us in creating the new human identity of the coming century. Structures of hypocrisy, fear, acquisitiveness, exclusion, poverty and bestiality are beginning to crumble under the gentle touch of love. Nothing can prevail against it. Release it in yourself, in your existing life situation, now.

Califer Hill
Near Forres

Appendix
The Findhorn Community &
the Western Mystery School

Unlike Eileen, Peter Caddy was trained in and had a great knowledge of esoterics. In the community's early years this esoteric background was a kind of spiritual seed bed, attracting interest and support from esoteric groups all over Britain and beyond. Power points, ascended Masters—especially St Germain—ley lines, flying saucers, the energies of crystals were all at various points themes of vigorous discussion among members. Both Roc and David Spangler, as well as Sir George Trevelyan, for many years one of our Trustees, had a deep knowledge of esoterics, and François Duquesne, the second focaliser, was well trained in them.

After Peter left at the end of the 1970s, such themes tended to become much more marginal. Eileen Caddy's guidance was not based on them. Yet our community jargon sometimes uses esoteric terms, and they are built into the language of the Game of Transformation to some degree. 'The Great Invocation' hangs on the wall of the Park Sanctuary. We tend to talk of the 'Christ Consciousness' to indicate the essence of Jesus's consciousness—something which is available to us rather than merely recorded in history. The use of the term 'glamour' to indicate a distortion in spiritual development stems from Alice Bailey's writings, and so on.

Esoteric 'study papers' are available to Orientees, if they want to read them. The nineteenth century spawned many esoteric schools, and they claimed their origins in various mystery traditions, some dating back to the Egyptians. Most of these schools agreed that there was a secret 'inner knowledge' which could be received only by initiates or be channelled by 'sensitives'. They tended to elitism and exclusivism, and were subject to splits similar to those that appeared in left-wing groups in the sixties and seventies of this century. A collective term for such groups has come to be the 'Western Mystery School', and there is a two-volume account, *The Western Way* by Caitlin and John Matthews, for

285

those interested in further detail.

In *One Earth*, our magazine, Vol. 2 (6), 1982, Nicholas Rose outlines this tradition and seeks to relate the Findhorn Community to it. He writes:

> *One of the main features of the mystery traditions is that they all come out of a consciousness of wholeness and a knowledge of the reality of the spiritual realms. All the maps that were produced—whether these were the Hermetic sciences, the astrological or alchemical symbolism, the Rosicrucian teachings or even some of the pre-Christian approaches—sprang from the idea of oneness and the inter-relatedness of the spiritual reality and the material world. Our culture has lost that awareness, but we are now trying to regain it in ways that are appropriate to our age. And certainly that is the consciousness that underlies the work at (the) Findhorn (Foundation) . . . . (It) represents a return to the essential core of the mystery teachings.*

(p. 14)

There is no doubt that in our language we owe something to the schools of Theosophy and Anthroposophy (Steiner), and to the writings of Alice Bailey. But the Findhorn Community has never had the exclusivist tendencies of groups following such teachings, nor their habit of separatism. The connection with nature energies first made by Dorothy Maclean and Roc has a resonance in pre-Christian pagan traditions, but also in those of the Essenes and St Francis. After reading accounts of Roc's visions of Pan, some fundamentalist Christian groups have accused us of being devil worshippers!

Yet Eileen's guidance is pure Christian mysticism and has much more in common with Meister Eckhart and Julian of Norwich than with any of the above. It is the teaching which has come through her that inspires the vast majority of those who come to the Foundation. It is a pure teaching of Divine Love, and has been expressed in many different ways through mystics in the post-war years. Of them all I have singled out two other sources for special mention in the text—the teachings of Sathya Sai Baba, stemming from the Hindu tradition, and those of *A Course In Miracles*. This is because both have had an influence on modern spirituality that is at least as powerful as that of the Findhorn Community, and also because both are now widely studied by our members and guests. But it is important also to acknowledge the esoteric background in our own history. Its research may provide a joyful hunting ground for theological scholars some day.